a&b

Detox Your Finances

The Ultimate Book of Money Matters for Women

Justine Trueman

Allison & Busby Limited
13 Charlotte Mews
London W1T 4EJ
www.allisonandbusby.com

This paperback original first published in 2009.

A CIP catalogue record for this book is available from the British Library.

10 9 8 7 6 5 4 3 2 1

13-ISBN 978-0-7490-7958-1

Typeset by Lara Crisp

The paper used for this Allison & Busby publication has been produced from trees that have been legally sourced from well-managed and credibly certified forests.

Printed and bound in the UK by
CPI Bookmarque, Croydon, CR0 4TD

JUSTINE TRUEMAN has 13 years' experience as a financial journalist working for the likes of Reuters, the *Telegraph* and *Time Magazine*. As part of her job, she spent many years interviewing top investors around the world and studying their techniques.

However, investing was a hobby before it became a job and she also has a lot of hands-on experience. She created her first budget at age 17 and began investing in the stock market when she was 20 years old.

She now works for an investment management company based in Paris. In her spare time, she runs a women-only investment club and shares her enthusiasm for saving and investing by speaking at investment conferences and women's associations.

author's note

All the statistics, fees and figures etc quoted in this book were correct at the time of writing. However, since financial markets can move very rapidly, they may have changed by the time of publication, so are given for illustrative purposes only. In most cases I have specified in which years the figures were published.

Although I was a financial journalist for many years and work for a finance company, I am not a financial adviser nor regulated to give advice. Anyone who is planning to invest should be aware of the risks of those investments, and take appropriate advice where necessary. Don't forget that past performance figures do not provide an accurate guide to future performance so in the short term you could lose money.

No real names were used in the case studies featured in this book.

Justine Trueman

To the women in my investment club,
for your inspiration and support

CONTENTS

INTRODUCTION

I'm pretty average really. I'm about average height and I think with average looks. I'm an average age (36), my family are neither rich, nor very poor and I've always earned around the average wage, which in case you're wondering is currently about £30,000 for full-time workers in the UK. Yet, one thing I do have that seems to be in rather short supply these days is financial independence. I can afford to live where I want, I don't worry about the monthly bills or my pension, I have no debts and quite a few assets and I can afford not to work for at least a year, possibly several. If something big were to happen tomorrow, like a large, unexpected bill or a death in the family that meant I had to take an international flight, it wouldn't be a problem. I could cover that expense without it affecting my life or my stress levels. Can you do that?

The reason I decided to write this book is because I realised that a lot of my friends are not in this position, but would like to be. Instead, they are constantly worried about how they are going to stretch their next month's pay to cover all the bills. Even friends earning high salaries feel extremely nervous at the idea of making an investment or even approaching someone in finance. They have no idea what to do about pensions and they worry about their credit card bills and their future.

I was a financial journalist for 12 years, but my financial education started a long time before that. It began when I was 17 and I read a book specifically about women and money. I don't have that book anymore, but I've certainly remembered many of the lessons it taught me. I hope this book will open your eyes in the same way that book helped me to see how, just by following a few simple rules in life, you can get on top of your finances and start building wealth.

aIMS OF THIS BOOK

The aim of this book is to improve your relationship with money so that you:

* Are less stressed.
* Improve the quality of your life.
* Feel in control of your finances.
* Stop fighting about money with your partner.
* Deal more effectively with your kids on money issues.
* Negotiate better.
* Recognise the psychological blocks that are preventing you from achieving your financial goals.
* Understand the key principles of building wealth.
* Know how to deal with people working in finance.

For many of us, our financial lives have become cluttered and inefficient. Like eating high-fat food or accumulating too much household junk, we have got into the bad habit of using high-interest rate credit cards and spending money in shops we can little afford. Even where we have built up savings or investments, they are often not working as efficiently as they should, wallowing in the land of weak returns and excessive fees.

It's time to clear out your purse, get back into the black, dust off those old share certificates and insurance forms, rid your life of that whiny stockbroker who keeps losing you money and commence a financial detox!

The first step is to get your budget in order and clear those debts. Once you are debt-free and have a sensible budget and savings plan, you can move on from a firm base. We'll also take a look at any negative thinking patterns that may be holding you back.

Then I will explain and walk you through the different types of investment products so you know what's out there, what the risks and rewards are, and what is best for you.

Later on, we'll look at developing your own portfolio, one that works as efficiently as possible and which you tailor-make so that your own unique requirements are met.

We'll also take a look at how you can improve your earnings at work, in your investment portfolio, and what you should reasonably expect from a financial adviser or stockbroker.

I encourage you to use this book as an opportunity to take a long, hard look at all aspects of your financial life. That way, you can decide what to polish up and revitalise, and what needs to be tossed. Whatever, or whoever, is cluttering up your finances, now is the time to take action. With the current state of the economy, there's no longer room for these unhealthy habits. It's time to detox your finances!

SECTION ONE – MONEY AND THE MIND

In the first section of this book I deal with the emotional or psychological aspects of our relationship with money: how our upbringing, our personal views and our habits affect the way we treat our finances. This has a direct impact on how much money we have, the problems we get into with it and even the way we fight about it with our partners or the money lessons we pass on to our children.

SECTION TWO – TAKING CONTROL

The second section of this book is more concerned with the practical aspects of saving and investing. This is the 'how to' part of the book. However, it's important not to skip over the first section, because I firmly believe that, unless you understand yourself and your attitudes to money very well, you are likely to make saving or investment mistakes. Even if you decide to delegate your investment decisions to a financial adviser, one of the first things they will try to determine is how much risk you are comfortable with. If you haven't even thought about your views on money, you won't know where to start when it comes to investing.

SECTION ONE

MONEY AND THE MIND

WOMEN AND MONEY

You may be asking yourself – why do women need their own separate guide to money? Surely we're just as smart and capable as men, so therefore should be able to read the same finance books.

WOMEN ARE DIFFERENT

I wrote this book because I find that a lot of women look at money in a different way to men. Although women are making more money than ever, the majority are still more likely to be driven by a desire for security rather than power. They want to be able to afford to take good care of their kids, have a comfortable retirement, live in a lovely home, and take luxury holidays – rather than be able to impress their mates down the pub with their flashy new sports car.

Many men simply enjoy the challenge of making money; it's like finance has become a game and winning it gives them respect in their community and a sense of control and power. In contrast, the game feels very dangerous for a lot of women. For us, the stakes are higher and we have more to lose. This is not some irrational fear; it is based on very real scenarios.

Women live longer, so our money has to last longer and we can't afford to 'gamble' it on a financial bet that may or may not pay off. Despite a great improvement in the last 30 years, we still earn less, so we don't have as much money to play with and are more concerned about losing it.

Also, we are more likely to be single parents, suffer financially after a divorce, take on the care of elderly parents and have lower pension benefits. The statistics speak for themselves: the majority of people living in poverty in the UK are women.

Women are more cautious

Given all this, it's not surprising that studies show women treat their savings with far more caution than men. Many women realise they are in a precarious position, but don't know how to move forward and are afraid of making a mistake if they do.

A study by the UK Financial Services Authority compared the savings products of men and women. It showed that women were less likely to buy financial products than men, especially if they didn't understand them, whereas men would sometimes buy regardless of their level of knowledge.

In particular, women were more likely to hold a savings account, but were less likely to hold riskier investments such as shares or managed funds.

Overall, 6% of women had not taken out any form of financial product – whether it be a current account, credit card, stocks or a mortgage, compared to 4% of men.

Similarly, when women do invest on the stock market, study after study has shown they are far more cautious. They trade less often, they are more likely to have a balanced portfolio with a wide variety of different companies chosen, they are less confident in their ability to make money from stocks (even when their returns are the same or better than men's) and they are more afraid of losing money in a stock market crash, which is more likely to put them off investing altogether.

A Financial Services Consumer Panel survey found 42% of men felt confident in choosing financial products compared to 34% of women. But in the same way that men will drive around for hours refusing to ask directions or even look at a map, studies show men are less likely to admit when they don't understand a financial product and less likely to ask questions or ask for help. In contrast, women will research each investment thoroughly, but may still be put off actually investing because of their lack of confidence.

Why do women lack so much confidence when it comes to the world of finance and managing money? Is it because of traditional roles where men were given the responsibility of taking care of the household finances? Or is it because of the confusing, elitist jargon often used by the finance industry? Perhaps it's because of the male-dominated and sometimes downright sexist nature of the industry? Maybe women are less competitive generally and more likely to view gambling as stupid rather than brave? Or perhaps the reason lies in our historically lower levels of education? The answer is probably a combination of all these factors.

Women are Better Investors

The good news is that, when women do pluck up the courage to invest, they usually do a better job of it than men.

Terrance Odean, a professor at the University of California-Davis, and Brad Barber conducted a study called 'Boys Will Be Boys: Gender, Overconfidence and Common Stock Investment'. It analysed investment patterns from 150,000 discount brokerage accounts over a period of 8 years and found that women beat men's returns on the stock market by 1.4%.

The study illustrates how women's cautious attitude to the stock market actually works in their favour. Odean points out that the main flaw in men's investment strategy is overconfidence, which leads them to trading (buying and selling) their stocks too often. Men change their investments at a rate of 77% per year, while women only trade 53% of the time.

Trading too much can reduce the returns on an investment portfolio. This is because every time you buy and sell you incur fees and charges which eat into your profits. Also, trading increases your chances of getting it wrong and buying a stock which falls in value, or selling one that will continue to rise in the future. According to Odean, those who trade the most realise by far the worst performance.

Other studies have shown similar results. A study by financial website Digital Look (**www.digitallook.com**) found women's share portfolios grew by 17% in one year while men's grew by 11%. This was not a fluke; studies in previous years showed the same result, that female portfolios outperformed male ones.

The study looked at more than 100,000 share portfolios, but women's were more likely to be diversified with a balanced mix of different sectors such as leisure, food and drink and utility companies such as electricity and gas firms. In contrast, men were more likely to buy 'fad' investments such as technology stocks or companies benefitting from rises in gold or oil prices. Jumping on the latest trend in this way shows how a little bit of knowledge can be a dangerous thing. By trying to time or outsmart the market, men often reduce their investment returns.

Characteristics of top investors

I'd like to show you how some typical female characteristics can work in our favour as investors. Our extra-cautious approach has already proved to be a benefit when picking stocks and it can be with other investments as well. A modest investor is more likely to do the proper research required and therefore reduce the risks of a loss. Secondly, women's longer lifespans can work in our favour too. The longer you invest in something, the more you increase your chances of a good return.

The most successful investors in the world tend to have certain characteristics that help them withstand the ups and downs of financial markets. Many of these are characteristics that women share, indicating that women have the potential to be successful investors.

Patience

Any woman who has had to take care of a screaming baby knows a thing or two about patience. Fortunately, top investors also tend to be patient, ignoring the fads and fluctuations of the market and holding on to the investments they have confidence in for many years. As Warren Buffett, one of the most celebrated investors of our time, put it, 'Someone is sitting in the shade today because someone planted a tree a long time ago'. Investing can be a lot like gardening, planting those little savings seeds and carefully nurturing them over the years. Investing for the long term and ignoring market fads takes patience, but it also reduces your risks while at the same time increasing your returns.

Persistence

Investors who trade a lot can be compared to sprinters; they might make good returns in the short term, but over the long term they often fail. It's just like the gambler who wins a lot of money, then gets too confident in his skill and bets it all on one spin of the wheel that goes against him – losing the lot. Good investors are more like marathon runners; they're in it for the long haul, regularly saving and reinvesting their profits over the days, months and years. Because they have their focus firmly fixed on a goal in the distant future they don't mind too much if the stock market falls one day; they know that it will go up again eventually, they just have to wait it out. Investors who stick with their principles over the long term are more likely to win.

Diversification

Buying a wide range of investments as well as different types of stocks reduces your risks. It's the old 'don't put all your eggs in one basket' line that you've heard a million times before. Knowing that you aren't risking everything on one bet that might not work out helps you sleep at night and limits your chances of a loss. This was part of the strategy used by Benjamin Graham, Warren Buffett's mentor and author of *The Intelligent Investor*. He bought small, growing companies at very cheap prices, but made sure he had lots of them so that if any of them went bust it didn't hurt him too badly.

Scepticism

Taking the advice of someone in the finance industry with a pinch of salt can be a good thing. I'm not saying distrust brokers, fund managers or financial advisers completely. If you do, you may never have the courage to invest in the first place and could miss out on some good advice, but a bit of scepticism can work in your favour. Many people in finance are simply salesmen trying to sell a product. Women can usually see a dodgy salesman from way off, so perhaps that's why the studies show we treat the world of finance with more scepticism than men. Taking a slightly critical view can lead you to research your options more thoroughly, so you buy a product that is good value with low fees, thereby improving your chances of success. Sometimes it takes courage and determination to ignore the buzz of stockbrokers, who constantly encourage investors to trade in and out of stocks – handing them fees in the process – but successful investors stick to their guns and aren't easily swayed by the 'noise' of the market.

Courage

This is one characteristic that successful investors display but which many women don't have when it comes to finance. Our lack of confidence makes us more cautious – and therefore more sensible investors – but too much timidity can mean you never invest at all. Unfortunately, by being too afraid to even dip their proverbial toes in the investment water, and relying solely on savings accounts, many women miss out on the security and good fortune that a bit of investing could have given them. Sure, it can be scary out there, but there are plenty of tricks that you can use to reduce your risks and ensure that money works **for** you rather than **against** you.

A Great Female Investor

It is sometimes difficult to find real life examples of how women can be better investors than men. There are currently only ten female managers of investment trusts in the UK against 190 male managers. Fortunately, if you're prepared to do some digging, wonderful stories of amazing women investors do exist.

Anne Sheiber's Story

Anne Sheiber, an American millionairess, used a cautious approach to investing and a long lifespan to her advantage. She began investing on her retirement in 1944 at the age of 50. After a lifetime of being chronically underpaid – she never earned more than $3,150 a year – she had nevertheless saved up $5,000. She invested the lot in large, quality companies on the stock market and when she died in 1995 at the ripe old age of 101 her portfolio was worth $22 million. She gave away all of it to help other struggling women by donating it to the Yeshiva University in New York.

Interestingly, Anne's initial attempt at investing had failed disastrously. In 1932, when she was 38 and working as an IRS auditor, she gave her life savings to her stockbroker brother and he lost all of it. It took her 12 years to save up another nest egg, yet despite this horrifying experience she hadn't lost faith in the stock market (only in her brother). The companies she bought were large, well-known brands and she researched them thoroughly, reinvesting all the dividends whilst living a frugal existence.

Why You Should Let Him Pay For Dinner

Several of my friends – successful and single, working women – hate the idea of a man paying for their dinner. 'Why should I let him?' they ask me. 'I can afford it.' For someone raised in a feminist era it seems downright old-fashioned to allow a man to pay for dinner, and frankly I used to feel the same way.

But these days I think about it in a different way. Imagine if you offered someone a gift and they turned it down; you would think they were quite rude wouldn't you? And if you look at all the depressing statistics on female poverty, it might make you feel a little less guilty about shifting some costs onto men.

Women now make up nearly half of the labour force in Britain. According to the Office of National Statistics (ONS), for the year to April 2007, the median weekly pay for women in full-time work was £394 compared with £498 for men. The gap between male and female earnings has certainly narrowed: we now earn around 80% of male full-time earnings and this is expected to improve further as more and more women achieve higher education.

Let's hope so, because unfortunately even a small gap in earnings such as this can add up to quite a lot over the long term. 'By how much?' you ask. Oh, around half a million pounds, that's all. According to the IDS Pay Report, the average earnings for a full-time male in the UK are around £31,515. For the average female they are £22,975. Over a 40-year career, assuming wages rise just 2% a year, that adds up to £1.941 million earned for him and just £1.415 million for her – a difference of £526,152 over a working life.

Part-Time Pay Gap

Even within female employment there is a growing gap between the very wealthy and the very poor. According to the Fawcett Society, an organisation set up in 1866 to campaign for equality between the sexes, this is partly due to the number of part-time female workers. Many poorer women in our society are only able to work part-time because of their responsibilities towards children or elderly relatives, or simply because that is the only work available to them. Women take up the majority of jobs in the five Cs – cleaning, catering, caring, cashiering and clerical work: this work is often low paid and requires few qualifications.

Even if you are a highly educated, successful woman you may at some point in your life decide to work part-time for any number of reasons, and the situation in part-time work is far less equal between the sexes.

Only 11% of male employees work part-time compared with 40% of female employees. Women working part-time earn 59% of men's full-time hourly pay, giving UK women one of the worst pay gaps in Europe. The UK part-time sector is not only larger than in many other European countries, but also has shorter working hours, leading to lower pay.

Since 1975, when the Equal Pay Act was introduced, the full-time pay gap has narrowed by more than a third, but the part-time gender pay gap has changed very little since the 1970s.

These jobs in part-time work are often low paid, low status, with little opportunity for training or advancement.

Broken work lives

It is because of women's broken work lives, as well as lower income, that we are likely to earn less over our entire lives. Add to this our longer lifespans – so the money has to last longer – and it is not surprising that women stand a greater chance of living in poverty in old age.

In the same way that a small amount, saved regularly, builds up over time to create a fortune, so these seemingly small stops and starts in our career, usually triggered by children, can erode our financial wellbeing over a lifetime.

So what is the solution? Not to have kids? No, but when couples sit down to work out if they can afford to have children, they often look at fairly short-term factors – the cost of childcare versus a taxed, part-time income that the mother could earn. Not surprisingly, some couples come to the conclusion that it's cheaper to forego the childcare and have the mother stay at home. But there are other costs associated with this decision. Neither she, nor her company on her behalf, will be making pension contributions. This could put her in financial jeopardy in retirement unless her husband is willing to match those contributions while she is off work. According to the Fawcett Society, the number of women who are saving for retirement halves when they have a baby, whereas the figure for men remains unchanged when they become new fathers.

Another thing to take into consideration is that a woman's career progression may suffer as a result of taking time out of the workforce. She might find it difficult to get back into her industry when the children are older and may discover she has missed the opportunity to learn new skills.

The statistics show that women reach their peak earning

period between the ages of 30 and 39 whereas men hit their peak between 40 and 49. This means that they are likely to be more experienced and thus able to demand higher earnings. So, while women are off having kids, their spouses are earning more than ever. Unfortunately, the statistics also show that once you have passed this peak earning period in your life your income is likely to decrease steadily. So, if you're still young, make sure you exploit this period of your life while it lasts and put something aside for when life gets more expensive with the kids around.

Although this point is much debated, one of the reasons we might want to stay at home to take care of our children has nothing to do with money. The idea that you don't have to drag yourself into the office to face demanding bosses or deal with the responsibility of making money can seem like bliss. I know I have certainly been attracted to this idea and succumbed to it a few times. It's not that being a mother isn't incredibly hard and legitimate work, it's just that we may be doing it partly to give up responsibility for our lives. The idea of allowing someone else to take care of all the financial decisions, and to take care of us, is incredibly attractive. It's like going back to childhood ourselves. No wonder many women (and increasingly men) are attracted to this idea. The trouble is, they then often find it difficult to get back into the workforce and start doubting whether they are able to handle all that responsibility again. The problem with this fear-based approach is that it doesn't help you in the long term. Whenever you give in to weakness and make a decision because you are afraid, or it seems easier than facing reality, you lose confidence in yourself and it becomes progressively harder to take any action. Your life becomes filled with fears and doubts about whether you can handle things – a job, surviving on your own, juggling your finances. If you have decided to take some time off for your children, do it by all means, but analyse the real reasons why you are doing it first and make sure you keep setting yourself small challenges and maintain your independence.

The Plight of Single Parents

If you have decided to have a child, whether you continue working or not, it is essential to ensure that you have enough life insurance. This should cover both parents so that if anything should happen to either of you the other is not left struggling.

This last point should not be underestimated. In the UK, more than half of all lone-parent households are poor. Lone-parent households are at a far higher risk of poverty than all working-age adults and there has been very little improvement in their plight in the last decade. Women are more likely to fall into this category; around a quarter of all families in the UK are headed by a lone mother. Female-headed households have a particularly high risk of poverty because of women's lower earning capacity. Worse, lone parents are more likely to have a long-term illness or disability that prevents them from working.

Given the breaks in women's careers, the increased likelihood that they will be a single parent and their lower earning potential, it is not surprising then that they are more likely than men to be reliant on benefits. Benefits make up 21% of the average woman's income and just 8% of the average man's income. Lone mothers and female pensioners are the groups most likely to receive handouts in our society. No wonder groups like the Fawcett Society say that poverty in Britain has a female face.

While women are more likely to receive their income from benefits, men are more likely to receive an income from investments and savings. If you add it all up, men have a much greater chance of building up wealth over their lifetimes: higher wages, self-employment, investments and higher pensions. In comparison, women earn less, are more likely to stop working, earn less from investments or savings, and live longer, meaning their money has to stretch further. Taking time off work in the UK also reduces a woman's government pension entitlement.

Female Pensioners: Where You Could End Up

Certainly, more women these days are working, building up state pension entitlement, and saving through private pensions and other investment schemes. However, the current situation is that many elderly British women are struggling financially and many of the life choices that created this scenario are still being made by young women today.

One in five single female pensioners in Britain lives in poverty. Only 13% of today's women pensioners have their own entitlement to a full basic state pension, compared to 92% of men.

Even women in pensioner couples receive less on average than their husbands, usually because they have lower entitlement to a pension if they haven't worked for as long. Women are also less likely to have a private pension to top-up their state benefits. Retired men on average have between £50 to £100 per week more private pension income than women of the same age.

If you are thinking you can just rely on your husband's pension when he retires, or even if he dies, think again. Women often only receive a small portion of a man's pension when he is in retirement and after he has passed away. Many elderly women discover that while their husbands are alive they are able to get by. But once the husbands pass away, their income drops, yet they have a very similar level of living costs, so their living standard plunges.

You might think that the circumstances your grandmother has gone through will not be repeated for you, but the reality is that many women are still making the same mistakes their grandmothers did. Sure, they are more likely to have a job, but this doesn't mean they're building up savings. Many women still assume that their spouse's income will mean they don't have to worry – ignoring the fact that they may get divorced, he may die prematurely, or that he may have lied or underestimated his pension entitlements.

Women's lifetime income gap and general poverty is caused by many factors. Sometimes this is the result of choices we make and sometimes it is simply bad luck, such as the death of a spouse, limited opportunities growing up, or someone in your family falling ill and leaving you to take on caring responsibilities. Here is a summary of some of the things that can lead to female poverty:

* Taking time off work for kids, study or to care for elderly parents.
* Doing part-time work.
* Lower education levels.
* Being a minority.
* Ending up a single parent (because of choice, death, divorce).
* An injury or illness.

Fortunately, there are steps that savvy women can take to prevent, or at least minimise the risks associated with these life circumstances.

SOLUTIONS

* Improved education.
* Regular savings. Start young so that investment income can provide a top-up or safety net in hard times.
* Ensure all savings and investments are working hard for you, i.e. earning a good enough return so they are not whittled away by inflation.
* Ensure equal financial status in your relationship, e.g. half-ownership of your home, even if he is the one paying the mortgage while you take care of the kids.
* Ensure you have a separate pension that still receives contributions while you take time off for kids.
* Take out insurance to protect yourself and your family.
* Learn to negotiate to increase your earnings potential (see chapter on this).
* If you are single, move in with other single women, so you can support each other.
* Ensure you keep taking responsibility for your own financial future, even if you stop work for a time, and don't simply allow your partner to make all the decisions.
* Finally, be careful not to jeopardise your own financial situation for the sake of your kids or their education. This will just make them feel guilty and they need you to be in as strong a financial position as possible.

WHEN THERE'S TOO MUCH MONEY

With all the talk about women living in poverty, it may surprise you to discover that some women feel they have *too much* money.

A report by the Centre for Economics and Business Research (CEBR), found that women own 48% of the nation's personal wealth and are projected to own 60% of it by 2025. This apparent turnaround in our situation and optimistic projection is partly based on increased home-ownership among women and improved levels of education.

According to the ONS, British girls outperform boys at all levels of education from primary school right through to university. The number of women gaining two or more GCSE A Levels (or equivalent) has more than doubled in the last decade, more women than men are awarded National Vocational Qualifications, and now more women than men are entering full-time undergraduate university or college courses (54%).

However, these statistics are based on averages and mask the widening gap between wealthy women in our society and the extremely poor, such as pensioners and single mothers. Nevertheless, for those of us who fall into the middle, these figures are extremely hopeful and show that women are already improving their financial situation and aren't afraid to take control.

Interestingly, the authors of the CEBR report also think that women's longer life expectancy can work in their favour because many women will outlive their husbands and inherit their money. UK millionaires over the age of 65 are more likely to be women because of this.

'The exciting thing is the accumulation of assets of women on their own,' says Douglas McWilliams, author of the report. 'Women are more sensible in their savings behaviour than men and have 2% more in savings. In particular, women below 30 are more likely to have savings and investments and if this trend continues it will build up to a lot of money over time.' He also points out that UK millionaires under the age of 45 are now more likely to be women.

According to Diana Chambers, a US-based financial adviser to wealthy women, the majority of wealth in the US is already in the hands of women. Chambers' clients are women who have built their own businesses, inherited money from their parents or spouse or won a great divorce settlement.

This trend of leaving money to wives or daughters is likely to continue. In the best-selling book, *The Millionaire Next Door*, authors Tom Stanley and William Danko found that the majority of millionaires interviewed were more likely to leave their wealth to their daughters, rather than their sons. They felt their daughters were already financially handicapped, because of their lower earnings capacity, so they would not hesitate to help them. In contrast, they wanted their sons to feel independent and didn't want to encourage them to rely on financial subsidies from their parents.

Poor Little Rich Girl

However, wealth doesn't always bring happiness. Rather than their wealth being a cause for celebration, many of these women are, unfortunately, deeply disturbed by the thought of so much money. Many have not been taught how to handle such a high level of assets and this weight of responsibility, and the fear that they could lose the wealth, terrifies them.

According to Diana Chambers, even when one is born into a family of substantial financial resources, carrying primary responsibility for significant wealth can be extremely difficult, especially if received suddenly and accompanied by a major personal trauma such as death or divorce.

A good example is all the wives of firemen and policemen in New York who received significant insurance payouts after the 9/11 disaster. Many of these women found themselves in a better financial position than before the attack, but under the circumstances it brought them no joy; they even referred to the payouts as 'blood money'.

Several worries crop up when you find yourself in this supposedly fortunate position. Apart from the stress of wondering whether you will be able to manage the money responsibly, there is also a fear that any new friends you make are really only there for the money, or that you will become used to a certain lifestyle and spend too much, finding yourself back at square one.

MONEY DOESN'T MAKE YOU HAPPY

In fact, some people who suddenly come into money – either because of a lottery win or inheritance – do lose their entire fortune quickly. Research from Camelot, operator of the UK National Lottery, found 44% of winners had spent their fortune after five years and in the US there is some research to show that as many as one-third of lottery winners become bankrupt.

Unfortunately, it can be difficult to analyse the results of studies done into the effects on people of winning the lottery because much of it is conflicting. In the UK, Camelot's research could be construed as biased; they are providing the lottery, so obviously want to create a good impression. Their research emphasises that the majority of lottery winners report feeling very happy after a win and, what's more, they haven't lost any friends. In contrast, some US studies conducted by anti-gambling religious groups highlight the number of people going bankrupt or turning to drink and drugs after a lottery win. In one example, a Florida widow, who had won $5 million on the US lottery in 1984, lost all her money, her mansion and cars within three years. Worse, she also owed the taxman $500,000. Eventually, she was arrested for trying to hire a contract killer to murder her daughter-in-law, whom she blamed for her lottery misfortune.

Studies from more neutral sources seem to indicate that winning a significant amount of money can make people happier in the short term, but in the longer term it has little impact, with most people reverting to whatever state of mind they were in before this life change. The Camelot study found that after five years 43% of UK winners claimed their win had no effect on their happiness.

Brickman, Coates and Janoff-Bulman at the University of California-Regents conducted a study into both lottery winners and people who had suffered a physical injury, then monitored their levels of happiness. They found that immediately after the event, the lottery winners were happier and the injured were unhappy, but after eight weeks or less both groups returned to the level of happiness they had before the event.

So, finding yourself with stacks of cash won't necessarily cheer you up if you are already quite unhappy. However, the way this money is gained can sometimes have a psychological impact, especially if you are a little vulnerable to begin with.

Oppressed by Guilt

Some people receiving money through inheritance or divorce feel guilty, that they don't deserve the money, and are overwhelmed by a desire to get rid of it as fast as possible.

Certain circumstances can even lead to depression, such as a death leading to an inheritance. At these times we are more emotional than usual, less rational, and this type of thinking influences the way the money is spent.

Eileen Gallo, a Los Angeles-based psychotherapist, conducted a study over two years into people who had gained sudden wealth. Unlike previous studies, these people were not solely lottery winners and came from a wide variety of backgrounds. She discovered that many people viewed their windfall as a positive experience, but that it did affect their lives significantly and their experience was influenced by three major factors – their childhood experiences with money, their adult experiences with money and the effect the sudden wealth had on their life.

Participants who were given positive messages about money as children and were taught things such as *save, don't spend*, or *save and spend responsibly* were more likely to adapt well and view an inheritance, for example, as positive.

Married people were also better able to cope than singles and, interestingly, those who took an active approach to managing their wealth felt more positive about the experience. In contrast, people who considered themselves helpless when making money decisions were more likely to have a negative experience and feel taken advantage of by advisers or family members. In particular, relationships with siblings often suffered.

People who adapted well were also more likely to be introspective, viewing this life-changing event as a soul-searching time and thinking hard about how they could use their new-found wealth to make a difference in the world.

Charity

The link between how good people felt about the money and how generous they were with it is intriguing. The lottery winners study by Camelot found 40% of people increased contributions to charity after their win. This generous approach does seem to help people overcome their feelings of guilt and create a rewarding experience.

Gallo discovered that there was a connection between altruism, either towards a charity or helping family and friends, and adapting positively to sudden wealth.

She found that 90% of people who viewed the experience as positive said they either wanted to help their children financially, or else expressed concern about the effect their money could have on their children. However, none of the participants who rated their sudden wealth as a negative experience even mentioned their children during interviews.

One of the ways wealth adviser Diana Chambers helps her clients is by utilising her background of working for charitable organisations. She is able to make these women feel better about their wealth by showing them how it can be effectively used in society to help others. In this way, they can overcome some of the guilt they feel for having received the money in the first place.

Dealing with a big win

I'm sure there are a million things you could think of doing with a lottery win or large inheritance. Holidays abroad, a new house, lots of lovely clothes – it's delicious just thinking about it. But, if you do find yourself in this happy position, what do most financial advisers recommend?

* Pay off all your debts, especially credit cards.
* Reduce your fixed living costs, e.g. cut your rent/mortgage by buying a house or paying off the house you live in.
* Ensure you have adequate insurance.

* Make sure you have an emergencies savings account.
* Put some of the money in a low-risk savings account or bonds to provide you with an income that would replace your regular income in case you lose your job.

This is all very sensible stuff and certainly aimed at reducing your risks. Camelot research shows that many lottery winners do follow at least some of this advice. Of course, more than 85% had taken a holiday abroad since their win, but also more than 40% have moved home, and of these, 75% moved to a detached house. Prudently, 10% now have private medical care.

If your wealth is received in a traumatic way, such as because of the death of someone close, then make sure you recognise that you may not be feeling completely rational about anything, much less your finances. Put the money in a high-interest account for a couple of months until you have had time to cope and are capable of thinking about the future calmly. After a major trauma the future may seem scary and distant, so you need to take some time to adjust to this new situation and the last thing you need are stressful financial decisions. Once you feel better, you can get some expert advice and should be in a better position to analyse your options. In a later chapter we'll talk about creating a financial portfolio and assessing different investments.

JUSTINE'S TOP 10 TIPS

1) Remember that, as women, we are often better investors - more patient, trading less and more diversified.

2) Women's modesty works to our advantage as we are more likely to do proper research.

3) Don't allow your fear to take over and invest too conservatively.

4) Use shopping skills and 'street smarts' when investing.

5) As women, we are becoming more influential economically but need to improve our understanding of finance.

6) Lower lifetime earnings and career breaks put us at a disadvantage, so start early to build up savings and investments.

7) Money won't make you happy and is not a solution to your emotional problems.

8) If you receive a windfall don't make any rash decisions when you are still feeling emotional.

9) Do your own research and take control of your situation, rather than letting others lead you by the nose.

10) If you receive a windfall pay off your debts first, put aside some savings and think about donating a portion of it to charity.

THE PSYCHOLOGY OF MONEY

'It's attitude not aptitude that counts.'
Kathleen Gurney, money psychologist

Although there have been a lot of studies done into what's known as 'behavioural finance' – the study of why financial markets behave the way they do – there has been less research into why individuals behave the way they do around money.

Many people in the finance world seem to believe that subjects like psychology shouldn't be mixed up with finance because they like to see money as something sensible and rational. It is supposed to be like mathematics, where everything adds up and there are no vague, emotional influences or subjective views. It's easy to see why people like to think about money this way: it means you can control it more easily! However, money, like humans, is a fickle, flexible medium that sometimes lands in your lap when you least expect it, or runs out the door at the worst possible time. Learning to understand why money behaves a certain way is really about learning to understand why we behave a certain way around money. After all, money is simply an inanimate object that is designed to be used as a tool for our own use. Just as a tool in capable hands can achieve amazing things, so money can be used skilfully if you have some knowledge and understand yourself very well. If you don't realise how your upbringing or emotional outlook on the world affects your behaviour towards money, then you are more likely to see it slip through your fingers and be left wondering why.

The old phrase 'a fool and his money are easily parted' holds true. If you know very little about money and act foolishly around it, you won't keep it for very long. Some people actually know an awful lot about financial markets, yet still find wealth elusive. I believe this is because their emotional history is undermining their attempts to reap the financial rewards they so desire.

Money attitudes

What I term the 'psychology of money', or the way people behave towards money, and why, is a relatively new field. Nevertheless, there have been a few studies done to try to analyse why some people seem to attract wealth so easily and others seem to struggle with their basic finances.

Many of the psychologists and financial advisers who have looked into this subject believe that our upbringing has a strong influence on the way we view money and therefore the way we behave towards it. People brought up in households where they were taught how to save from an early age and were encouraged to spend carefully, seem to be better equipped to stay in control of their finances. However, there are many examples of people brought up in very poor households, or where money was spent unwisely, who went on to become millionaires. So, while your childhood experiences will *influence* you to some extent, they can't *dictate* your future. Ultimately, how you treat your money depends on your own personal choices and, even if your history has been riddled with examples of poor money management, this can be turned around. The secret is understanding what your current attitude is, why or how you developed it, which aspects of it make you unhappy, and then formulating a plan to change things and develop new habits that will help you reach your goals. As with many things in life, until you can recognise and correctly diagnose a problem it is difficult to fix it.

You're unique

The objective here is not to mould you into a money-mad entrepreneur who works ridiculously long hours to build up a fortune – that is simply one type of 'money personality', and not necessarily a healthy one. Rather, the aim is to discover what your unique money personality is and how it is affecting your life. Armed with this information you can then navigate the best way forward. You may decide that, in fact, you like the way you view money and don't want to change a thing, or you may just make slight adjustments.

Many of the studies done on our attitudes to money use glaring stereotypes to illustrate how some people behave towards their finances. However, every individual is unique and we all have our own perspective on the way we view money. Certain themes do seem to crop up, but you may find that you don't fall completely into one category. Our ideas about money are very closely tied to our beliefs. So, in the same way that you may consider yourself mostly left-wing, but agree with some of the ideas offered by a right-wing political party, so you may discover that you mostly have a carefree attitude to money, but are positively miserly when it comes to certain expenses. Therefore, don't look at these categories too strictly. The aim is simply to get you to think more about your attitudes and behaviour towards money. Sometimes, by identifying what you are not, you can see what you are.

HOW YOU BEHAVE DEPENDS ON HOW YOU THINK

In the first part of this chapter we're going to look at some of the studies that have been done into our thoughts about money and what has influenced our ideas. Later on, we'll look at what our behaviour towards money is and the many different ways that people act.

Many factors influence our views on money, such as:

* Parental influence.
* Life events (losses or windfalls).
* Our own poverty or prosperity thinking.
* Our personality (submissive or aggressive).

PARENTAL INFLUENCE

The beliefs and attitudes towards money that our parents held are crucial to understanding our own beliefs surrounding our finances, and in fact many other aspects of our lives. Because they were the first people to influence us and teach us, we absorbed many ideas from our parents without realising it. Phrases that our parents used such as 'money doesn't grow on trees' or 'waste not, want not' were soaked up by our sponge-like childhood brains, so that we often find ourselves repeating them to partners or children without thinking.

As adults, most people either mimic their parents' behaviour towards money or rebel against it. If you are trying to escape a poor upbringing, or disagree with the way one or both parents treated money, you are likely to swing to the opposite extreme in your behaviour towards your finances. By becoming aware of your own attitude and where it comes from, it's easier to see how conflicts with your friends, partner or children can arise, and how you can manage this and perhaps moderate your views or reactions to become more balanced. In a later chapter we will look specifically at how to resolve money conflicts with your partner and children.

LIFE EVENTS

Along with our upbringing, adult experiences can also influence our attitudes towards money. This is especially so if you experience a significant event such as losing your job or your business, get divorced or go bankrupt.

Losses

One famous example of someone who was strongly influenced by a financial loss is Benjamin Graham. He is considered by many to be the father of modern investment theory and wrote the book *The Intelligent Investor*. He was also the mentor for one of the world's richest and most successful stock market investors, Warren Buffett. But Graham may never have come up with his revolutionary investment theory if he hadn't been brought to the brink of bankruptcy by the great stock market crash of 1929.

After losing so much money on the stock market, Graham decided to stick with investing, but to take an ultra-cautious approach. He would only buy stocks that were at the bottom of the investment barrel and extremely cheap.

His protégé, Warren Buffett, later dubbed these 'cigar butt' stocks because they only had one puff left in them. Graham bought stocks that were valued very cheaply by the stock market, but which had assets such as factories or buildings which could be sold off at a higher price than the value of the whole company. He also made sure he didn't pin all his hopes on one investment and was well diversified in case some of these bets didn't work out. Throughout his life Graham stuck with this investment strategy which had been so highly influenced by his personal experiences. However, his protégé, Buffett, soon recognised that it was an overly fearful approach to investing, and that having a more rational view could lead to even greater profits.

Perhaps you know of other people in your life who have suffered a financial loss which has affected the way they look at money? Perhaps you watched your own parents suffer financially and that has affected your outlook. It's important for you to acknowledge these viewpoints before you can address your own financial health.

Windfalls

As discussed in an earlier chapter, a financial windfall can also have a major impact on people's attitudes and even have a negative affect on their state of mind. This doesn't have to be a million-pound lottery win. Even a relatively modest inheritance, business success, divorce settlement, insurance payout or company stock option payout can lead to stress if the person receiving the money has little or no experience of handling large sums of money.

These people may feel guilty and unworthy of receiving the money, or they may be terrified of losing it all because they know they don't have the skills which can be acquired by building wealth gradually. As motivational speaker Jim Rohn said: 'If someone hands you a million dollars, best you become a millionaire, or you won't get to keep the money.'

Dr Kathleen Gurney, a US money psychologist and author of *Your Money Personality: What It Is and How You Can Profit From It,* says that people can have blind spots when it comes to certain areas of their finances – habits that they repeat over and over again without realising it, or that the habit may be destructive. As she points out, it's only when you become aware of your blind spots that you can change them. So, take a long look at all the things that have influenced your attitudes towards money over the years, write down the sayings you heard your parents use and that sum up your beliefs about money, and any particular life events that have contributed to how you feel today.

POVERTY/PROSPERITY THINKING

Another US-based money psychologist, Dr James Gottfurcht, has spent many years researching this topic and building up a consultancy business to help people overcome negative financial habits. He believes that our childhood experiences have a deep and lasting effect on our adult behaviour, and that this is especially true when it comes to dealing with money.

Whether it's because of childhood influences or a later event, some psychologists split our resulting attitudes into two broad categories – poverty thinking (or a poverty mentality) and prosperity thinking (or abundance theory). Of course, humans are a little more complicated than that, and attitudes can be split into several more sub-categories, but for now let's examine these two.

Poverty Thinking

Poverty thinking is unfortunately very common in our society and most of us look at money in this way at least to some degree. It is a pessimistic and mistrustful way of looking at the world, and finances in particular. It is a belief that things will not work out and that disaster is always hovering on the horizon. People with this type of thinking assume that they are not capable of handling their finances well and that things will go badly for them. Deep down they don't believe they are either capable of amassing riches or that they deserve them. Even people who seem to be very wealthy and earn high incomes can be vulnerable to this type of thinking, particularly if they grew up in an environment where their family or those around them thought this way. This is what is known as the 'bag lady syndrome' in the US, where highly successful and wealthy women feel dominated by the fear that they will spend their retirement in abject poverty living on the streets.

The main emotion controlling the actions of these people is fear. With a poverty mentality you can be extremely fearful of any dealings with money which can lead to bad investment decisions and acting in an irrational way to market movements or economic events. According to Dr Gottfurcht, this extreme lack of confidence in their ability to handle money can make such people very difficult as clients for financial advisers because, even when they are given perfectly good financial advice, they don't believe it or are incapable of following it.

Of course, thinking of yourself as poor, and that you always will be, and not having confidence in your ability to manage money, will lead to exactly that result. It's not until you accept that you can manage your money effectively, and really have the desire to change and take control of your situation by learning as much as you can about money, that you will see success.

Prosperity Thinking

Prosperity thinking is something many people find hard to grasp. It's about putting your trust in the universe, having faith that things will work out and that God, or the universe, will provide. It's letting go, but also believing in yourself and that no matter what happens, if you lose your job or your business fails, everything will work out OK. The skills you have learnt will remain with you and enable you to build up your fortune again, perhaps even to a greater extent.

To many people, these ideas sound downright flaky. Yet, if you read the biographies of countless successful men and women you may be surprised to find that many had this ultra-optimistic attitude. Many also failed before they succeeded and went on to greater success.

By refusing to give up, and by having a strong belief in their own ability and right to wealth, these people were able to overcome incredible difficulties and eventually reach their goals. People with prosperity thinking have an optimistic state of mind and their beliefs influence their behaviour, so that everything they do (no matter what their present situation) leads them towards a clearly defined and visualised goal. These people also believe that they create their own future. So, if something negative happens in their lives they attribute it to the fact that they didn't work hard enough (not just bad luck). Similarly, if something good happens they take credit for it.

Act and Then Believe

You might be thinking, 'Well, that's all very interesting, but how on earth can I achieve this prosperity thinking?' It's a strange quirk of nature that what you believe affects what you do, but the reverse is also true. If you can do something regularly, you will eventually find yourself believing in it. For example, if you start going to the gym regularly and forcing yourself to eat a healthy diet, you will eventually start seeing yourself as healthy. All the evidence proves that you are, no matter how overweight you felt in high school or what your deep-seated beliefs might have been. It's similar with money. If you pay off your debts and start saving regularly, eventually you have to recognise that, no matter what your upbringing, your behaviour towards money is quite sensible. By constantly questioning our beliefs and taking action we can change them.

Every day you face challenges where you have to decide whether you are going to take a fear-based approach and let things overwhelm you, or whether you are going to tackle things head on. Often, when I've put off the fight, it has grown to become an even bigger problem that is harder to overcome later. As women, we tend to be quite cautious and fearful when it comes to money, often underestimating our abilities. Yet women consistently show that they are brilliant managers of other people's money, so there is really no reason why they can't manage their own money just as well. The good news is that taking control of your finances will not only give you increased confidence in your ability to manage your money, but it will also give you confidence in other areas of your life. Being able to control your finances means being able to control your destiny to a certain extent.

It means knowing that you can provide for yourself and don't have to become dependent on others. That's an amazingly powerful strength to have.

Creating Abundance Thinking

Studies have shown that if you think obsessively about a certain goal, such as becoming a teacher or buying a Porsche 911, and you really believe in the possibility of achieving this goal, you will eventually put yourself in a situation where it will come to you. However, this can also work in reverse. People who worry obsessively about how little money they have can actually perpetuate their weak financial position.

Therefore, attracting abundance has to start with recognising what you already have in your own life, realising how rich you already are, and then opening yourself up to more of these good things. It's not simply a case of acting as if you were rich, but recognising that you really are wealthy if you compare yourself to the millions all over the world less fortunate than you.

The second step is to clearly visualize yourself in the life you want to be leading, living in the house you want, surrounded by the things you want. In his book *Change Your Life in 7 Days*, Paul McKenna recommends creating a scrapbook or even a wall chart covered in cuttings and pictures of the things you want drawn to you. He even recommends creating a 'fake' bank statement with a fat balance so you can literally see how rich you want to become.

Another way that psychologists and assertiveness trainers categorise people's thinking is to label them submissive, aggressive or assertive.

Your Personality

A Submissive Tendency

When it comes to money, many people are submissive, particularly women. These are the people who say things like ‘Oh, don’t mind me’ or ‘You choose, I don’t care which film we watch’. They constantly say yes when they really want to say no. Submissive people are usually very ‘nice’, but they also get walked over. They find it hard to ask for what they want and end up feeling resentful when they don’t get it or others are rewarded instead. They are also terrified of any type of conflict and have a ‘nice at any price’ attitude. They’re the type of people who are likely to say things like, ‘If you can’t say anything nice, don’t say anything at all’. The trouble with this attitude is that if you continually repress your desires and needs for the sake of others, you end up feeling resentful and can even subconsciously attack other, often innocent, people because you feel badly done by.

Submissive behaviour can be quite destructive for the way you deal with money. Submissive people are less likely to ask for a pay rise even when they deserve one and rarely have the courage to really go for the things they want in life. They are the people who complain bitterly that their boss doesn’t appreciate them, or that they work for a terrible company full of greedy, rich executives. They take the position of victim and often expect others to take care of them financially, and may also end up in debt. They blame others for their situation, rather than taking responsibility for their future.

According to Robert Bolton in his book *People Skills*, being submissive can be hazardous for your health. ‘If repressed emotion does not escape…it remains to wreak destruction on the mind and/or body of the "nice" person. Diseases sometimes caused or aggravated by submissive behaviours include migraine headaches, asthma attacks, many skin diseases, ulcers, arthritis, chronic fatigue, hypertension, and high blood pressure.'

Studies of cancer victims have also found that people described as 'nice', but who are inhibited or bottle up their emotions, are more likely to fall victim to this disease.

An Aggressive Personality

In contrast, an aggressive attitude can often put people in positions of great wealth or power. These people have a tendency to continually put their own needs before others and even try to control or overpower people. They can be abusive and dominating. However, although this behaviour can achieve results in the short term, it is not a healthy way to live or to achieve financial success. It is the opposite to submissive behaviour, but neither response is appropriate. Such a greedy attitude to money does have a negative psychological affect on the person exhibiting this behaviour. They often feel out of control of their emotions, and their aggression may be the result of deep-seated insecurity where they need to prove themselves by overpowering or dominating others. They are likely to have extreme swings in their emotions and end up feeling very guilty for their behaviour afterwards. Also, other people distrust and dislike aggressive people and often do things to undermine them, or simply refuse to comply with their demands. This can leave the aggressive person feeling very lonely. Their health can be affected badly by such negative emotions and they are more likely to suffer from heart attacks or coronary disease.

The Middle Ground – Being Assertive

Standing up for your rights, refusing to let others push you around, but respecting other people's views and not trying to dominate them, is obviously the best solution. Not only will a more mature approach to life and relationships improve your health and sense of wellbeing, but it can also fill your purse.

By asking for what you deserve, and not being too ashamed or shy to allow wealth into your life, you make yourself happier and that benefits others around you.

Studies have shown that the happiest people in the world are those who are doing something for other people.

Psychologist Abraham Maslow, who devoted his life to the study of psychologically healthy people, found that these people were involved in causes that forced them to deal with other people's problems rather than focusing on their own.

You don't have to give up your day job and go and become a Buddhist monk or work full-time for a charity to benefit others and the community around you. As I've shown, extreme reactions can have negative side-effects. Taking a calm, middle path will not only ensure your own financial and emotional needs are met, but also ensure that you are a benefit to, rather than a burden on your family and community. Greater financial security, achieved in an ethical way, makes you happier and means you can afford to give more to charities. As Abraham Lincoln said, 'You can't help the poor by being one of them'. Many rich, successful business people in our society have used their wealth to retire early and devote themselves to charitable activities.

Money Behaviour

According to psychologist Eilleen Gallo, our thinking or our feelings about money colour the way we act towards it. So, if you don't already have an idea about what your money attitudes are, then ask yourself these questions.

* Does having money make you feel: secure, free, anxious, dependent or guilty for having too much?
* Do you see money as a measure of your self-esteem?
* Do you consider yourself thrifty or a spender? Do you feel like there's never enough money to go around and worry about not having enough, or feel like you will always be fine and that, when you need money, it will come to you?
* Do you feel secure or insecure in your relationship with money? Do you find it worrying and a drain on your life and happiness, or do you think there are a couple of things you'd like to improve, but overall the situation is OK?

The following definitions may help you answer some of these questions and see where your attitudes lie on a scale from one extreme to another. It breaks down our behaviour in terms of how money is acquired, how we use or spend it and how we manage it. Most people will no doubt be in the middle somewhere, or you may find you are more focused on one aspect of money – such as earning it – but are more lazy when it comes to managing your finances.

Making Money

First have a look at your attitudes to earning money. Imagine a scale where, at one end, you have the extreme example of someone who is insatiable in their desire to earn money. For example, you may picture a businessman or woman who is so obsessed with acquiring money that they are prepared to work very long hours, sacrificing family life and even health, in the pursuit of their goal. It doesn't matter how many millions they make, their desire for money is insatiable and they judge their ability to make money as a measure of their self-esteem. Losing their job or business is the worst thing for these people. They may have been taught as a child that financial success would bring approval, or that it was possible to 'buy' love.

At the opposite extreme is someone who actively dislikes money and thinks it is the root of all evil. Like religious followers in times gone by, these people shun all symbols of wealth and live an austere existence, even suffering to prove that they are not under the control of any financial incentives. Even when opportunities are offered to them to make more money they walk away, or refuse a promotion saying that money isn't important to them. In fact, these people may simply be terrified of the responsibility that having money brings, so label it as evil because they are afraid of it. Now think about where you might fit on this scale.

Spending

This is another scale. At one extreme is the shopaholic who compulsively overspends. For them, spending has become like a drug where they crave shopping and buy themselves little presents whenever they feel down. Going on a spending spree becomes like binge-eating – handing over credit cards or piling up lots of purchases gives them a rush of exhilaration, but afterwards they experience the come-down. They may rush home and guiltily hide their shopping bags or bank statements, so that their partner doesn't find out. They may even come up with ingenious ideas on how to fiddle the figures, or take out credit cards in secret to give their partner the impression that they haven't spent as much as they really have.

The opposite of the shopaholic is the miser. This person may earn a lot of money but finds it difficult to spend it, perhaps because they are fearful of losing all their wealth and ending up in poverty. These people may be so obsessed with scrimping and saving that they make irrational decisions.

Millionaire Hetty Green was born in 1834 to a wealthy American family and inherited $7.5 million at the age of 21. Despite being born with a silver spoon in her mouth, she was obsessed with budgeting and investing. Her careful investing allowed her to build up her inheritance to $100 million by the time of her death in 1916.

However, her penny-pinching sometimes came at a cost. She famously refused to pay for medical care which resulted in her 15-year-old son losing his leg.

Managing Finances

At one end is the micro-manager who watches where every penny is spent. Unlike the miser, they may be prepared to spend money when necessary, but you can be sure that it is recorded in a little book or on a computer somewhere. These are the people who buy financial software programmes and meticulously calculate any gain in their investments. They may also collect coupons or discount vouchers, even when they can easily afford to pay full price.

At the other end is the extremely disorganised and chaotic manager of money. They avoid opening bank statements or put off paying bills until the last minute, so that their credit record is harmed or they end up paying fees for late payment. Even when they have the money to pay off a credit card bill, they may become frozen with indecision or simply put it off so that they end up paying large amounts in interest. Larger financial decisions such as buying a house are too terrifying to contemplate. They may follow their partner when they view properties, but leave all the decision-making and effort up to them. Again, fear may be behind this disorganised behaviour, because often these people can be quite organised in other areas of their life.

Taking control

So how does it help to understand what your money personality is? I believe if you can recognise where your money habits are coming from and realise how you are behaving – sometimes irrationally – towards money, you are on the first step to changing any habits you are unhappy with.

How many times have you met someone who seems to have everything – looks, personality, intelligence – yet they continually fail to make themselves happy or get what they want from life? Often, it is a person's feelings about themselves that influence how they behave. The trick is to turn that situation on its head and start doing things that are positive, so that you will eventually start to believe in yourself and your own ability to manage your money, and your life, effectively.

Jessica's story

Jessica was an intelligent woman who earned a decent living and had plenty of opportunities to receive all the things in life that she would have liked. However, she consistently earned below her potential and was nervous about asking for a pay rise, so allowed her employer, and others, to exploit her. When her pay did come in, she spent it quickly and was often in overdraft and had lots of credit card debt. She also had a student loan that she felt was looming over her head and felt incapable of ever being able to pay it off. Jessica felt she was simply bad with money and avoided looking at her credit card bills every month, shoving them in a drawer or under the bed so that she didn't have to face financial reality. Jessica's mother had also been 'bad with money'. She often frittered away her husband's pay on little gifts for herself and there were never any savings left to pay for family things. Jessica felt her mother's approach to money was irresponsible and she was angry with her for this, yet she felt destined to follow in her mother's footsteps. She assumed that being able to handle money was something hereditary and no matter what she did, she simply didn't believe she would be capable of change. Every time she tried to save and do the right thing, something would go wrong. An unexpected bill would come in, or she'd be tempted out by friends on an expensive night on the town, or she would get depressed about her job and buy herself something to cheer up.

Jessica was very unhappy with her relationship with money, her job and even her marriage. She felt life was spiralling out of control and longed for the days when she had been a child and adult things like money were someone else's problem.

Things came to a head when her husband left. It was a

painful shock, especially as he had always managed the household finances, but Jessica used that opportunity to change cities, change her job and start a new life. For the first time she had to start taking responsibility for her finances, her health and her life. Her new job, in a completely different profession, paid less than her previous one, but her living costs were lower in the new town, so she found, miraculously, that she was able to start saving. She had managed to get a decent settlement from her divorce, so that helped pay off some old debts and she could have a fresh start with her new life. Little by little, the more Jessica saved each month, the more she started to realise that not only was she capable of handling money, but she even enjoyed it. Being responsible and having some control over her finances gave her a new-found sense of achievement and pride. She realised that she didn't have to treat money the way her mother had, and that she was perfectly capable of saving and even investing. Before long, she also met someone new and now she is happily married and, finally, happy with her relationship with money too.

MONEY AND SPIRITUALITY

'Do not value money for any more nor any less than its worth; it is a good servant but a bad master.'
Alexandre Dumas fils, *Camille*, 1852

There is no point to having wealth if it doesn't make you happy. I believe that it is not enough simply to feel prosperous, you also need to have a healthy attitude towards money and feel in control of it, rather than feel it is controlling you. One way to achieve this is to ensure your money is used efficiently and for a good purpose. Take what you need for yourself and your family, and use what's left over to aid your spirit and the community around you. Being financially independent means having choices; it can also mean being able to afford to give to your favourite charity on a regular basis.

In the West there is a lot of guilt surrounding money. We are brought up to believe that it's bad to be too interested in money. But you don't have to love money to use it well, you just need to respect it. In the same way that you might respect the weather and not take it for granted, so money must be respected before it can be used effectively. In Asian societies, wealth is seen simply as good fortune. Buddhism considers wealth as one of the pillars underlying happiness.

> 'In Buddhism . . . there is a reference to the four factors of fulfilment, or happiness: wealth, worldly satisfaction, spirituality, and enlightenment. Together, they embrace the totality of an individual's quest for happiness.'
>
> Dalai Lama

MONEY IS LIKE WATER

For me, money is a bit like water – it's a valuable resource that we all need, but which a lot of people waste. In the right hands, it has the power to do a lot of good, just as in the wrong hands it can be used badly. People with too much money sometimes don't use it efficiently and waste it on crazy things like six sports cars. Yet there are plenty of people literally dying because they don't have enough of it.

Getting involved with charity and helping others not only improves a wealthy person's relationship with money, but it can also aid those on much smaller incomes.

If you always feel like there is never enough money to go around and have a deep-seated feeling of lack, then a good antidote is to visit a Third World country, or even a very poor neighbourhood near you, and observe how others less fortunate than you manage to survive. Sometimes we are so busy worrying about how little money we have in comparison to our neighbours that we don't realise how rich we really are. One of the reasons you may be feeling poor is because you are comparing yourself to a rich neighbour, friend or relative. Trying to compete in this way is a futile business and can damage not only your wealth, but also your happiness.

If your goal is to improve your relationship with money and start feeling good about it, instead of bitter or lost, then there are a couple of hurdles you may need to jump. The first is to recognise that your situation may not be as bad as you think. The second is to take responsibility for your situation and promise yourself that you will make the changes necessary so that your future is brighter. The third and last step is to take that action and stick to it persistently. Taking control, even if you are afraid to, will dramatically improve your confidence and mood. By feeling angry or victimised by our financial situation, we not only suffer ourselves, but can also hurt those around us.

By changing the way you look at money and changing the way you deal with it, you will not only feel more positive and hopeful but your new outlook on life will make you kinder towards others, attracting many new friends.

'There are people who have money and people who are rich.'
Coco Chanel

JUSTINE'S TOP 10 TIPS

1) Take the quiz and figure out your own attitudes towards money. How have these been influenced by the events and people in your life?

2) Although we are all unique, it's likely that you will fit into a certain category. Are you a spender or saver? Are you obsessed with earning money or think wealthy people are greedy?

3) If you have a very negative view of money and it has caused pain in your life, try to figure out which specific influences may have contributed to that, and whether or not you want to continue behaving in the same way.

4) If your parents had a destructive attitude to money it doesn't mean you have to as well. You can build a different kind of life.

5) Change your behaviour first and your beliefs are likely to follow.

6) When you step outside of yourself and focus your thoughts on helping other people you often forget your own problems.

7) Form an investment club or even a money bookclub to talk to other people about your experiences and attitudes. You may discover you are not alone in certain behaviours so will feel less guilty about them. The support will help you put an end to any further self-destructive behaviour.

8) Log on to one of the money chatrooms on Yahoo or the Motley Fool website (**www.fool.co.uk**) to chat to people anonymously about these issues.

9) Remember, you are not alone. There are plenty of people who are just as bad if not worse; don't be afraid to talk about money.

10) Focus on the good things you have in your life and learn to appreciate the abundance that is all around you. In the same way that, when you go on a diet you suddenly start craving pudding, if you feel miserable and poor, you will suddenly get the urge to spend. Therefore focus on all the great things you have already.

BUDGETS

'We can tell our values by looking at our chequebook stubs.'
Gloria Steinem

Once you have worked out what psychological influences are affecting the way you treat money, you can begin to form some positive habits that will improve your relationship with money.

First work out where all the money is going with a budget.

* Then clear your debts.
* Build up some savings.
* Invest your savings.

First you need to create an easy-to-follow budget, so that you know where your money is coming from and, more importantly, where it is going. This doesn't have to be difficult; the trick is to keep your budget as simple as possible, so that you don't have to spend a lot of time on it. Then, if you have a lot of credit card debts that are making you uncomfortable, you will need to create a plan for how to clear those. We will look at debt in more detail in the next chapter. Third, if you haven't started already, set up a savings account that can provide not only a 'buffer' for hard times, but that will also lead you to the fourth and final step – investing. By building up an investment portfolio, you can provide yourself with a second income that will supplement your regular job and could eventually replace it.

WHY BOTHER?

As we saw in the first section of this book, women's situation in society, our lower earnings and the increased likelihood that we will take a career break, mean that we need to be better with money than men. You might think you are doing OK at the moment because you are earning decent money, making all your debt repayments and perhaps have some assets. But things can, and usually do, go wrong.

A few years ago, I had just bought myself a new flat with my partner. It was a complete tip and, as he didn't have any savings, I poured any spare cash I had into renovating and furnishing it. With an older property, things are always going wrong: the boiler breaks down and you are without hot water and heating in the middle of winter; the roof starts leaking after a storm and the insurance company decides it's somehow your fault; the builders you get in steal your bicycle. All of this happened to us. Then, my partner got ill and, as the NHS was no help, I ended up forking out a significant sum to help him get better. Not long after this, perhaps it was even prompted by this traumatic event, we decided that our relationship wasn't going to work after all and decided to split. Suddenly, I was living in a half-renovated property, paying two mortgages with one income instead of two.

It felt like overnight I had gone from feeling content about my financial situation to full-blown panic.

Thank God I didn't lose my job as well, or things could have become really nasty, but throughout it all I had one consolation: my savings account or 'buffer' as I refer to it. This was some money I started saving when I was still a teenager and had never – and still haven't – dipped into. I knew that if things really came to the crunch I would at least have those savings. In the end, I didn't have to dip into my savings because I just massively cut back on my outgoings. I walked to work, packed a lunch, became positively anal with my food shopping, invited friends to dinner instead of going to restaurants and made sure I never had to catch a taxi. Eventually, I was also able to rent out a room which really helped.

My point with all this is to remind you that many of the people who end up at the Citizens Advice Bureau over debt counselling are there because of a change in circumstances just like I went through. Whether it's divorce, job loss, pregnancy or ill-health, these sudden changes in your life (and believe me, you never see them coming) can have a radical effect on your finances. That's the main reason why I save and stick to my budget, because I know these things happen, that insurance and other safety nets don't always help, and I don't want to ever find myself on my knees financially because of them.

YOU DON'T HAVE TO BE A 'NATURAL' TO LEARN HOW TO BUDGET

I wasn't always good with money. Sure, I started young (at 17), but when I was in high school I was never able to save a penny. We were given around £20 a semester, but mine had always disappeared within the first few months of school, while my best friend Melinda always had some cash left over at the end of term.

While I was swept away by the colours, the smells and the sheer novelty of being in a shop and having money to spend, she would calmly and carefully choose only what she really desired. I always seemed to buy more, and eat more, than I needed while she seemed magically able to restrain herself. From her example, I learnt how to do a budget and my life changed. I amazed myself with my ability to build up savings. Watching all that money accumulate was incredible and filled me with a sense of pride and achievement. I could suddenly start making calm, rational decisions about money the way my friend Melinda had.

IT'S HOW YOU LOOK at IT

Some people may argue that a budget isn't really essential. That it's OK to take a more relaxed attitude as long as you are still saving. If that works for you, and you consistently save a set amount each month without the discipline of a budget, then that's fine. But for most people a budget ensures you have a clear idea of exactly where your money is going, and personally I don't think I would be able to save, especially in tough times, if I didn't keep track of my expenses.

The trouble is, budgets are a bit like diets: just the mere mention of them and people quail in terror. I like to flip this thinking on its head and look at it as simply a means to an end. A strategy to control your spending so that you can save, and that leads you to all the fun stuff like holidays, the home of your dreams, and being able to afford to buy something really wonderful once in a while.

Rather than thinking of budgets in terms of denying yourself something and saying you are not allowed to spend 10% of your earnings, you tell yourself that you are paying yourself 10% for your future. And surely your future is important enough to you that it deserves this investment?

The best-kept secret about money

Budgets are important no matter what your age or income. It doesn't matter that you have thousands of pounds pouring into your account if you are spending it all just as quickly as it comes in. What's the point of working so hard to learn about investing and make your money work for you if you have a leak in your pocket and all the money is draining away because you don't have a proper budget and can't control your spending?

This is the great secret of money – the more you earn, the more you are tempted to spend. As your level of income rises, the amount you think you can afford to spend on little luxuries floats up too, in direct proportion.

For example, when you were a student, you probably didn't mind having parties at a friend's place where you all brought your own alcohol and sometimes food as well. Living on pot noodles was almost an adventure because it's what all your friends were doing and you didn't worry so much about your waistline. Tracking down bargains at the local Oxfam was part of the experience as well. Once you started work and were earning a reasonable amount though, your expectations suddenly skyrocketed. All your friends were going out to cool clubs and eating at fancy restaurants, so you wanted to as well. You justified all that extra money you were spending on clothing as a necessary investment to ensure you kept your job.

As you get older these expectations just keep building. Suddenly it's essential that you have a car, go on foreign holidays, buy a flat and then a house, put your kids into day care and then a private school...and what about buying a holiday house overseas? All your friends seem to be doing that these days. Perhaps you've even been attracted to stock market investment simply because it's something everyone else seems to be doing.

This is natural really. Humans are ambitious creatures, if we didn't always dream about having more, we would never have evolved. However, sometimes when you justify this increased spending, because you decide that now you can afford it, you put off saving yet again. Somehow savings stay elusive, we put them at the bottom of our list of priorities, as if we don't deserve this one luxury that could change our lives so much.

What money has in common with chocolate

There is a law in economics called 'The Law of Diminishing Returns'. It sounds very impressive, but it always reminds me of the way some people spend money. Imagine you have a box of chocolates. The first one you eat always tastes amazing, particularly if you're very hungry. After that, each one tastes better and better until you reach a certain point, sometimes called the *satiation point*. After that, each chocolate you force yourself to eat is less and less enjoyable. If you continue eating, you will literally make yourself sick and won't want to look at another chocolate again in your life. Sometimes, it's difficult to figure out where this satiation point is, and whether or not we've reached it. You may have noticed that sometimes you just get into a spending frenzy where you waste lots of money, but it doesn't bring you much satisfaction, and afterwards you feel a bit sick and depressed. You've passed your satiation point! You probably had too much money to spend, so you blew it. Often, having less money means we are far more efficient with it and therefore get more enjoyment out of each penny spent.

FOCUS ON THE BIG THINGS

If you tell yourself that your savings are really just deferred spending for something bigger – a house, a year or two off to study, your retirement – then it is harder to justify spending money on the little things like lattes and fashion magazines because they get in the way of your big dream.

The trick is to get into the habit of saving as soon as you can. Then it doesn't matter what life brings your way. You will still earn more, as you have more experience, and spend more as well, but it won't come at a cost to your future. You'd be surprised how easy it is to live on 90% of your income instead of 100%; in fact, you may not even notice the difference.

I started saving when I was at university and living on around £40 a week. A lot of my friends were on the same amount and found it a real struggle. They complained bitterly about being a 'poor student' and were always asking their parents for more money, which was mostly spent on beer. Instead, I looked at managing on a limited income as a challenge and tried to track down all the bargains I could. Besides, in those days £40 seemed like a small fortune to me because I had previously had to scrounge pocket money from my parents or from odd jobs. Even though £40 sounds like a small amount now, at the time it was more money than I'd ever had before in my life.

Think about how you managed to get by when you were younger, or during a period when you were earning less. Did it feel like a chore then? Do you remember being happy at a time when you had a lot less money?

See it as a challenge – not denial

Once you start to look at budgeting in a positive light, it actually becomes enjoyable. You have to use your imagination to come up with meals that are cheap as well as healthy; dinner parties that are fun without breaking the bank; and enjoyable days out that don't cost a penny. Abide by the saying that the best things in life are free, and you will find it can actually be quite liberating to detach yourself from this consumerist society of ours and do yourself some good at the same time. Besides, it's great watching your money pile up in a bank account and you can pat yourself on the back every month when you take a look at your statement, instead of hiding it under the couch where your partner won't see it.

Take a long, hard look

The most difficult part for most people is forcing themselves to take a long, hard look at their finances rather than ignoring the bank statements when they come in, and seeing where all the money is actually going. It's amazing how much can be wasted on tiny things like buying newspapers and magazines, grabbing a coffee on your way to work, always buying lunch or dinner out. Little things that really don't make a great difference to our life (like just one extra cigarette/drink/chocolate) can really add up to a lot over time. Just as every little percentage point of extra return on your investments makes a big difference in the long term, so every extra pound wasted now doesn't have the chance to be invested and whittles away at your financial health. It might not seem like much at the time, but the result is that you are held back, don't reach your financial goals and feel stuck in a hole.

HOW TO BUDGET

Start by taking out your bank statement, receipts and anything else lying around to try to figure out what you have been spending your money on. If this doesn't help much, start keeping a money diary where you write down everything you spend during the week.

Again, make sure you look at this little book in a positive way. Don't beat yourself up about what you are spending your money on, just write down everything in a non-judgemental way, no matter how tiny the amount and use it as a tool for self-observation. This tool doesn't just help you get an idea of where all that money is going, it also gives you an idea of what you value in life. We all have things that we choose to splurge on. For me it's indulging in bath products at Boots. Every time I walk in there, I know I'm going to come out with far more things in my bag than were on my shopping list. Other friends spend all their spare cash on shoes, or fancy lingerie or countless magazines. We all need some luxuries in life – the trick is making sure you are controlling them and not going overboard with treats. Don't let them control you.

You may also find that the things you really value in life are not what you spend your money on. Are you stopping yourself from buying a lovely bunch of flowers that would cheer you up no end because they're viewed as too expensive, but frittering away a lot more money on cappuccinos or things that don't really add much to your life?

Budget Table

ITEM	PER WEEK	PER MONTH	ANNUAL
Savings			
Mortgage/Rent			
Gas/Electricity			
Phone			
Council Tax			
Transport			
Food			
Holidays			
Entertainment			
Clothes			

Prioritise your life (and your spending)

Once you have a clear idea of where your money is going, you can draw up a table putting your expenses in categories like the one shown. You can split the figures up by week or month, but I find it easier to keep track of things if I am looking at it on a weekly (or even daily) basis. Normally, I split up the big things (rent/mortgage) over the month, but then break down the more frequent expenses like food shopping and entertainment, so that I keep track of them on a weekly basis. Keep it simple! If you know you can only spend say £50 a week on the fun stuff (which I categorise as 'entertainment') you will be much more choosy about whether you should buy that particular handbag/ magazine/coffee etc. Take your weekly allowance out of the cash machine on Monday, then you know that when you run out you can't do whatever has just been proposed. It doesn't matter if you go over a little bit one week, just ensure you make it up the next week.

'They who are of the opinion that money will do everything, may very well be suspected to do everything for money.'
George Savile

This is the very simple budget I use. I try to keep it as short as possible, so that I can remember exactly where my money is going. When things like birthdays or postage costs crop up, I just make sure I cover them from my entertainment allowance. When I am really tight on money, I cut my clothes allowance completely and cope by asking for certain items for my birthday or Christmas. At other times, I add certain expenses like education/training. Budgets are very personal. Your budget may differ or need to be longer, especially if you have children and need to cover things like school fees and their clothes. It's true children are not cheap, but you don't have to spend a fortune on them. The average cost of raising a child in the UK is around £8,000 a year – most of which is due to childcare. So, if you can somehow reduce childcare (for example, by getting your family to help out), you can massively cut your costs. Many other savings can be made as well without harming your child's upbringing.

Certain expenses, such as utility bills, arrive monthly, but others, like food, I like to work out on a weekly basis because it helps me keep a closer eye on them. By looking at the annual cost of things, it gives you an interesting perspective. I particularly use the annual column for things like holidays and clothes.

DON'T LET EMPTY POCKETS HOLD YOU BACK

'But I can't afford it!' you cry. 'You don't understand, Justine. You probably earn a lot more than I do and it's just impossible to scrape by on my earnings.' Hmm, if this is how you feel, then the best advice I can give you is to go and speak to your grandmother and ask her how much she used to live on and what she did to get by. A few stories about making soup from old bones might make you see things differently. People didn't always have all the things we take for granted these days. I lived without a TV for several years, made my own lunch and walked to work, but was more happy in my life than a few years later when I was earning more money. We all know money doesn't equal happiness, but still let it control our lives and dictate our moods. When you're feeling low it's important to remember that it's not money itself that is the source of all evil, it's how we treat it.

The best lesson I ever learnt on how to get by on very little was when I went to Russia. I stayed with a lady who was quite well-off by Russian standards, yet she never wasted a thing. If I didn't finish my meal, which would upset her greatly as she was an excellent cook, she would feed the leftovers to her cat or find another use for it. The really ingenious thing was how little rubbish she threw out. She could minimise her rubbish to a bag the size of a packet of flour. Which was just as well, as refuse collectors were pretty thin on the ground in Russia and she had to walk a long way to get rid of it. I also noticed that, in Russia, unlike London, you never saw items discarded on the street. In London, one morning on my way to work I saw an old jumper, a broken umbrella, a half-eaten box of chips and an entire cooked chicken. You would never see these things in Russia; they couldn't afford to waste things like that. Many old *babushkas* were so poor that they would stand at the entrance to the metro selling kittens, or mushrooms picked from the forest. When I gave them my spare change, they literally wept with gratitude.

If you really think you're not earning enough to survive, then perhaps you should focus on what you can do to improve your situation. It might sound harsh, but thinking of yourself as a victim won't get you anywhere. The only way to fix things is to look for solutions, not excuses. Can you take evening classes to improve your qualifications and get a pay raise? Can you get another job that pays better? Can you get a part-time job? Are there welfare benefits you could be taking advantage of but don't know about or are too proud to accept? Once you really put your mind to coming up with a creative solution it's amazing what opportunities appear.

The stigma of poverty

In the UK, there is a great deal of stigma about being poor. People are naturally proud, and if they are really feeling poor the last thing they want is for their neighbours, or anyone else for that matter, to know about it. This kind of adult peer group pressure can be incredibly destructive. It can lead people into high levels of debt, just so they give the impression that they are as well off as their peers or living the way they think everyone else is. A study was once done in the UK to see if people bought unbranded products at the grocery store. The surprising result was that many of the poorest people, such as single mothers, refused to buy these much cheaper products because they didn't want anyone looking into their shopping trolley and knowing that they were poor.

Peer group pressure

We can all be affected by this kind of peer group pressure. It isn't just something that affects children and highly strung teenagers. Someone I know recently bought a brand-new sports car, one that I have dreamt about owning. At first, I was green with envy, but then he told me how much he was paying a year in insurance and my envy fizzled. I don't currently have a car, but my partner drives a very sensible, if less sporty, car that is exactly right for his needs and easily affordable. Thinking about how sensible his decision was, and how I probably would have done the same thing, gave me a feeling of moral righteousness which, thankfully, wiped out any feelings of greed I might have been harbouring before. Besides, when people buy fancy cars or very expensive clothes it is often because they are trying very hard to give the impression that they are doing well, even when they're not. The strange thing is that this acquaintance is quite scared to drive his new car too often. It is quite difficult to handle, and he's terrified of having an accident and paying for all those expensive repairs. Perhaps one day I'll feel rich enough that buying such a car won't feel like an outrageous expense. In the meantime, I'm happy to resist temptation and treat my finances more sensibly.

Keeping up with the Joneses

Katie is a successful marketing executive I know who works for a large, multinational firm in London. She earns above the average wage and lives with her boyfriend, Mike.

Although Katie seems to have it all, she is miserable, even desperate. Recently, she complained to me that she feels poor, like she is struggling to make ends meet, and wanted to know how she could make more money. She has become obsessed with money and buys every financial or get-rich-quick book she can find.

The trouble is that getting a pay rise won't solve Katie's problem. Her issue is not her income. In a way, the source of her problems are her friends.

Her best friend works in the City and earns far more than she could ever dream of, while her boyfriend works in the media, where he is also paid an exorbitant salary. The reason Katie feels poor is because she is constantly comparing herself to these richer friends and trying to 'catch up' to them. When her friends invite her out to dinner, followed by a concert and then an expensive night of clubbing, she finds it hard to refuse. She wants to join in the fun even though she knows she can't really afford it. So she goes out, has a great time, and the next day wakes up feeling miserable. Like a lot of people with credit card debts, Katie's desired lifestyle far exceeds her real income, but blaming her friends or peer group pressure won't solve anything. She has to be honest with herself and stop trying to live a life that doesn't make her happy, just because she's too afraid to say no to her friends. She has to decide what is more important – trying to live a glamorous life she can't really afford, or taking care of her own peace of mind, living within her means and building something for the future.

If you are honest with your friends and admit that you really can't afford to do something, they'll understand, especially if they are true friends. Whenever I've done this with some ridiculously wealthy friends, they have always been completely sympathetic and simply proposed something more affordable. I try not to waste my time wishing I was as rich as them; instead, I focus on enjoying all the benefits I get from having such wonderful friends in my life. I know the price they've paid to achieve those riches, and in many cases, I wouldn't be prepared to pay the same price, so I am content with my situation. If you are feeling resentful towards your friends for being too rich, perhaps it's because you are dissatisfied with your career or lack of savings and investments. Instead of becoming bitter, focus on what you can do to improve your lot.

'I am opposed to millionaires but it would be dangerous to offer me the position.'

Mark Twain

Justine's Top 10 Tips

1) There will always be someone richer than you, just as there will always be someone who seems prettier. So don't waste your time comparing yourself with rich friends.

2) Compare yourself to those who are less fortunate. Speak to your grandparents or people who have been through a difficult time financially and made it eventually. Learn from their money management techniques.

3) Avoid temptation. Find a new route into work so you don't walk past shops you know you will just 'have' to step into.

4) Find activities to do on the weekend that don't involve shopping. Join a community garden, find a hobby, go for a jog or do some charity work.

5) Don't punish yourself every time you go over budget, just resolve to spend less the next week.

6) The more positive you are, the more effective you will be. When you're depressed you often want to spend more to try to cheer yourself up so do things that make you happy.

7) If you are spending because you are feeling down, look at exactly what is causing this unhappiness and what you can do to improve the situation.

8) Stop ignoring bills and statements. Sit down now and work out exactly what your financial situation is. Put a figure on how much debt you are in or how much savings you have.

9) Once you know exactly where you are, then you can start to work out an action plan. Keep a diary of all your expenses for a month and then create a simple budget.

10) Stop looking at magazines that make you feel poor or greedy for possessions you don't have. See your situation as a challenge, not a problem, and make a list of things you can do to earn more or cut your expenses.

DEBT

Over the years, many of my friends have found themselves in trouble with money and come to me for advice. Usually, they are stressed and worried, they feel like their lives are spinning out of control, the bills are stacking up and they're not sure how they are going to meet all their expenses. Time after time, I've sat down with them and we've worked out a budget together and I've told them all I know about saving and investing. They nod their heads obediently and then go away and ignore everything I've said. Budgets are forgotten and good savings habits, like New Year's resolutions, never get off the ground. Although frustrating, this has finally led me to realise that motivating people to take good care of their money takes a lot more than teaching them how to do a budget. Your attitude to money, how you feel about it and what your parents believed about it, have led to patterns of behaviour that can't be changed overnight, or with a simple demonstration on what a budget looks like. If you really are sick of being in debt and genuinely want to sort it out, then I believe you can do it. However, first I think it's important to sit down and ask yourself some questions about how you really feel about money and what benefits you might be getting from staying in your current situation. Otherwise, you could end up sabotaging all your good efforts before they have a chance to work.

'We can loan you enough money to get you completely out of debt.'
(Advertising poster for a bank)

NOT ALL DEBT IS BAD

There are a lot of different types of debt. There is nothing wrong with borrowing money in itself – whether it's borrowing for a house, putting money on a credit card or taking out a car or personal loan. Obviously, the problem is when debts get out of hand and it seems like they are controlling you, rather than the other way around. If you know how to handle debt sensibly it can be an interesting tool to boost your wealth. Unfortunately, for many people this increased choice and flexibility has been used to destroy their wealth as high interest charges and late fees mount up.

The total amount of personal debt held by people in the UK stands at £1,421 billion. Most of this money is due to mortgage borrowing, but total consumer credit lending for things like credit cards totalled £227 billion in February 2008. This was a 6.6% increase on the previous year.

According to Credit Action, consumer borrowing for credit cards, motor and retail finance deals, overdrafts and unsecured personal loans (excluding mortgages) is around £21,166 per household in the UK. Britain's personal debt is increasing by £1 million every five minutes.

Causes of debt

There has been some research to show that having a chronic level of debt may be due to economic factors. Chronic debtors are usually a small group with limited economic and social resources. They may have a job that pays poorly and no family or friends they can fall back on in a crisis.

However, psychological factors have also been shown to have an influence. Many people in debt tend to focus on the short-term in their thinking, rather than plan for long-term goals. They may also find it difficult to control their behaviour in many aspects of their life – not just with money. There is some evidence to show that people in debt are more likely to smoke, drink and be overweight, although this could be a result of being in debt rather than one of these factors contributing to their debt.

One worrying trend in recent years has been the influence of these more psychological factors when it comes to insolvency.

When debt levels get beyond control, one option that some people look at is bankruptcy or declaring yourself insolvent via an Individual Voluntary Arrangement – which is a common alternative to bankruptcy. Traditionally, people succumbing to this blamed the effect of losing their job or a breakdown in their marriage. However, with personal insolvency rates now at an all time high in the UK, more people are citing 'living beyond their means' as the reason for their situation.

Many of the people who find themselves in debt view it as a temporary situation. Perhaps they lost their job or had their income reduced in some way, so continue living at the same level by borrowing on credit cards. These people fully expect to turn their situation around in the future when their income levels return to normal. Studies of people living on the street have also found that these people often view their situation as temporary and expect to be back on their feet in a short time.

IT'S NOT ALL YOUR FAULT

However, recent statistics show that, if anything, the debt situation for the majority of people in the UK is actually getting worse. Rising council tax rates and food prices are making it increasingly difficult to get by.

Figures from the Citizens Advice Bureau show debt enquiries have hit a record high. The number of debt problems the Bureau looks at has doubled in the last ten years. Debt is now the number one issue accounting for one in three enquiries. The average client with the CAB has around £13,000 in debt which is 17.5 times their monthly income.

Unfortunately, the deregulation of the UK credit market has led to some questionable practices by banks. With stories in our newspapers of debtors finding themselves in such dire straits that they are prepared to commit suicide it is not surprising that many people have started to ask questions. Why were people with obviously limited means allowed to build up such astronomical levels of debt in the first place?

Meanwhile, people who take out a new credit card in a desperate attempt to cover their expenses are charged exorbitant rates. The average interest rate on credit card lending is currently 17.4%, far higher than the base rate which at the time of writing was just 4.5%. Experts say the financial crisis has meant banks are trying to make money any way they can, so some have pushed up their rates to as high as 40%

A study by uSwitch found that nine out of ten credit card

borrowers were issued cards without the lender carrying out any checks to verify that they could afford to repay the debt. There are now around four credit cards circulating for every UK adult.

The majority of people (around 80%) who are granted credit cards are not asked for proof of their annual income beyond the figures stated on their application, and around 95% are not asked to show evidence of their outgoings in order to provide a true picture of affordability.

The role of the government

It doesn't help when the UK government is often encouraging consumers to get out there and spend in order to boost retail sales and the economy. Even in the current difficult environment, government ministers are encouraging consumers to prop up the building industry! In other countries in the European Union borrowing is much more difficult and inflexible because regulators recognise that it's easy for ordinary people to get themselves into trouble. People taking out a mortgage in France, for example, must ensure that their repayments are no more than one-third of their monthly after-tax income and there are far more restrictions on credit card use. It's not surprising, then, that UK consumers are twice as indebted as those in Continental Europe.

A report by Paul Webley and Ellen Nyhus at the University of Exeter (Representations of Savings and Saving Behaviour, 1999) found that, historically, the amount of debt people get into or the amount of savings they have can be influenced by the fashions of the time or the encouragement the government gives to a certain type of behaviour.

For example, in Victorian England, when Samuel Smiles wrote

his best-seller *Self Help,* there was a strong emphasis at the time on thrift and having savings. Similarly, in early American society, the protestant work ethic emphasised frugal behaviour. In the 18th and 19th centuries, Americans were saving around 15% of their income, yet today the average American has little or no savings. The authors blame this on a turnaround in the 1920s, when it became fashionable to spend rather than to save. The stock market crash of 1929 and the Great Depression reinforced the idea that saving was pointless, and since then conspicuous consumption has ruled, with the support of a government that is hardly leading by example with very high levels of national debt. Britain is not much better. Although our national accounts have been cleaned up a bit, the government still encourages consumption at alarming rates.

In addition, people have started to compare themselves with much richer people whom they see on TV, rather than their immediate neighbours. The authors showed that sometimes these social needs are stronger than people's motivation to be financially sensible. For example, a study of working-class people in Britain found they did not always buy financial products that gave the best return, rather those that gave them status. So, getting into debt to buy a car that is the envy of your neighbours could be more important to you than saving for a rainy day.

The role of your parents

Don't get me wrong, I'm not saying it's your parents' fault if you are in a lot of debt. Ultimately, the responsibility lies with you. However, many psychologists will tell you that shopaholics are just like any other addict. They deny that they have a problem, they feel like the addiction is controlling them rather than the other way around, they are more like to shop when they are feeling depressed and, crucially, they often don't recover until they have hit rock bottom.

If you have a parent, friend or partner who regularly lends you money to bail you out of financial problems then, although they think they are helping, those people are actually stopping you from hitting rock bottom and getting on the road to recovery.

Parents are, understandably, often the people doing exactly that. They see their children in trouble and they want to lend a hand, but sometimes they give them the wrong sort of help. After all, giving someone money seems far removed from handing an alcoholic another drink, yet in a way the two actions are similar. Some parents, particularly wealthy parents, also get a certain amount of satisfaction out of having their children economically dependent on them. They are not deliberately trying to sabotage their children's financial health, but sometimes it's an instinctive reaction to want to take over. As babies, children are completely dependent on their parents, making them feel needed and important. As children grow up, they become more independent and some parents find that difficult to cope with. On some level they like still having a role to play. They might complain loudly about their economically crippled youngsters sponging off them but deep down they are getting some satisfaction from being in the 'provider' position. The solution, of course, is to be incredibly strong and cut off that financial umbilical cord by saying 'no' when parents offer to pay your debts, buy you a house next door etc. Difficult though it may be, you may find that the real cost of accepting these monetary gifts is more than you thought.

Debt-related stress

Perhaps you haven't hit rock bottom yet because you don't think there's anything wrong or unusual about having lots of credit card debt. All your friends are doing it, even celebrities have been branded shopaholics, so why not? The trouble with having a lot of debt, even if you view it as a temporary situation, is that it can be incredibly stressful and harm your health.

A survey by debt counsellors found that 63% of people with bad debt problems believe their health has suffered as a direct result of their debt. This has been described by some as 'Money Sickness Syndrome' and it is estimated that almost half the UK adult population is affected by money worries or have experienced MSS symptoms.

Psychologists say one of the worst feelings for people is to feel out of control of their lives. Too much debt can give you a sense of feeling out of control of your finances. Taking back that control often means doing scary things that are difficult to face – like calling creditors or peering at bank statements that show lots of negative numbers. Many people spend hours worrying about these problems, rather than taking action that could alleviate some of their stress, because they are just so afraid to do it. Of course, worrying about your problems uses up far more energy than actually solving them.

Taking control

It doesn't matter what your fears are in life – being alone, losing your job/degree/partner, not being able to cope in certain situations. We all have fears, they are a part of life.

Often, we recognise that certain fears are holding us back. We know that the right thing to do is to face up to our credit card debt for example and start paying it off, but this would mean facing something quite uncomfortable. However, when you don't face your fears, they have a tendency to grow and can take over your life. We spend far too much time and energy worrying about the things that we need to do, rather than actually going out there and doing them.

The good news is that once you start attacking your fears, by taking small, measured, achievable steps, you suddenly put yourself back in control and can start reclaiming your life. Sometimes it takes years for people to:

a) Identify their fear.

b) Admit to this fear.

c) Have the strength to change it.

Be kind to yourself and acknowledge that these fears are there and that they are affecting your life, and then start to take small steps to overcome them – whatever they are. If it's credit card debt, set yourself the target of paying off the debt with the highest interest rate first. Don't worry too much about the others yet, just focus on that one.

If things have been spiralling out of control for a while and you feel very overwhelmed and frozen by your fear, then just do something very small like making a phone call to the Consumer Advice Bureau or someone who can help you. This small act can leave you awash with relief.

Don't be afraid to share the burden of your troubles. As they say, a problem shared is a problem halved. Professional debt advisers can help you, and they don't know or care what you look like or what family you're from. They've seen lots of people like you before and they know exactly how to fix things, so don't be too embarrassed to tell them your story. Alternatively, log on to one of the many financial websites such as The Motley Fool, MSN Money or the Consumer Counselling Service's website. These sites not only have information on how to get out of debt and loads of savings tips but you can also find chatrooms where you can speak to other people in similar circumstances and who will cheer you on in your efforts to clear your debts.

Most importantly, forgive yourself. OK, so maybe you haven't handled things well in the past, but that doesn't mean your whole life has to be like that. You can take one small step today that will put you on the path to changing your life and making you happier, so take it.

Do One Difficult Thing a Day

One of the little tactics I like to use is to do one difficult thing every day. Sometimes, that difficult thing is just getting out of bed, but once you've done it you can pat yourself on the back for achieving something and stop worrying about all the other things on an impossibly long list that you should have done.

Another good idea is, instead of writing down your New Year's resolutions (stop smoking, lose weight, get out of debt), rather focus on your achievements for the previous year. For example, you may have run 5km, cut drinking to two nights a week, gone on an exotic holiday, made new friends, broke up with that dodgy bloke, got a pay rise, made your gran happy. It doesn't matter what they were, as long as they made you proud and happy.

Cheering yourself on is far more productive than beating yourself up over your shortfalls. Often the problem is that you have set yourself goals that are too big, too ambitious and so you feel paralysed to move. If your debts are large, most likely you won't be able to pay them off in one year but that doesn't mean you shouldn't start.

When you're depressed, you waste money. It's like you purposely hurt yourself financially in some sort of masochistic way because you are already hurting in other areas. You buy yourself little presents to cheer yourself up, but they don't work. It's time to stop this destructive behaviour and instead start doing things today that are kind to both you and your purse.

1) Make a list of five of your greatest fears. For example:

* Being alone.
* Not being able to cope.
* Being made bankrupt.
* Being eaten by a shark.
* Losing a loved one.

2) List something difficult that you are going to do today and then go and do it. Hint: the best time of day to do your difficult thing is as soon as you get up in the morning – then it's over and done with.

3) Do something kind for yourself – have a bubble bath, listen to some nice music, do something pointless and childlike that you haven't done for years like making a drawing with coloured pencils, cook your favourite dish, pick some flowers, make a mural of pictures or photos of your favourite things (it's amazing how this can cheer you up).

4) Imagine yourself as an old lady and write a detailed description of what you want your life to be like when you are 85. What kind of person are you? Where do you live? What have you achieved in life that you're proud of? What are the things around you that make you happy?

Maybe the reason you're spending so much is because you're depressed, but you're depressed because you have lots of credit card debt. What do you do then? Usually the reason people are unhappy with their lives is because there is something that they are afraid of and that they are not facing. Something they know they should do, but are just too scared to do – end a relationship, quit their job, leap over the precipice on a ski slope. Thinking about it for a long time doesn't help! Whenever you feel fear, you have to just ignore it and take action anyway. Admittedly sometimes it can take years before you have the courage to do something really big like get out of a bad relationship, but eventually you know you just have to do it. And the sooner you do it, the sooner you'll be happy again. In the meantime, there are little things you can do on a daily basis to improve your mood:

* Wear brighter clothes – this works, believe me!
* Do some sport or exercise.
* Make time to spend regularly with good friends who you trust and can be yourself with.
* Make a list of the things that really make you happy in life and then try to do one a week or even one a day. E.g. walking in the park, buying flowers, doing something creative, burning scented candles, going dancing, listening to lovely music.
* Make a list of all the things in life that you have to be thankful for.
* Read positive books designed to cheer you up – whether it's a self-help book or a trashy romance novel.
* Do something for someone else. This doesn't have to be charity work, but when you help someone else who is really in need it makes you feel all warm inside and helps them too so there's a double effect.

The Victim

Sometimes being out of control and the victim is a state you've become used to over many years and are comfortable with, so it's difficult to start taking responsibility when you have 'benefitted' from being helpless.

You may get sympathy for being a victim, which may comfort you more than the idea of being financially independent. You may think: 'Why would I want to be independent? I'm getting all my needs met right here.' But are you happy?

If you start to change, you may suddenly feel overwhelmed and sabotage yourself just when you're close to achieving success. Perhaps because you don't really believe it's possible or that you deserve it. You may try to convince yourself that paying off debts doesn't matter (all your friends are in debt too), or that your achievements so far are too small to make a difference.

Regular, small steps are sometimes more difficult to take than one big, dramatic clearing of all your debts, but they are nevertheless the most practical way of taking action and therefore overcoming fears. You have to keep chipping away at that debt stone. Persistency is the key. If you have started paying off your debts, then you are already a long way down the road to success, even if it doesn't feel like it. Just by starting you have become a different person. You owe it to that person to continue.

> ***'Life shrinks or expands in proportion to one's courage'***
> **Anais Nin**

Often, there are little signs to encourage you – a kind word from a friend, or some unexpected money. Grasp hold of any of these little positive signs and hold them close or repeat them to yourself.

Although it's scary, you should also tell other people what you are doing, as it helps you stick with the plan. Believe that the universe wants you to achieve this goal, and all you have to do is keep chipping away and not give up.

Be sympathetic to yourself. Yes, this is scary. Yes, you have a right to be afraid – but just being afraid doesn't mean you can't still do it. That's what bravery is, being afraid but doing it anyway. If you're not scared of something then doing it isn't brave (no matter how terrified other people might be of doing it).

If you are hitting one of those emotional snags where you feel like giving up, you can pause for a bit to figure out the best way to overcome it. Maybe you've been pushing yourself a bit too hard or trying to pay back too large an amount at once. Scale back your efforts to something a bit more achievable, but keep going.

YOU CAN DO IT!

Some people make a big deal about cutting their spending and keeping track of all their expenses. But keeping to a budget is certainly no harder than sticking to a diet, and a lot easier than giving up smoking.

Besides, most women are natural-born shoppers. They know how to get a bargain and that's half the skill. When I walk into a supermarket, I enjoy the challenge of working out how I can get the most meals, or the most delicious ones, out of a limited amount of money. I'm sure you have enough imagination to think up other ways of stretching your pounds to get what you want. It's a strange phenomenon, perhaps, but usually if you want something very badly, you can figure out a way to get it even if you don't have the resources at hand.

Many of my friends tell me they are 'bad with money'. If they continue to believe that, they will be. However, there is no rational reason for them to really believe this. They are just as good as anyone else at finding a bargain and sticking with a programme when they really want to achieve something. So, try to trust yourself a bit more. One of the simplest ways to save is to ask your bank to deduct a certain amount from your pay each month. It's like getting a pay cut, only the money is going towards a better future for you. It doesn't take long to get used to living on a slightly smaller amount, so why not use this trick to help pay off debts? Then later you can use the money as savings.

When I first met my friend Rebecca, she was in debt to the tune of £12,000. Most of this had been built up gradually by taking small actions which didn't seem important at the time. In the same way that 'every little bit counts' when you are building up savings, the same can happen with debts. Rebecca was convinced that the reason for her debt was because she was born with a natural ability to lose money. However, when we sat down and looked at where all the money was going, she realised that the problem hadn't arisen because she was spending an awful lot of money on herself. Rather, it was because she had made one or two unwise decisions in the past and was also spending a lot of money on helping to support her parents. To her complete surprise, today she is in much better shape, financially. I wouldn't say she's rich, but, most importantly, her thinking about money has changed. She has now successfully run two businesses and proved that even someone who's 'bad with money' can turn a profit, manage accounts sensibly and even pull up the Inland Revenue when they make a mistake.

Life coaches will tell you that one of the best ways to develop self-confidence is to slowly expose yourself to the thing that really terrifies you. For example, if you're really afraid of spiders, start out by just looking at a photo of a spider and thinking positive thoughts. After a while its effect on you is decreased. Similarly you need to start doing the things that you are afraid of doing, in a small, safe way. Once you have proved to yourself that you can do them, and have built up a record of successful experiences behind you, you will overcome your fear.

Once my friend Rebecca was forced to handle money for her business she realised she wasn't so bad with it after all. The first hurdle is always overcoming your psychological barriers.

Learning how to get in control of your money can be just as rewarding as other activities, like learning a new sport. Once you overcome your fears, in whatever form they come, nothing seems impossible. However, unlike sports, where it is sometimes difficult to see if you are progressing, it is easy to measure your success with money and get a record of successful experiences behind you that spur you to keep going. Every time you reduce your debt or build up your savings or get a good return on your investments, you can see the results in black and white before you.

SHOPAHOLICS ANONYMOUS – HOW TO GET OUT OF THE DEBT HOLE

Spending can become an addiction. In the same way that people become addicted to alcohol, drugs, food or sex, people can be addicted to shopping.

The treatment for any addiction is usually awareness, acceptance and then action. The first of these is often difficult, especially in the UK where many people are too proud to admit they are having financial problems. It can also be difficult to get the kind of emotional support you need at this time. Some debt agencies simply show you a budget and then leave you on your own, but this may be only part of the work necessary to overcome a long-term habit of living beyond your means.

Like other addicts, debtors may follow a binge cycle. This involves feeling some sort of tension or depression, spending, feeling relieved immediately afterwards, but then feeling remorse for spending, abstaining for a period, then feeling tension and beginning all over again.

> **'*The waste of money cures itself, for soon there is no more to waste.*'**
> **MW Harrison**

Changing old patterns

Keeping track of where your money comes from and how you spend is one way you can care for yourself and stop participating in this form of self-abuse.

No matter how painful your troubles have been, they are in the past now. Just deal with the present and the future. You are not your money problems and you don't have to define yourself that way. You are better than that; you've just hit a bit of a snag, but you will get over it and change. There's no rule that says that because your parents were bad with money that you have to be. This is learned behaviour; it is not in your genes. You simply have to rewire your brain.

I understand that facing these problems is very difficult. Indeed, you may find yourself getting angry or frustrated with this book while you are reading it. You may even start to feel ill. This could be displaced anger or anxiety about your money problems. Don't worry too much about it. The best way to get through those feelings is to take some action. By following the measures below consistently for three months you will form a habit and these actions will get easier and easier to do.

1. Write Down Everything You Spend

Many people resist this exercise, saying they don't have time or simply don't like doing it. Like physical exercise, writing everything down forms a discipline and forces you to be aware of where your money is going. You can no longer use the excuse that you're not paid enough when you can see that the reason there's no cash left for groceries is because you spent it on other, less important things.

The first four weeks are the hardest; you are changing old habits and forming new ones so there is resistance. But stick with it.

2. Create a Budget

Follow the guidelines given in the previous chapter on how to construct a budget. At the top of your budget, write your monthly income and then take amounts off that. If you have a fluctuating income, keep track of it in the same way you keep track of your outgoing expenses.

3. No New Debts

During this time you must:

* Not put anything on your credit card.
* In particular, avoid incurring any big new expenses.
* Talk to creditors and inform them of your intentions to pay and stop hiding.

This is like going cold turkey, so you can get a clear view of your situation and learn how to recover.

Once you have a bit of distance, it's important to start replacing old habits with new ones. In the same way that a garden needs to be filled with desirable plants so that there is no space for weeds to grow, try to replace your spending ideas with saving ideas. That is the only way I have found to be successful – play tricks on your mind and stop spending. If you obsess about how little money you have or how unhappy you are with your situation, you will spend. If you replace those ideas constantly with happy, motivating ideas on how you can go out and have fun without it costing a fortune, you are more likely to stick to your aims.

TIPS FOR SURVIVING YOUR DEBT DETOX

* Start writing down everything you spend – but don't judge yourself.
* Cut up your credit cards, so you stop incurring more debt.
* Avoid any major new expenses.
* Talk to your creditors and tell them of your intentions to pay – i.e. stop hiding.
* Keep a diary of your emotions and note how you felt just before, during and just after any binge spending. See if you can find a pattern.
* Write down your favourite quote or mantra that makes you feel inspired. Stick it somewhere you will see it regularly, like on the fridge or your mirror.
* Join a money chatroom or look at sites with ideas on how to save money so that you don't feel alone.
* Cut stories out of newspapers or magazines of people who got badly into debt and came to harm so you can see that there are other people worse off than you.
* Create a montage of how you would like your life to be in

the future with pictures of things you want to have or goals you want to achieve.

* Create a fake bank statement with no debts and lots of money in savings, so that you can visualise your future clearly.
* Get regular exercise and fill up your time doing cheap or free things that make you feel happy without any guilt. Organise a picnic with your friends in the park or go for a walk.
* Take care of yourself by eating properly and getting enough sleep.
* Do a summary at the end of each week. Give yourself lots of praise for any achievements, but don't beat yourself up too badly for mistakes.
* Make a list of all the things in life that you enjoy and that are free.
* Write down a list of reasons why you want to get out of debt, and how it will change your life and your relationships with others.
* Write about how your relationship with money has hurt you in the past.
* Make a list of any money that is owed to you and do one thing to get it back.
* Make a list of your skills that could earn you extra money.
* Make a list of things you would be prepared to sell.
* What's usually your main excuse for sabotaging yourself financially? Do you say it's because your efforts aren't appreciated or you're spending because you are unhappy and deserve it?
* List ten ways you are stingy and ten ways you are extravagant.

Prince Charming

Sometimes women put off getting out of their financial problems because they are hoping that they'll meet some rich, handsome man who will sweep them off their feet and out of all their credit card debt. Apart from the fact that not taking responsibility for your life in this way is likely to have negative effects long term, the Prince Charming syndrome is also very unrealistic.

In the best-selling book *The Millionaire Next Door,* the authors came to a number of surprising conclusions about the behaviour and attitudes of America's millionaires. Among them was the finding that the average millionaire had a wife who was more careful with money than he was. The conclusion many of these men came to was that they would never be able to become wealthy in one generation if they were married to someone who was wasteful. For this reason, many ensured they chose wives who didn't have lots of credit card debt and were very frugal.

So, if you're daydreaming about marrying a wealthy man who'll take away all your problems, think again. Even if he's a rich footballer when you meet him, if you are both too loose with your spending, the money will drain away quicker than water and you may find yourself facing real difficulties when you're older and are less able to cope with it. By then, you may have missed out on the chance to improve your qualifications and build up work experience and savings. 'Rich' and 'famous' are two words that don't necessarily go together in the real world.

Sexually Transmitted Debt

Unfortunately, even when you manage your own finances perfectly well, you can get into some trouble if your partner, or former partner, racks up debts and then leaves you with the bills.

If you own a home in joint names or have a bank account or credit cards in joint names, you could be asked to pay for the whole debt. This also applies to household bills that are in both your names. If your partner has moved out, you should get those changed as soon as possible into your sole name. You may also find some bills will be lower, such as council tax, if they are only held in one name.

If your partner started a business and you were a signatory for that business (you signed cheques or had director's responsibilities), you can also be held accountable. If the business fails and your partner goes bankrupt, you could end up losing your (jointly owned) home to pay off the creditors.

Even if you are the one who moves out, you will be held responsible for your share of the council tax while you were living in the home.

Of course, if there are debts solely in his name, you are not liable for those and creditors cannot ask you to pay for them, even if you were or are still married.

If there was a County Court judgement against your ex and bailiffs or other creditors come knocking, they still have no right to take your belongings if the debts are in his name.

You should never invite bailiffs into your home, or even leave the door open so they can enter. If creditors are sending you letters or calling you, you should tell them that the person they are looking for no longer lives there, that they should not call you again, and pass on a forwarding address if you have one.

The Office of Fair Trading's debt collection guidance prohibits unfair practices by collection agents. They cannot pursue third parties for payment when they are not liable, or demand payment when they are not sure that person is the debtor, or force that person to supply information to prove they are not the debtor.

Some Helpful Numbers & Websites Related to UK Debt Issues

* National Debtline (**www.nationaldebtline.co.uk**) 0808 808 4000
* Information Commission 01625 545 745
* Data Protection Helpline 01625 545 700 (general)
* Experian 0870 2414297 (leaflet order line) 0870 2416212 (helpline)
* Callcredit 0870 0601414
* Credit Industry Fraud Avoidance Scheme (CIFAS) 0870 010 2091
* Citizens Advice Bureau (**www.adviceguide.org.uk**)

JUSTINE'S 10 TIPS

1) Analyse what has influenced your behaviour and attitudes towards money.

2) How do you feel about your level of debts? In denial or going crazy with worry?

3) Analyse your health and emotional wellbeing; do you feel you are in control of your debts or are they controlling you?

4) Once you've decided there is a problem, it's time to take control and face up to your fears.

5) Every day do something to reduce your debts. This takes you another step closer to freedom.

6) Forgive yourself for getting into this situation, but then resolve to also be firm.

7) Spend some time helping people who are worse off than you.

8) Make a list of all the wonderful things in life that are completely free!

9) One of the most important tips is to ensure you have no new debts. This will show how determined you are.

10) Analyse whether you are putting off fixing your debt problem because you are simply waiting for someone else to come and rescue you.

relationships and money

The last taboo

In a world where sexual positions are discussed openly in magazines and on TV, money has become the last taboo. Discussing how assets will be split or who will pay the bills when one of you is out of work, or looking after the children, or taking time off to study, seems somehow unromantic. You're supposed to be together for better or for worse, in sickness and in health, so it's assumed that we're above these petty ideas about who will pay the bills and how much taking care of each other really costs.

For many couples, talking about money is incredibly difficult, yet researchers tell us it is the main subject that we fight about. Why is money such a trigger point in our relationships and how can we use it to improve, rather than harm, the interactions we have with our loved ones?

Parental influence

When you get into a fight with your partner, it's not just you and him in the room. It's also your mum and dad, his parents and plenty of other people besides, who have influenced you both.

In her book *Stop Fighting About Money*, Corinne Sweet explains that before we can solve our money problems in a relationship, we first need to analyse our own attitudes towards money and how they have been influenced by our upbringing. It's a question of 'know thyself first' before you start to work out if you really know your partner and his feelings about money.

To start with, look at the way your parents thought about money. When you were growing up, they would have been the primary example of how to behave on financial issues. Was your mum a spendthrift, or did she watch every penny? Was your father obsessed with never paying too much for something and earning a decent return on his savings and investments, or did your mum shout at him for being a layabout and not earning enough? When you were a child, did you feel like your family was rich, even if you weren't, or was it hammered home to you that 'money doesn't grow on trees' and that you'd better pull your weight around the house or you'd all end up in financial ruin? What things were seen as sensible to spend money on, and what things were seen as a waste – and did you agree with these opinions? Take some time to think about these questions and perhaps write down your views, bearing in mind that many people either mimic or rebel against the attitudes their parents had towards money.

Family Communication

The way your parents discussed money in their relationship will also have a significant influence on how you discuss (or don't discuss) money in your own relationship and the type of role you see for yourself or your partner. If money was never mentioned, you may feel uncomfortable talking about it at first. But it's important to push aside these feelings, as communication is incredibly important in any relationship and it's the things you don't talk about that can cause the most problems. Analysing your experiences and feelings could lead to interesting discoveries about yourself. Perhaps you had a father who was quite frugal and now you are terrified of your partner acting similarly. Perhaps this is the reason you overreact when he innocently asks you how much something cost. If you can talk about these feelings with your partner, he is more likely to be sensitive towards you on certain issues. If you don't say anything, he will keep making the same mistakes and upsetting you unnecessarily.

Whilst some people mimic their parents, others do the opposite. I always felt that my parents were great at making money, but terrible at keeping it. They seemed far too spendthrift for me. I've no idea where my frugal attitude came from; perhaps it was from reading books about money, or perhaps it was a reaction to my parents' attitude. However, I'm glad that, unlike some families, we were pretty open in our discussions about money at home.

I have met some people who are terrified to even mention how much certain things cost. They don't know how much their partner or any of their relatives earn and they don't care to know. Asking such a question is seen as bad-mannered. Likewise, they think it's rude to ask how much someone paid for their home. Who cares if you're about to buy a property and are trying to get an idea of the market – you simply don't ask.

The trouble with this lack of communication is that it can make it difficult for people to learn about money and be able to use it more effectively. If getting into debt was taboo in your family, you may feel incredibly guilty about even using a credit card and too ashamed to tell your partner if you go into overdraft. Such secrecy might help your pride for a while, but few relationships can withstand lies, deceit and misinformation, even if there are innocent reasons behind it all. If you can't trust your partner enough to share this hyper-sensitive information, then who can you trust? By opening up a little, you may find that, in fact, they won't be as harsh with you as you fear, and it could even deepen the intimacy in your relationship.

Pam's Story

My friend Pam has a mother who has always been a bit of a spendthrift with money and does things like guiltily hiding shopping bags or things she's bought on a whim, so that her husband won't find them. In contrast, Pam's Scottish father has always been rather severe and has a 'waste not, want not' attitude to money. This caused a lot of fights at home. Her parents' conflicting views on how money should be handled and what it should be spent on, coloured Pam's childhood. As an adult, she feels she follows her mother's behaviour more and considers herself 'bad' with money, overspending on credit cards and then feeling guilty afterwards.

A few years ago, she found herself in a relationship with Dan, who was a bit like her father in his attitude to money. He earned a decent income as a marketing manager and was careful with his spending. It didn't take long for friction to develop between the two. Dan felt Pam was irresponsible; she thought he was too mean. Living with such a money-perfectionist made Pam even less confident in her ability to manage money and she felt she would never live up to his expectations. Dan worried that no matter how much he earned, it would never be enough to support the two of them because Pam seemed to spend money so recklessly.

In the end, these conflicts were too much and, unable to reconcile their differences, the couple separated. Fortunately, Pam then met Steven. The two of them had many things in common: the same movies, the same type of food, Sunday morning lie-ins, but best of all, similar ideas on what type of things money should be spent on. With their values in sync Pam also felt more comfortable speaking to Steven about money and didn't worry that he would treat her like a naughty schoolgirl if she overspent. In fact, Steven trusted Pam straightaway when it came to money. Although she protested that she was 'bad' with money, he nevertheless handed over his pay packet for her to manage each month, as his own father had done. Being given this responsibility terrified Pam but also inspired her to be more responsible. After a while, she started to realise that she wasn't quite as terrible with money as she had previously thought and was actually capable of managing things in an efficient way. Before long, Pam and Steven decided to set up their own business, and with Steven working hard on attracting sales, it was Pam's job to manage the accounts. Again, she was terrified but surprised herself (and some of her friends) with her ability to take on this task responsibly.

Are you financially compatible?

With people marrying later in life – in the UK the average age for tying the knot is 31 for men and 29 for women – we are more likely to bring large assets or large debts into a relationship. That means financial differences can be exacerbated.

Today, it's more important than ever to find out if you and your partner are financially compatible. Some people like to keep a tight rein on their spending and get anxious if they don't have any savings, or don't know where their next pay cheque is coming from. Others have a 'the universe will provide' attitude, spend freely and believe people should live life to the full in case they get hit by a bus tomorrow. This can create huge problems if you are the 'cautious saver' type and want to buy a home, or renovate the one you're in and start saving for your children's education, while your partner has lots of credit card debts and dreams about going on a round-the-world trip.

As we've discussed previously, we are all unique individuals with different experiences in life and different influences that affect the way we approach our finances. It's inevitable that some conflicts will come up in your relationship that have to do with money. The secret to resolving these conflicts is knowing your financial self very well, knowing your partner's attitudes towards money, ensuring that you have open communication with your partner and learning to accept each other's differences. If you understand why your partner feels a certain way, and can recognise the real underlying fears that are influencing his behaviour, it can go a long way to preventing arguments.

Sadly, many people jump into relationships without knowing anything about their partner's ideas on money. You know their favourite colour, football team, the fact that you both love the same TV shows, that you have mutual attraction and both want 2.4 kids but there are still plenty of unanswered questions, even if you seem perfect for each other at this stage.

It's important to ask yourself the following questions and discuss them with your partner too, if you feel comfortable doing so at this stage of the relationship.

* Is he a saver or a spender?
* Does he have savings?
* Does he have debts – and if so what kind are they (i.e. student debts or credit cards)?
* How does he feel about debt – does he see it as evil or a necessary part of life?
* What are his short-term and long-term financial goals?
* Are they the same as yours?
* Do you know how much each other earns?
* What financial lessons did he learn from his parents and grandparents? Was money ever discussed in the family?
* Does he think money should never be spoken about – among the couple and/or with the children?
* What's his price? How rich does he think is rich enough?
* What are his beliefs with regards to giving and charity?
* Do you consider him generous or overly miserly, and how does this differ from his own beliefs about himself?
* What does he think about your attitude to money? (Don't try to guess, ask him.)
* What is his approach to risk and how does this differ from yours? E.g. Does he think a bank account is the best place to keep money, or is he happy to gamble and take high risks regularly?
* Do you have a similar vision for your future?
* Is he as ambitious about his career as you'd like him to be?
* Do you ever feel like you are competing with him financially, or in your job?
* Does he have the same approach to money as your father did? If not, does that comfort or worry you?

Once you have identified what 'type' your partner is, and also understand your own feelings about money, you can start to analyse the underlying factors that have led to this and how he differs from you. If you understand why he is a certain way, you may not get so offended when he does something different from you. Similarly, if he understands that you have certain trigger points, like freaking out when your bank account is in the red, he may be able to manage his behaviour so that he doesn't upset you so often.

Which are you, a spendthrift or miser? Of course, these are very broad categories, but most of us lean towards one or the other. If your partner is the opposite, you may find it very difficult to understand his or her attitude. It helps if you can see beyond these stereotypes to understand what is going on underneath. For example, someone who spends a lot of money may be doing it because they are essentially unhappy and trying to buy happiness. On the other hand, someone who is very miserly may be terrified of being poor. Perhaps they grew up in a family where money was hard to come by and they see earning lots of money as a way of proving themselves and controlling this fear. If you can see what is motivating someone's behaviour, it shows you a way towards helping them.

Even if you are money opposites, your compatibility can grow if you take the time to discuss your different attitudes to money and why certain things your partner does trigger a particular money-related fear for you. One of the most important things is having the same goals in life, so that even if you take a different approach to getting there, you both still end up at the same place.

resolving conflicts (new couples)

If you have not been in the relationship very long, you may have noticed certain things that concern you. For example, if he seems overly obsessed with money and becoming rich, look at the underlying fears causing this. Perhaps he grew up in a poor household and he feels insecure and that people won't take him seriously unless he is wealthy. Maybe he is competing with a sibling or parent - or even yourself. Get him to think and talk about these issues – he may not have ever thought about it himself.

When analysing your compatibility, look at what he does, not just what he says. For example, what type of car does he drive? It may sound shallow but this can tell you a lot about the values a guy has. Look at the things he has already spent his money on, to give you an indication of where his real sentiments lie.

It may be flattering to go out with a guy who showers you with gifts, but if you are the 'saver' type his spending may become a source of conflict at some stage. Similarly, if you have a more laid-back attitude towards finances, his controlling habits may make you feel restricted.

once you're in a relationship – working through problems

If you are too afraid to speak to your partner about financial topics, any problems you may have could be suppressed temporarily, only to emerge – much larger – at a later date. Having different ideas doesn't mean your relationship is doomed as long as you are both prepared to be flexible and meet halfway. Your biggest problem is not having a partner who is your financial opposite, but in having one who won't make any efforts to resolve these issues – especially if you are trying hard to find a compromise and not simply criticising his different behaviour.

When couples have any differences, and don't talk about them, fights can erupt easily. If you discover that you have different priorities but don't do anything about resolving this, you could end up trying to sabotage each other financially, focusing on individual wants rather than joint responsibilities. Women might start writing large cheques or spending more than they know they should on the joint account; men might start building up separate investments that they don't tell their wives about. Before you know it, his little slush fund has become a *pied-à-terre* in the city where he keeps his mistress and your shopping frenzy is out of control.

In the beginning, you may be tempted to turn a blind eye to your differences. After all, it sounds positively unromantic to talk about money when you're in love. Bringing up the subject of prenuptial agreements, for example, can make you feel a scrooge and give your partner the impression that you don't trust that the relationship will work out. But, as just about every relationship counsellor will tell you, open communication and honesty are essential in a healthy relationship. That applies to money just as much as other topics. Sometimes, it's even more important to talk about money because that can be where we hide our deepest fears about ourselves. For example you may have a spending addiction where you buy yourself lots of presents because it helps you overcome your fears of being abandoned and unloved.

Sometimes, the reason you may be avoiding financial topics with your partner is because you feel guilty about your own spending habits, or you are trying to hide from yourself. Perhaps your partner has tried to speak to you about money, but instead you just hide under the duvet and pretend everything is fine when you know it isn't. Carefully analyse the influences in your own life. Write down how your mother and father looked at money and how this may have affected you. Identify any fears or worries you have about money and talk it all through with a supportive partner or friend. This way, you can not only improve your relationship, but also find some peace and happiness on a subject that has been nagging you for years. Examining how you relate to money can force you to examine yourself honestly – something that many people find scary.

DON'T TRY TO CHANGE HIM

I went through a very painful experience which illustrates how differing attitudes to money, and trying to force your partner to change, can help to wreck a relationship. I used to be with a wonderful man who was very kind and loving and incredibly patient with me. Unfortunately, we had completely opposite views when it came to money. In retrospect, our differing views on money were not the only things that drove us apart, but it was certainly a factor. We saw the world in very different ways and, consciously or not, we were both trying to change each other. In the beginning, I thought it didn't matter that I was ambitious and wanted to be financially independent and he didn't, but eventually these things did matter because it meant we had different long-term goals. I started to feel like he was holding me back instead of encouraging me and supporting me in those areas. But why would he have supported me? He didn't believe in those things. It wasn't a goal he thought was worth striving for. The trouble with this is that unless you support each other, even if you don't really believe in what the other person is doing, eventually things start to crumble.

For us, life became a tug-of-war with him trying to make me more like him and me trying to force him to act more like I did. Instead of appreciating our differences and accepting them, we struggled and even competed. Whose ideology was going to win? In the end, neither won and we both lost a lot.

What made the situation worse was that we didn't discuss these differences; we just ignored them and hoped that eventually the other person would change. I've also realised that sometimes when we fought about money it was because I was trying to give up responsibility for my own finances or achievements. I was scared that I wasn't good enough, so I tried to force him to make more money so he could support me (in case I failed), or I tried to force him to do something he didn't want to do that would help me achieve my goals – not his. For example, I'd tell him we had to buy a flat together because then I would be able to get a bigger mortgage and make more money from property investing – even though he didn't want to buy a flat, or even believe in property ownership. Using someone else to achieve your aims is, needless to say, not healthy for your relationship.

I don't believe that you have to find someone who believes in exactly the same things you do. That's impossible anyway, because we are all unique and there are always going to be things we disagree on. However, you have to at least be prepared to allow your partner to be who they are and not try to change them. If you are an ambitious woman, then don't try to force your partner to be ambitious. He either will or he won't, but it's nothing to do with you. Support him in whatever he wants to do but don't tell him what to do or how to do it. Men can be remarkably capable and self-reliant if we let them.

My current partner is lovely and we're very happy but I've learnt my lesson the hard way. He is a very intelligent and capable man, so I don't try to tell him what to do. Happily, we also have quite similar views on money. We certainly disagree on some areas but we have the same short- and long-term goals and are both incredibly open about money and our opinions. Whenever conflicts arise, we sit down and work out what the real reasons are behind both our own and the other person's views. If you understand why your partner feels a certain way, it somehow makes you more sympathetic to their views. Being sympathetic to your partner's values also ensures that you support them in whatever they want to do, even if their plans are a little different from yours. Having this type of support enriches your relationship and strengthens the trust between you.

If you think your partner needs lots of changing, then that's a pretty bad start, whether money comes into the equation or not. Don't stay just because you're scared to leave or you think he'll be lost without you. Set him free to be with some other woman who will appreciate him for all he is already.

Tips for resolving conflicts

If you have been in a relationship for a while, or are living together but have never discussed money issues clearly and find you are already fighting about it, then it's important to also look at what your financial stress points are.

* What subjects are you most likely to fight about and when?
* Can you identify the underlying causes or fears behind these fights?

* Are you fighting because you are tired or stressed, or because you truly resent something your partner does?
* What hidden fears or anxieties are triggered by certain actions?

For example, your husband comes home with a gift for you after a drunken night out with the lads and you find yourself getting angry because he is wasting money yet again and jeopardising your chances of feeding, clothing and educating your kids or meeting your mortgage payments. Your need for financial security and fear of not having enough to survive, explodes with force. It reminds you of your impoverished upbringing when your family really had to struggle. You may actually have plenty of money in the bank now and earn a good living, but these inbuilt fears can take years to go away – if ever.

Talk About It

It's important for you both to let the other person know your own views on money, what you think influenced these opinions and the types of things that upset you and why. Try not to criticise him, or tell him he has to change. Rather, focus on your own behaviour and feelings. Analyse why certain things he does might trigger a memory from the past that upsets you. Use the 'When you do this…I feel like that…' approach and try to be as non-judgemental as possible. Simply try to explain your feelings and what you think has led to them. Sometimes talking doesn't work, so letter-writing is an alternative that many counsellors recommend. It gives people time to think about what they want to say and how they really feel.

Speak to Your Parents

For instance, if he questions your purchases after a day of shopping, this might remind you of arguments your own parents had where your penny-pinching father restricted your mother's spending. If your parents fought a lot about money, this may have prompted some irrational fears in you, so that you are terrified of even broaching the subject in case it turns into a fight. In this instance, it may be helpful to go and speak to one or both of your parents and try to figure out why they were really fighting. Sometimes, the perspective of a child is slanted. You may not realise the subtext that was going on in your parents' relationship. Perhaps the real reason for the fights was something you had never considered before or, with the perspective of an adult, you may be able to see how certain insecurities in your parents provoked arguments unnecessarily. Although you are influenced by your parents, you are a different person, so you don't have to have this knee-jerk reaction in your relationship every time your partner does something that provokes a childhood memory.

Set up a Joint Account for Bills

If you are having conflicts on a daily basis over little things like household bills, it's a good idea to sit down and work out a solution that will defuse tension in the relationship. For example, if you know you always fight over who pays for the groceries, set up a joint account where an equal amount of money is direct-debited each month, and use this only for joint purchases such as groceries and things for the house. Either have no overdraft facility on this account or, if you must, make sure it is minimal so that neither of you can act irresponsibly with this joint money and run off with the other person's savings.

Allow for Independence

If you are the partner who is more responsible with money, try to accept that your partner's money is his or her own, and that it's a personal choice how they spend it. Don't try to tell them how to spend their own money – this is the same as telling them how to live their life. Allow them this independence and learn to respect your differences. People don't change very much, and only if they want to anyway, so if you love them your only option is to learn to accept what you can't change. The secret of happiness is changing what you can and learning to accept what you can't.

Find a Compromise

If you are feeling sympathetic towards your partner, rather than angry, it will be easier to think more creatively so that you are able to come up with compromises. For example, you want to buy a flat now but he wants to go travelling. You can either argue until you're blue in the face over who is right, or you can sit down and work out how both of you can achieve your goals. You may discover that he wants to buy a flat too, just not yet. Perhaps, as a compromise, he could shorten the length of his trip and you could put off your property purchase for a little while.

are you really fighting about money?

Sometimes in a fight we use money as a cover-up for something else. We fight about who paid for what because we don't want to admit to these other, more sensitive, fears.

There's a lovely description of this in a novel I once read by a French author. A man is shouting at his wife for spending too much money on a new pair of high heels which, like the good French woman she is, she considers absolutely *de rigueur.* So, she fires back with a comment about all the ridiculous ties he spends his money on. Before long, it becomes apparent that these two aren't fighting about clothes, or even money, at all. He thinks she looks far too sexy in her new heels and he's jealous that she'll attract other men. She's scared that he's buying all those ties to impress the new PA in his office. Stop blaming money! If you can talk honestly and openly in your relationship, you'll soon find that money may simply be a mask for these deeper emotions. After such fights, think hard about what your real emotions were. Why did what your partner said hurt quite so much? If you can identify what your real fear is, you are halfway to resolving the problem and overcoming this fear.

There are lots of easy ways to reduce the chances of you arguing about money. If you haven't come up with any of the above ideas, or are baulking at putting them into practice, perhaps there's a reason for that. Perhaps you would prefer to argue about money rather than face what is really troubling you.

JUSTINE'S TOP 10 TIPS

1) Work out how your parents or certain events have influenced your views on money. Then work out how your partner's views on money have been formed, so that you understand exactly what and who you are dealing with.

2) Analyse the way your partner behaves with his money, rather than just what he says he plans to do with it.

3) Communication is key in all good relationships, so don't let money become a taboo subject or problems are likely to grow, not go away.

4) When speaking about money try to avoid blame or nagging. Instead explain to your partner how certain behaviour makes you feel. Use the 'when you do this...I feel that...' formula then work together on a compromise.

5) Listen, listen, listen. If someone feels listened to and understood, they will open up and be more willing to compromise.

6) Make sure you are prepared to compromise as well. Admitting your own faults first often helps ease the tension.

7) Don't keep score in your arguments. The goal is to improve your relationship, not win points.

8) If you have very different approaches to saving and spending, at least identify if you both want to head in the same direction financially (i.e. if you have the same long-term goals or values in life).

9) Learn to accept your differences. The key to happiness is changing what you can and learning to accept what you can't. If you can't accept him as he is, you have more to worry about than financial compatibility.

10) Analyse yourself – are your fights really about money or are they being used as a cover-up for deeper issues?

KIDS aND MONeY

'Children today are tyrants. They contradict their parents, gobble their food, and tyrannise their teachers.'
Socrates 470-399 BC

Conflicts between parents and children over money can occur at all stages of your life: from when you have very small children asking for pocket money, to economically dependent adult children, and even beyond the grave if you plan on leaving an inheritance to your heirs.

At all points along the way, a sensitive approach to managing these situations will help you, as well as a willingness to genuinely see things from your child's (or grandchild's) point of view. At the same time, it's important to realise when you need to be strong and say no to them for their own good and the development of their independence and self-esteem. Obviously, walking this emotional tightrope can be very difficult at times.

Set a good example

One of the best ways to teach children how to manage their money well is to make sure you are managing your own finances effectively. Children usually learn from the example you set, rather than from what you tell them, so if you ever needed an incentive to sort your finances out, this is it. Studies show that the messages we receive about money early on in life influence the way we handle it as adults. The earlier chapter on discovering your own money attitudes should have helped you to recognise your strengths and weaknesses in handling money. Fortunately, even if you are a terrible money manager, it doesn't mean your kids will turn out like that – in fact, it may spur them to become brilliant financiers because they are so sick of living in a family where there never seems to be enough money to go around. The important things are the subtle messages they receive about money, influenced by your own beliefs. Do you believe, and therefore give your children the impression, that money is evil or bad in any way? Do you encourage saving and thrift, or have the attitude that 'you can't take it with you'? Do you take part in charitable activities and encourage your children to do so as well? Be aware of the messages you are sending because they could have a lasting impact.

Talk about it

If you are unsure how your children feel about money, a good start is simply to talk to them about it. Many people send their children very strong messages through their actions but never actually broach the subject in conversation. It's a bit like not talking about sex. If you don't ever talk about money, your children may grow up with the impression that it is wrong to do so, and fail to ask for help when they need it. Often, the only time parents mention money is when they are saying 'no you can't have that, we can't afford it'. Even in families where money is occasionally discussed, parents may not explicitly teach children about how you actually manage it.

Four key elements

When discussing the financial world with your kids, there are four key elements you can look at covering:

* Spending
* Saving
* Investing
* Donating

Spending

Most children are very familiar with this element – spending. In fact, they probably think they know more about it than you do. Marketing companies have made an art of bombarding our children with advertisements designed to entice them into spending as much as possible. Unless you are sending them some alternative messages, children can grow up with this rather limited and naive view of money that could get them into all sorts of problems with debt. Use any opportunity to drum home your views when issues about spending come up. One man I know, when his grandson asked for a £1 bag of chips, gave him a long lecture on how that £1, if it were wisely invested, would add up to a fortune by the time the child reached his age.

Perhaps the next time your child asks for something, you could say to them, 'Well, can you afford it?' This gets them thinking about how there's a price for everything and that issues such as affordability have to be taken into account before making a purchase. It also takes the pressure off you as ultimate provider and gets them thinking about becoming more self-reliant. A friend of mine did this with her three-year-old. Unfortunately, she made the mistake of adding: 'Do you have a credit card?' This not only sent out the message that a credit card was a magic wand that could buy him anything he wanted, but also inspired him to steal his grandmother's credit card and stow it away in his toybox for the next time his mother asked the question.

Saving

The way to 'sell' the concept of saving is to demonstrate how children can achieve their goals – a new bike for example – by saving small amounts regularly. One trick is to ask them to write down their short- and long-term financial goals and then to sit down with them and work out how they are going to achieve them. Many children enjoy this problem-solving game, especially when the end reward is something they really want. You may be surprised to find that they are motivated to take on part-time work or offer to do extra jobs around the house to meet their goal earlier. Also, if you take the time to work on these goals with your children and then perhaps post their list of goals, or a picture of the goal they are aiming for, somewhere visible in the house, they are more likely to continue working towards it and not give up.

Another idea is to give them a little quiz to teach them about compound interest. Ask them: 'At age ten, you decide to start saving £1 a day in a savings account earning 5% interest a year.

At age 20, approximately how much do you think this money would be worth?'

a) £1,000
b) £2,000
c) £3,000
d) £5,000

The answer is, of course, (d) £5,000. If the money was kept under the mattress it would only amount to around £3,000, the rest of the return comes from interest.

If your children are a bit older and perhaps already earning a small income, teaching them how to do a budget from their very first pay packet could start a habit that helps them for a lifetime. The famous Rockefeller children learned from a young age, through a family tradition, to always save 10% of everything they earned and to donate a further 10% to charity. The other 80% was theirs to keep.

One way to encourage saving is to promise to match pound for pound any savings that your children build up, particularly if the idea is that they are saving for a very long-term goal, which they may find difficult to visualise. This incentive plan will help them meet their goals faster and also show them the power of compounding.

Many British children are already showing an avid interest in saving. A study by NatWest as part of its 'Face 2 Face with Finance' programme for schools found 76% of youngsters understood the importance of savings and were amassing more than £107 million a year in their piggy banks and bank accounts. The study also found that 68% of 11 to 18-year-olds thought they should be learning about how to manage money and save while at school.

Don't Kill Off Their Initiative

For parents who have already started a savings or investment programme on behalf of their child, I would add one note of caution. It can be very tempting to want to do too much for your kids and help them out financially as much as you can. Of course, I can understand this sentiment but sometimes the more you do for someone the less they do for themselves, so you could find you are inadvertently stripping them of initiative. My parents didn't give me any pocket money until I was in high school, so I had to come up with my own ingenious ideas on how to pay for the things I wanted. This kind of creative thinking can be a very valuable lesson for children. I've heard many stories from now extremely wealthy men of how they first learnt about money as children when they started delivering newspapers, created a lemonade stand, sold second-hand comic books or broken fortune cookies and even rented out pinball machines. This last idea was from a 13-year old entrepreneur, who grew up to be Warren Buffett, one of the wealthiest men in the world.

Another risk is that some parents put themselves into financial trouble in the name of helping their children. If you grew up in a family where you had to wear hand-me-downs or your parents couldn't afford certain things, it may be very tempting to give your children all the things you never had. Be careful not to go overboard with this idea. If you put yourself into debt so that your children look just as cool as their schoolmates, you may risk not being able to afford to pay for their university education. It's surprising how many people get into all sorts of problems with credit card debt in the name of 'helping' their kids. Few of them realise that the message they are sending to their children through these actions is that credit cards are not 'real' money and that it's OK to spend more than you earn. When it comes to helping your kids, the rule is the same as the safety instructions on a plane, where they say put the air mask over your own mouth before you attach your child's. Make sure you take care of your own financial health first, otherwise you won't be able to help them out in the future, when they may really need it.

Linked to this is the idea of building up a savings pot for your child when they are born. Although I love this idea myself, as children are perfectly positioned to benefit from the amazing effects of compound growth, it too can be dangerous if you go overboard. Why bother to learn to save for yourself if your parents have already done it for you? By always saving for your kids, and telling them you are doing so, they may never learn how to save for themselves. Most people know that we often learn to do something by doing it. Saving for your child's university education or helping them onto the property ladder is one thing. Handing them a lump sum at 18 to do whatever they want with could be quite different. Generally, people don't appreciate the things that have come to them too easily, so don't jeopardise your own financial future trying to pull together savings for your child. It's a type of martyrdom they may not appreciate anyway.

Don't Hide Your Failures

If you are open about the financial difficulties you come across in life, your children are much less likely to have the impression that 'money grows on trees' and will be better prepared for adult life. As I discuss later in this chapter, one of the reasons some adult children stay at home for longer than expected is because they feel unprepared to face the financial realities of modern day life. They may have been raised in comfortable surroundings and are fearful of experiencing the drop in living standards that comes with leaving home. In the same way that some people don't like to talk about money, they may try to protect their children by never revealing the financial problems they experience. This can be a huge mistake, because then your children never have the opportunity to learn the same lessons you have learnt from this experience and may be doomed to repeat it.

INVESTING

There are a number of board games, like Monopoly, which teach children about investing in a fun way.

Additionally, for several years now, the Share Centre has run an annual Shares4Schools competition, where school children build up a portfolio of stocks and compete against other schools. The idea is to teach them how to invest in stocks, and there have been many instances of these children not only beating the performance of the overall stock market, but also of many professionals in the industry.

One very successful fund manager I know in London told me how he started his career this way. He made his first stock market investment at 13 and was so successful that it spawned a love affair with the market that helped him build his own funds management company and later retire early. Many teenagers are keen to learn all they can about the magical world of high finance. Encourage them in these endeavours, while at the same time pointing out that it isn't necessarily the route to instant riches they may think it is. As with your own forays into the stock market, any early failures could be extremely beneficial if they teach your children that it's not always as easy as it looks, but persistence is the key to long-term success.

DONATING

If you are involved in a charity yourself, then don't be afraid to drag your child or sullen teenager along to these events. They might not think it's a 'cool' thing to do at the time, but many studies have shown that involvement in a charity can be a huge boost to self-esteem and also help them develop their own identity. This is particularly important if you come from a fairly wealthy family and are worried about your children becoming too spoilt from having everything their hearts desire. Donating and charity work have been the route to happiness for many dissatisfied children from wealthy families. Try to pick a charity that might interest your child, rather than just one of your own pet projects. For example, if your young teenager has suddenly announced they want to become vegetarian, it may be because they are concerned about animal welfare, so a charity related to animals could fire up their enthusiasm.

ADULT CHILDREN – CROWDED NESTS

Nowadays, grown-up children refusing to leave home is a common scenario for baby boomer parents. Laddish 20- and 30-something boys spend their days lounging around their parents' home, extending their degrees and seducing women. They are still living the student life long after they should have grown up and moved on.

The idea that their children wouldn't want to grasp hold of their independence as early as possible is a source of consternation to parents who grew up in the 1950s and '60s, when many young people were leaving home straight after school to enter fairly good jobs. Their own experiences at this age were of joyfully embracing their new-found freedom and financial independence. The baby boomer generation as teens became a significant and influential consumer group and created a previously untapped market.

The current generation of young people has quite different views on financial independence. Rather than being something exciting and adventurous, many young people find it terrifying.

As sociologists Schnaiberg and Goldenberg pointed out in their study, young people today have many more reasons than their parents not to leave home.

These incentives include material comfort, economic security and emotional support. With such strong financial incentives, young people today are increasingly prepared to delay the benefits of privacy and increased sexual freedom that living independently brings.

According to the Office of National Statistics, the number of young people still living at home has increased in recent years, particularly among males, with one in four men in their twenties still living with their parents.

In 2005, 57% of 20 to 24-year-old men had failed to flee the nest, up from 50% in 1991. Among 25 to 29-year-olds, 23% were still at home compared with 19% in 1991.

Women were more likely to leave home at an early age with only 38% of 20-24 year-olds still at home in 2005, up from 32% in 1991. Among slightly older women, 11%, up from 9%, were still benefitting from this free accommodation.

While their fathers might have been able to land a well-paid job that could support themselves and a wife with just a high school certificate, today's youths need higher qualifications of degrees and even post-graduate degrees if they want to be able to compete in the workforce.

People are also marrying around a decade later these days. The average marrying age in the UK for women is 29 and 31 for men. This means there is less need for privacy and more time to live a glamorous single life trying to find your perfect mate, rather than starting to build your own nest.

In many cases, the wealthier and more successful their parents have been, the more comfortable a person's life at home is and the less incentive they have to leave. Additionally, the more protective parents have been in giving their children the best they could, the more the idea of economic self-sufficiency is unattractive.

Why leave home when you are in a comfortable, familiar environment with loved ones around you? Moving out would mean a substantial drop in lifestyle, not to mention all the uncertainties of a fickle job market, likely lower standards of accommodation and taking on difficult financial responsibilities. Some may even be afraid of taking on emotional responsibilities, given the high divorce rate.

Despite these many apparent benefits, it is of course in the child's best interest that they let go of the apron strings and assume adult responsibilities and economic independence.

A Way Out

The way to wean children off the idea that staying at home is best is to gradually reduce the financial benefits while continuing to maintain, or increasing, emotional support. Adult children these days need more emotional and psychological support than ever, particularly if their parents have been very protective of them in the past.

It's important to build self-confidence and learn to listen to your children rather than simply directing or giving them orders. By allowing them to make their own decisions, they will have more faith in themselves and feel more capable of venturing out on their own. If you give a man a fish, you have fed him for a day, teach a man to fish and you have fed him for a lifetime.

If they don't feel prepared for adult economic life perhaps it's because they haven't been given enough instruction on how to deal with it. Many families don't talk about money, but by actively showing them how to manage a budget and juggle responsibilities, rather than protecting them from these things, you will help them much more.

One way of teaching children about money is to share your own financial challenges. Children may be under the mistaken impression that life has always been this easy for their parents and not realise the financial struggles and difficult times which had to be encountered before their parents finally reached a comfortable lifestyle. They may have entered adulthood with unrealistic optimism, expecting the same comforts as their parents, only to be shocked by the difficulties they face. By sharing economic difficulties, children are more aware that life has its ups and downs but success can be achieved eventually and it doesn't have to be scary.

If you are embarking on a plan to 'phase out' economic dependency, you will likely come up against tears and even hostility in the initial stage. However, with continued emotional support, and as children get a taste of financial independence, they will begin to enjoy it and the self-confidence that comes with it.

INHERITANCE PLANNING

'Power in the hands of one who did not acquire it gradually is often fatal to success.' Napoleon Hill

History is littered with examples of men, and sometimes women, who inherited riches without any effort and promptly squandered it. There's an old Chinese saying we would do well to heed: the first generation creates the wealth, the second generation builds it up and the third generation loses it all.

However, there is no reason to go back to the history books to find examples. Just pick up any newspaper or entertainment industry magazine and you can find examples of wealthy rock stars, actors or sports heroes spending extreme amounts of money and often doing damage to their health in the process.

'Cocaine is God's way of telling you that you have too much money.' Robin Williams

It is not uncommon for men and women to be inspired to create great fortunes following a modest upbringing. These rags-to-riches stories make great reading because they inspire us all with hope. It makes you feel all warm and fuzzy inside reading about the determined efforts of a man of humble origins as he battles against all the obstacles to reach the top of his pile. The greatest challenge these men face, however, may be in ensuring that their wealth is retained and not thrown to the winds by their offspring. As Andrew Carnegie, a mighty steel baron and one of the richest men of his time wrote: 'The parent who leaves his son enormous wealth generally deadens the talents and energies of the son.'

In the same way that having poor parents can inspire you

to become wealthy, having rich parents can kill off the urge to earn and, if handled incorrectly, can even lead heirs to destroying themselves with the wanton use of their parents' wealth.

What the rich do

As our society has become wealthier, so have an increasing number of families. One of the major concerns these days has become how to, or whether to, leave money to your heirs. In the past, this perhaps wasn't such a big issue for the majority of people as families simply didn't have significant assets to leave behind. Those assets that were inherited weren't large enough to cause major problems. However, today many more people are millionaires.

In the UK, it is estimated that there is an increasing number of property millionaires and, as we discussed earlier, many of them are now women.

Studies on the world's richest women show that these include women who head their own billion-dollar businesses, such as many of China's new female entrepreneurs or women like JK Rowling. Others are active directors or major shareholders in their husbands' companies – like Cristina Green, wife of Philip Green the owner of Topshop and the Arcadia clothing group.

Even where women have inherited their wealth, it's more likely to be from their husband or father rather than 'old money' from generations ago. For example, France's Lillian Bettencourt, whose father founded L'Oréal, is one of the richest women in the world.

The studies show, quite clearly, how difficult it is to make money last over the generations, even if you have a great fortune. Many wealthy parents, rather than see their children blow all their hard-earned dosh, prefer to leave their money to charity.

Famous millionaires like stockpicking guru Warren Buffett and Microsoft's Bill Gates have stated that they plan to give the majority of their wealth away to charity. They, like many others, are concerned that their enormous fortunes could prove to be a burden to their children and kill off the incentive that money often provides to become a productive member of society. The idea is to give them enough money so that they feel they are able to do what they want with their lives, but not so much that they are inspired to do nothing. Certainly, there is a real fear that with too much money heirs could succumb to the behaviour of overly rich movie stars and football heroes who spend their time on fast cars, fast women and too much alcohol or drugs. In addition, most people want their wealth to be used for a good purpose, rather than simply be splurged, and if the family is already well-provided for, then the next avenue is to help the poor or something like the environment.

Nevertheless, if you have decided you would like to leave some money to your heirs, what is the best way to do it?

Tax, Wills and the Queen of Hearts

When Princess Diana died in August 1997, her will, which had been signed in June 1993, had not been altered to take account of the £17 million divorce settlement she had received from Charles in 1996.

Her level of wealth estimated in the will was much lower than the approximately £20 million she eventually left behind to her sons, William and Harry.

As a result, a large chunk of her divorce settlement,

more than £8.5 million, went to the tax man in the form of an inheritance tax bill.

The executors of her will also had to negotiate with the tax authorities to try to exempt her famous wedding dress from death duties.

Prince Charles considered trying to get a court to overturn the settlement. He wanted the money to return to him, so that he could put it in a trust for his sons, but in the end the princes paid the tax. Incidentally, the princes won't receive their full inheritance payment until they turn 30.

If Diana's will had been altered before her death, no doubt her advisers would have put in place measures to reduce the amount of inheritance tax her heirs would have to pay. The Queen is not subject to inheritance tax – she didn't pay any when her mother died – but the rest of the royals and other lords and ladies are affected by the same rules as you or me.

This story highlights the importance of making a will and, even if you have already made a will, it may need to be altered to take account of any major change in your circumstances. You may consider yourself too poor for things such as wills. However, it's very important for women with children, whether married or single, to make a will so that they can name a reliable person as guardian to look after their children in the event of premature death.

For example, Diana didn't want her husband to have the sole responsibility for bringing up her sons and specified in her will that her brother, Earl Spencer, and her mother be guardians if both she and Charles died early.

In the UK, you need to leave behind total assets of more than £285,000, before your heirs are affected by the 40% inheritance tax. In the past decade, rising property prices have made it fairly easy to go over this amount – and even with the current troubled market, house prices are still very high. Fortunately, there are a number of ways your estate can be managed before death in order to minimise this tax bill.

Tax

Briefly, the main inheritance tax rules in the UK at the time of writing are:

Nil-rate band: If you were to inherit £200,000 from your mother and this was her entire estate – i.e. the value of her home plus all her possessions – you wouldn't have to pay any tax because the amount is below the threshold (in the tax year 2008-2009 this was £312,000. This threshold will rise to £350,000 by 2010-2011). You won't even have to report the money to the Inland Revenue on your tax form because it will be reported by the executors of her estate. Nor should you have to pay any income or capital gains tax on the money, but if you invest it you might have to pay tax on the interest or other gains you make from this investment.

Between spouses: If you are married, you can transfer your entire estate to your spouse and they won't have to pay inheritance tax on it. However, when your spouse dies, your children would be eligible for the tax on whatever is left. Therefore, it usually makes sense to ensure some of your money is left directly to your children, in case you die first, so that you can both utilise your personal nil-rate bands.

Gifts: You can give a gift, money or items to your heirs before you die, as long as you live for another seven years after making the gift. If you die before, your heirs will have to pay tax on the gift.

Annual gifts: In addition, you could give your children or grandchildren up to £3,000 a year in tax-free gifts. There are also special provisions for weddings, where you are allowed to give them more if it's a wedding present.

Also, you can give any number of £250 gifts to different people. So, in theory you could stand on a street corner and hand out £250 to each passer-by until your wealth was used up and none of them would have to pay inheritance tax on the money.

If you really hate the idea of the taxman getting any of your money then you can give all your assets to charities like the National Trust, or even a political party, and there won't be any tax on it.

Ruling from the grave

Money can also be held in trust so that heirs don't receive it straightaway, or only receive income, so that the main assets can continue to grow. Investments can be structured in a variety of ways, but this is a constantly changing and complex area of finance with governments often altering the rules, so it is wise to speak to a professional adviser to be sure you are structuring your assets properly.

Some people are so determined not to leave any money to the taxman that they would rather give all their assets away to charity or the National Trust. Of course, if you are the person who has built up the money, then it's not you but your heirs who will have to worry about the tax bill, but most people want to ensure their heirs are not put under any financial pressure needlessly.

But what if you have significant assets and would like to control how the money you leave behind is spent? Perhaps one of your children or grandchildren has always displayed signs of being a spendthrift, despite your wise counselling, and you are concerned that they would fritter away their inheritance, or worse, blow it on alcohol or drugs.

Alternatively, you may have a son or daughter who you believe is in an unstable marriage and you are concerned about their spouse gaining access to your wealth or continuing the relationship purely for financial reasons. In other cases, one of your heirs may be disabled and need significant financial resources to support themselves, or simply be young and immature in the ways of money, so you'd like them to inherit the money eventually, but perhaps not just yet.

In many of these cases, a good financial adviser or estate planner can set up a trust, perhaps with older heirs having power of attorney, which puts in certain criteria (e.g. they may only benefit when they reach the required age). Or you may want money to be left to pay for your grandchildren's university education. Bear in mind though, that they may not decide to pursue higher education, or perhaps they will and then drop out. Does that mean only those heirs following the required route benefit? And what if they study something unproductive simply to take advantage of the inheritance? These are all difficult questions which people with money will need to think long and hard about when deciding how to divvy up their assets.

At the end of the day, there is no point trying too hard to control how your family spends the money you leave them. If you have taught them well and trust that they are responsible people, then that should be some comfort. At some point you just have to let go and learn to trust them. They may waste some of the money, or not use it in a way that you would have preferred, but once you have given it to them, it is a gift and theirs to do with as they please. There is no point trying to rule from the grave or complaining after the fact that the money wasn't spent in a way you would have liked: it's not your money anymore once you have given it to them.

JUSTINE'S TOP 10 TIPS

1) Make sure you set a good example to your children by managing your own finances well – children often learn from watching you.

2) Talk about money, don't make it a 'taboo' and be open about your successes as well as failures.

3) Make saving and investing a game so that children see it as enjoyable and positive.

4) Don't blow all your assets on your kids: they won't thank you for it in the long run.

5) If you have children who won't leave home, gradually reduce the financial benefits while increasing the emotional support you give them.

6) Make a will, even if it's only to specify who will be the guardians of your children, and update it as soon as any major changes occur in your life.

7) If you are wealthy, think carefully about what effect a large inheritance could have on your children psychologically and consider whether leaving some money to charity, and less to your heirs, might actually be in their interest.

8) It pays to get a will done professionally, as there are many things that you might not foresee in the future, but which a legal professional will make provision for, and to get financial advice to reduce inheritance tax.

9) Think about whether you are trying too hard to 'rule from the grave' and control the future, which may not make your heirs happy.

10) Think carefully about how you split any assets between children so that they don't end up squabbling over it after you are gone.

SECTION TWO

TAKING CONTROL

Career Development and Negotiating

Pay Tactics

If you want to know how to get rich, there are two methods. The first is to reduce your spending, and the second is to increase your earnings. Personally, I like to do both: reduce my spending, and then increase my earnings by investing those savings.

However, when I speak to most people about increasing their earnings, they think of their job and about increasing their pay. Certainly, this is one way to get more money. For most of this book, I've focused on the saving and investing strategy, but it's also a good idea to exploit your job. By negotiating well, you can keep doing the same thing but get more money for it, and that certainly makes financial sense.

Some researchers believe that the reason many women are paid less than men is because they don't negotiate well enough. While men expect to be paid well, and often demand it, women feel privileged just to have a job and focus more on work conditions than pay.

A study by Linda Babcock at Carnegie Mellon University in the US, found that the starting salaries of men who graduated in her year were 7.4% higher than the women's, simply because they asked for more and didn't just accept the first offer they were given.

Personally, I have come across people who don't meet these stereotypes – men who negotiated very badly and subsequently were paid poorly, and women who talked their way into 'movie star money' – so don't let the statistics put you off. As W Somerset Maugham wrote in *The Treasure*: 'It's a funny thing about life: if you refuse to accept anything but the best, you very often get it.' The above study shows that even if you are a graduate with no work experience, you still have the power to negotiate a higher salary.

TIPS FOR IMPROVING YOUR NEGOTIATING ABILITY

Power

Negotiating is often about power. Many women feel quite powerless in a negotiating situation, especially if it is with their boss, who can decide their future and usually has more experience than they. It is crucial that you are psychologically prepared before you go into any negotiation. The more confident you are, the more power you have, and the stronger the position you are in when negotiating. This is regardless of your level of skills or intelligence. It's important to believe that you deserve a pay rise, otherwise you won't dare to ask for one. As the above study showed, even a young graduate, with no experience, can talk their way into a well-paid job if they are cocky enough. If you are already employed, remember that your employer should want to have happy workers who stick around. High job turnover makes them look bad, and is costly.

Negotiating is a Process

If you get very stressed about negotiating pay, it may ease your concerns a little to remember that negotiating is a process, not a single meeting. There are lots of things you can do beforehand to prepare yourself so relax and take your time working out a deal. If you are in a hurry, it puts you in a weaker position, so at least give the impression that you want to take your time. Don't let someone force you into agreeing to a deal when you haven't had time to evaluate your options properly.

Do Your Homework

You have to know what you want to get out of any deal before you go into it. Write down your objectives in terms of what you need, what you want and what would be nice – usually three figures. Ask for something outrageous that you don't think you'll get and work backwards from there – you're then more likely to end up with what you really want. Let's say you are currently being paid £30,000, so that's how much you 'need' to be paid. What you want from a new employer, to compensate for moving jobs and all the unknowns that entails, is £35,000. Is that what you ask for? No, ask for £40,000 and let them talk you down. Your 'needs' can also be certain perks that you must get to accept the job. Your 'wants' could be things that you are prepared to let go of, but only if you get something else in return. And your 'would be nice' list is filled with things that are less important but can be used as bargaining chips. The person you are negotiating with shouldn't know which of these things you are willing to part with. If you are very well prepared, you should also know what things the other party is likely to have on his or her list of needs and wants.

Know Your Opponent

The better you understand what your negotiating opponent wants to get out of a deal, the better prepared you'll be. If you can see things from their point of view, you'll be able to explain how you can help them get what they want, and at the same time achieve your own objectives. If people feel listened to and understood, whether it's your boss or your partner, they are more likely to accept a situation they wouldn't have come up with themselves.

If you have done your homework well, you will know what the other person is looking for. One idea is to ask your boss for a very brief meeting, before the actual pay negotiation takes place. The idea of this is not to reveal any of your objectives, but to find out some information on what they are looking for. If he asks for your objectives, say you will discuss that in the proper meeting, this is just something casual to give you an idea of what they want. Take notes and really listen to them, so you are sure about what they want. That way, in the official meeting, you can concentrate on what you're trying to say and also have time to read their body language. If this pre-meeting is not possible, try to find out from other colleagues what your employer is like to negotiate with, or how other meetings have gone. In some companies, there is a procedure that more long-standing workers will be aware of. Don't be afraid to talk to your colleagues about pay and conditions; they are a vital source of information and the more information you have, the stronger the position you are in.

Conflict

Conflict is a natural part of negotiation – this is quite difficult for some women to deal with, as they usually try to avoid conflict in life. Don't allow this inevitable tension to upset you. Of course you will have different objectives – you are different people. Just think of it all as a kind of game and try not to get too emotional about it. Some people may try to use underhand tactics (as I will explain later) to get their way, so just look at these as the immature moves they are. Rise above it all and stick firmly to your objectives.

Know Your Strengths and Weaknesses

Employers often ask you to list your strengths and weaknesses. Rather than listing all your weaknesses, tell them the areas where you would like to improve and how you are going to do it. If you know where you are going and how you want to progress in the company, your employer is more likely to see you as a good investment and may even offer to pay for training.

Have an idea before you go in where you want your career to go and what shorter-term goals you have set yourself. If you can show you have a clear map planned out for the year ahead (especially one that fits in with their objectives) they will be in a much better mood with you. It shows you have enthusiasm for the job – which is a key characteristic that employers look for. Of course, make sure you follow through on these plans.

Don't Reveal All Your Cards at First

In the initial stages of a negotiation, you shouldn't reveal all your interests and you should try to listen more than talk. The person who talks the most usually has the most to lose. One boss I had was extremely good at this and used to stare intently at you so that you got nervous and chatted away, revealing all sorts of things that you didn't want to. After you had said one thing, he would just nod and say *hmmm*, so that you kept talking. If someone asks a question you don't really want to answer, try to be vague and turn it around so that you ask them a question instead. Another trick is to say something like: 'Oh, I think the more important issue is this…' and then explain it. I was once asked for a very specific statistic in an interview – which I didn't know. I simply explained that I didn't think this figure was so important and that there were other issues (such as…) that were more interesting. The interviewer looked a bit taken aback at first, but it worked, because I got the job. Later, I found out that this was a standard question he asked everyone and few people ever knew the answer, but many of them got flustered and nervous by it – weakening their position.

However, if you are involved in a long negotiation and have built up some trust over time, you may want to reveal more and be more honest as a sign of goodwill. It will help the other party see that you are after a win-win situation and they may be more willing to compromise on certain things. Make sure you keep an open mind as well and are prepared to compromise on certain things – though of course not everything. If you compromise on too much, your opponent will not respect you and also just think you're a bit silly.

State That You Want a Win-Win Outcome

As I explained, understanding what your counterpart wants puts you in a better position to come up with a compromise that suits you both. Although there will always be some conflict, you can arrange a good deal that you are both happy, with if you use your imagination and listen well. That way, you both get what you want and the time you spend together in the future will be more satisfactory. If you negotiate badly, you may feel bitter afterwards and not work as hard as you could.

I once worked for a man who negotiated quite badly. When I went in for my pay review, he basically threatened to sack me, saying that I had a very good job and should be pleased with how much I was getting paid. This completely shocked me because I knew I had done an excellent job and that my more immediate boss was extremely happy with me. I didn't realise it at the time, but in fact he was struggling to pay all his staff and couldn't afford to give me the pay rise he knew I was expecting. In fact, he had promised an increase in pay after a set period when I was first hired and his time was up. Unfortunately for him, I was so offended by his attitude that I left the company not long after for a much better job (on more pay). He was hopping mad about that and then tried to make me feel guilty for leaving him short-staffed. If he had been more honest with me, I might have stayed, despite the pay, as long as I felt appreciated. For him, the first rule of negotiating was not to reveal his real motivation and to just go after his own objectives, ignoring the idea of a win-win outcome. This cost him the deal.

Be Prepared to Walk Away

As anyone who has ever dated a 'bad boy' knows – if you are too attached to something, you will be in a weaker position in a negotiation. If you really like him, you'll let him turn up late for dates and forget flowers on Valentine's Day and when you complain, he won't take you seriously because he knows you're head over heels and he has the upper hand. Don't let yourself get into this position with money! You always need to be prepared to walk away if the conditions are really not satisfactory. Quite often, women put up with pay and conditions that are far worse than they deserve simply because they are too scared to walk away or stand up for their rights. Have a little confidence. If you know you have certain skills that are valuable, then you should be paid for that. Speaking to as many prospective employers as possible will also help you realise your value and make it easier to say no to the ones that come up short.

The objective for many bosses is to get away with paying their employees as little as possible, while getting as much productive work out of them as possible. Your objective is to get as much money as possible while working in an environment that you enjoy. A lot of people seem to expect their boss to simply know how much money they want and pay them what they deserve. It might sound fair, but unfortunately, reality is not like that, so don't waste your time wishing things were different. Instead, focus on learning how to play the game better.

Watch Out for the Following Underhand Negotiation Strategies

* Writing up the contract, signing it and then sending it to you, assuming you will agree to it, without allowing for any negotiation.
* Similarly, not giving you appropriate time to review a contract thoroughly (or show it to a lawyer) before asking you to sign.
* Claiming that certain terms are 'standard practice' – this may or may not be the case, so you need to do some research first before agreeing.

* Claiming that this is their company policy, so you have to agree to certain terms. In this case, just tell them you would like to agree to a contract that is 'outside normal policy'. This can, and often does happen. You can have an agreement letter, which is outside of the normal contract.
* Offering you an interview, but only with their Human Resources department (initially). They are there to screen out weaker candidates, so be careful, and say as little as possible. A person from HR is not able to discuss money so you need to get to the next level for the real negotiating.
* If you are on a tight deadline and the other party knows this, they can use it against you.
* Inflating the importance of a minor issue, so that you overlook something else they are more interested in pushing through – a common ploy among politicians.
* Pretending to walk out on the deal in favour of someone else, so that you reduce your terms.
* Playing 'good cop, bad cop', with one person negotiating in a tough way, while the other smoothes things over.
* Saying they don't have the authority to agree to certain things and would have to refer to someone higher. In this case, you should stop negotiating with the person making this claim and insist on only negotiating with the more senior person.

Finally, if someone uses too many dodgy tactics you may want to reassess whether you want to do any business with them – particularly if this is a prospective employer. Is that the sort of company environment you want to spend the majority of your day in?

LISTENING

Studies have shown that women usually have a higher level of conversational skills than men, are less likely to have speech impediments, and find it easier to get their ideas across. Unfortunately, our knack of being able to chat away can work against us in a negotiation, if we fail to listen. By talking too much, you can give too much away and miss what your employer, or whoever you are negotiating with, is really looking for from you.

I have always been a bit of a talker. My dad used to say that I could talk underwater with a mouthful of marbles. Although I thought I was being smart and savvy by jabbering away about how wonderful I was, or what excellent points I had to put across, this often worked against me. There's an old saying from Proverbs, 'Even a fool is considered wise when he keeps silent.' It always amazed me at school that certain girls, who may have simply had very little to say, seemed shrouded in a mist of wisdom just because they were able to keep their traps shut. I have been making the mistake of talking too much and not listening enough for many years, but the older I get, the more convinced I am that this approach simply doesn't work and often does more harm than good.

Running off at the mouth can not only harm your career prospects, but it can also damage your relationships. We all know how hurtful words can be and sadly the person saying them may not even mean to be so harsh; they may simply be speaking and not thinking. Once said, those cruel words are difficult to take back, particularly if you are in a sensitive situation where emotions are highly charged. I've seen a flippant remark end careers and do untold damage to marriages. So, if you have the gift of the gab, take some advice from someone who has learnt the hard way and try to listen more and think carefully before you open your mouth.

When you are in a negotiation situation, you must listen hard, not just with your ears but with your eyes as well. Body language can give away a lot, so before you begin make sure you are clear on the main points you want to get across and then try to spend the rest of the time in focused listening mode. If you do this well, the other party will likely appreciate that you are listening to them and that will improve your chances of success.

Make them like you – negotiating

Judith Merians, a top-notch negotiator and US lawyer, maintains that your goal in any negotiating situation is often to get the other party to like you. We all know that you catch more flies with honey and this doesn't just apply to an interview situation. You will help your career enormously if you spend some time networking and getting to know as many people in the office as possible – particularly the important people. Know who the movers and shakers are, and if someone in a higher position compliments you or notices your work, make a point of thanking them personally or taking them out to lunch. If you have a personal connection with someone, they are more likely to think of you when an interesting opportunity arises.

This is particularly important for women, as men often do this sort of networking without realising it. They might go for drinks with their boss or senior colleagues or join in a sporting event which is mostly played by men. This puts them in a much more attractive position than their female colleague who might not be into drinking or competitive sports.

A good idea is to take someone to lunch whom you respect and admire, and then pick their brains about how they got to where they are. People always love talking about themselves, so this shouldn't be too difficult. If you get on quite well, you could also ask them what they think you should do to enhance your career. Often, they will have insights you hadn't even thought of.

If you find yourself being asked questions you don't want to answer, or feel put on the spot, it's often a good idea to say 'That's interesting, but I'd like to come back to it later.' This way you don't say no or finalise anything and give yourself time to think and work out a solution that better fits your needs.

Job Interviews

There are some particular tips for negotiating for a new job which women in particular need to be aware of.

1) Negotiate for the whole package. Don't just focus on the salary. Other benefits such as a car, insurance, pensions, client entertainment, travel expenses, bonuses, commissions, healthcare etc are just as important, and becoming increasingly so. Often, these things don't cost the company that much – they may even be tax deductible – but would make a big difference to your lifestyle. The employer may not bring up these other benefits but you should. Men always ask for an expense account.

2) Research the company. Go online and find out the salaries of all the top personnel, what profits the company is making, who their main competitors are. You will get a better package if you target jobs in a department that is growing. Similarly, it helps if you know someone who already works there and can give you an introduction. A personal reference is always preferred.

3) Make a list of your skills showing how you would be an asset to this company. Do your homework on the company, so that you have a clear idea of where they are making most of their money and their growth areas. If your skills could help them to grow, you will be far more valuable. For example, let's say you are a personal assistant applying for a job with a multi-national company. You also learn French at night school and, lucky for you, this particular company is thinking of expanding its operations in France. Although you might not feel comfortable putting French on your CV yet, you should definitely mention this area of interest.

4) Never get emotional. If something comes up which really upsets you and you think your emotions might get the better of you, excuse yourself from the room and come back later.

5) Network, network, network. Make friends with other people in your industry, as well as important people within your company. You never know when your company might decide to retrench people and those industry friends will come in handy. Ideally, the majority of people in your industry should know who you are and, importantly, respect your work. As I mentioned earlier, if they have a personal connection with you, they are more likely to recommend you.

6) Don't accept a fancy title without any salary increase. This is a common trap for many women. They like the titles because they make them feel appreciated, but you should always say, 'Thank you, that sounds lovely. What comes with that title?'

7) Don't bring up money until late in the negotiation process. Wait until you are sure they really want you and are very keen, then start working out the money.

8) If someone says no, try to find out why. Figure out a way to address their needs and meet your own. I was once turned down for a job, so afterwards wrote to the employer offering my services if any other positions came up. The employer was so impressed, he immediately rang me and said he'd never received a letter like mine and would certainly keep me in mind.

9) Don't answer inappropriate questions. You don't have to answer questions that are too personal or offensive. For example, if an employer asks if you're planning to get pregnant just say no and leave it at that. Don't add any more details. Similarly, you don't need to mention if you are married, living with someone or have three kids. That's none of their business and, as long as it doesn't affect your work, it shouldn't be an issue. If they find out you have lots of kids, or suggest you are too old for a position, just tell them you are a remarkable woman with an incredible amount of energy. What they really want to know is if they can rely on you when there's a tight deadline, so you should make this clear. This way you respond to them in a positive way, without answering the question directly.

JUSTINE'S TOP TIPS

1) Being able to negotiate is an important skill, whether it's for a job or an investment, so learn as much as you can about these techniques and don't be shy about asking for what you deserve.

2) Build up your confidence and you will improve your ability to negotiate.

3) Never be afraid to walk away from a deal, and don't let your opponent intimidate you.

4) Be prepared! The more homework you do, the better. It will also help you deal with underhand negotiation techniques.

5) Don't finalise anything in the meeting. If there is a new subject that is brought up and that you haven't researched, ask for more time to look at it before taking a stance or agreeing to anything.

6) Don't get emotional unless you are using emotion as a tool.

7) Get someone else to negotiate for you for very important deals, or at the very least get some good advice from someone who knows the industry or the people involved very well.

8) Your goal is to make sure the other person likes you – or at least doesn't dislike you.

9) Don't reveal anything you don't need to. In interviews answer sensitive questions simply and then just stop talking.

10) For work situations, do lots of networking ahead of time so that you can get a personal introduction and become well-regarded in your industry.

THE SAVING HABIT

'The difference between poor people and rich people is easy. The poor spend their money and then save what's left over; the rich save their money and then spend what's left over.'
Jim Rohn

My first lesson in saving came at the age of 11, when my Seventh Grade teacher talked to us about controlling our spending. I can't remember why she brought this topic up, but I know that she had been a poorly paid school teacher and single mum for most of her life and was still pretty careful with what she spent.

What she taught us, and it's the most memorable thing I learnt from her, is that you have to analyse everything before you buy it and decide if it is a 'want' or a 'need'. At the time I was getting pocket money from my parents of about £20 a semester – that's the grand sum of £40 a year. At first, it had seemed like a fortune, but I soon realised how quickly a hungry teenager can use up that kind of money once the sweet shop opens. Nevertheless, ever since then I've taken her advice to heart and it has certainly served me well.

Every month or so, I sit down and work out if I'm still on track with my financial goals, if I'm overspending or underspending, what my assets are now worth and how much I have in savings. If I'm doing well, it gives me a nice glow of satisfaction. If I haven't been so good, I work out where I can spend less, or how I can rearrange things to get more money. It takes a bit of creativity but not much.

I find that when I know I've been overspending, I start to get a bit stressed and act worried a lot. Usually, I let this sensation drag on for a few days, or even weeks, annoying the hell out of my friends and family, whingeing about my predicament to them. Eventually, though, I pull myself together and start working hard at cutting unnecessary expenses. Sometimes, this just means cooking at home more, getting a DVD/video instead of going to a movie, walking rather than paying for transport (or the gym!). At other times, it means coming up with creative solutions for Christmas and birthday presents or making sure I hunt down the lowest plane or train tickets for any upcoming trips. Other times, it's stuff like changing my phone or gas provider. If things are particularly bad, you may need a larger change – such as renting out a room in your home, selling off old books or having a car boot sale, quitting smoking or cutting down on alcohol, buying second-hand or making things, going to the library more often, or even selling your car.

I could give you a long list here of ways to save money, but I think the best source is your own imagination. It's amazing what you can come up with when you sit down and think about it. Besides, the things you are prepared to cut back on are not the same things another person would be prepared to do without. My mother used an old basket as a cradle for my older sister when she was born because she couldn't afford a proper cot at the time. I've heard of people even using old drawers, but when I suggested these ideas to a friend who was worrying about the costs of a new child, he was horrified. I'm sure I've done things in the name of saving money that have shocked or surprised my friends and family, but it didn't bother me to do them. I was often so firmly focused on a long-term savings goal that these small sacrifices seemed worth it. It didn't feel like it was a chore to walk 40 minutes in to work for example. In fact, I discovered that it became the most enjoyable part of my day. However, if you asked me to cut back on certain bath products, I would really feel like I was suffering.

If you are struggling for ideas on how to save, there are plenty of websites, books and even articles where people swap savings tips. Check out the following: **www.thisismoney.co.uk**, **www.moneysavingexpert.com** or **www.fool.co.uk**.

Alternatively, borrow books from the library such as: *How I lived on a Pound a Day* by Kath Kelly, *Thrifty Ways for Modern Days* by Martin Lewis, *The Thrift Book* by India Knight and *The New Spend Less Revolution* by Rebecca Ash.

The path to riches

'He that wants money, means, and content is without three good friends.'
William Shakespeare

A study by economists Steven Venti and David Wise called 'Choice, Chance and Wealth Dispersion at Retirement', proved that earning money is only half the job; the other half is how you manage it.

They found that income level and investment choice did not make a big difference to how wealthy people became. The main difference was due to the amount households saved. Two families with the same lifetime income can end up with vastly different levels of wealth at retirement simply due to the amount they save and the assets they are therefore able to build up.

Some families with low levels of lifetime earnings may accumulate substantial assets by retirement, while other families with high lifetime incomes may have very few financial assets. The authors found that certain things that are out of our control, such as unexpected medical bills or inheritances, have very little to do with this result. Similarly, investment choices, from conservative to risky, didn't have much effect on the level of assets at retirement. Instead, most of the money people had built up by retirement was due to the difference in the percentage of income those households chose to save.

I used to live with a friend who earned roughly the same level of salary as me. At the end of each month, I always had savings and he seemed to have somehow built up debt. The strange thing was that we weren't living radically different lives. Our rent and other household bills were the same, we spent the same amount on holidays and we lived a similar lifestyle. Yet most of his money was whittled away on little things like newspapers and magazines, books, snack food, coffees and little gifts he would buy himself. It's amazing how those little things added up to so much over time. Additionally, he wasn't very careful with the fees his bank (and other people) charged him. He would go over his overdraft by mistake and get hit with a £20 fine. I could understand this happening once, but it happened repeatedly. He also never got around to switching credit cards, even though his bank was charging almost 20% in interest.

Every individual has their own priorities when it comes to

money and we can't ask or expect the other people in our lives to change, just because we have a different view on what money should be spent on. People will decide for themselves if they want to change and if they don't, they won't. It's as simple as that. However, if you are the person with no savings and you're not happy with that situation, then it's much simpler. It's ten times easier to change your own behaviour than someone else's.

Taking control

Taking control of your money is a bit like being a parent. You have to be strong and disciplined and say no to the child within you a lot. If you take control of your money and handle it responsibly, it will treat you well and do your bidding and help you make more money. But if you spend it needlessly, it will get out of control and could destroy you. Every time you look at a purchase ask yourself the question: *Is it a 'want' or a 'need'?* Do you really need those gold pumps, or are you just spoiling yourself because you feel tired, hungry or emotionally needy and you think this purchase will comfort you?

How much should you save?

Most books about money and saving say you should try to save at least 10% of your earnings. I think this is a good level because often you discover that it's not that difficult to live on 90% of your earnings – you end up with a similar lifestyle to if you were living on 100% of the money. Personally, I have saved much more than this, between one-third and a half of my earnings at certain times. However, I wouldn't necessarily recommend this. At the time, I wasn't earning a particularly large salary, but I was just so excited about the idea of saving and investing that I was highly motivated to cut back as much as I could. I saw it as a challenge to see how far I could push myself and how little I could live on. A family friend used to say that I lived on the niff of an oil rag – which was, of course a complete exaggeration. Not surprisingly, though, it meant that my life wasn't terribly exciting at times (and my partner and friends found me quite a drag), but I was simply so focused on my goal that I didn't care. Besides, I discovered that many of the things in life that are really enjoyable are quite simple and don't necessarily involve money. Often, people are the real source of our joy in life, so just sharing a simple meal with good friends or spending time with loved ones can give you far more fulfilment than a trip to the shopping mall. These days, I'm happy to say I have a lot more balance in my life. I still save, but it's a more reasonable amount – 10% to 15% of earnings – and I make sure I get the best of both worlds with a mixture of controlled consumerism and spending lots of time with friends and family.

WHY WOMEN ARE LUCKY TO LIVE LONGER

'When prosperity comes, do not use all of it.'
Confucius

Women can benefit from the fact that they live longer than men if they take advantage of the amazing effects of compound growth – described by Albert Einstein as the greatest mathematical discovery of all time.

This concept is fairly well known in finance circles, but it is worth explaining for the sake of those who have never come across it before.

Basically, the idea is that every pound you save earns interest but if you also save the interest it starts to work for you too. That's your interest earning you *more* interest. In *The Richest Man in Babylon*, the author, George S Clason, describes it as putting your gold slaves to work for you. Every time you save a coin of gold, it is like having your own slave. The money (interest) that this slave earns turns into another slave that can also do your bidding. After a while, the money builds up and builds up until you have a fortune. The key is reinvesting all your interest and utilising the benefit of time.

Here's an example: Sally has £5,000 in savings at age 20. Assuming her money is earning her around 7% a year (either in interest from the bank or from share dividends or property rent), her money should double about every ten years.

At age 30, her money will have grown to £10,000.
Age 40, it grows to £20,000
Age 50 – £40,000
Age 60 – £80,000
Age 70 – £160,000
Age 80 – £320,000
Age 90 – £640,000
Age 100 – £1.28 million

This is assuming that Sally has not bothered to save any more money her whole life, other than that first £5,000. Because she started young, invested over a long time and didn't touch the money, it just kept growing for her. Notice how most of this growth came in the last few years, when the amounts doubling are much greater. In the early years it can seem like saving doesn't make much difference, but in the long term it makes a huge difference.

Let's say that Sally is too poor at 20 to have a lump sum, so instead decides to save £100 a month, or £1,200 a year.

By age 50, assuming she is earning 7% a year, she will have accumulated £121,287.65.

She then stops saving and just leaves the money to grow without spending any of it. By age 60, just another ten years later, her savings would have jumped to £256,331.48 and by 80, she will be a millionaire with £1,044,560.17.

However, if she was too conservative with her investments and was only able to achieve a 5% annual return by 80 she will have less than half that amount with £445,515.48.

John has the same idea but doesn't start saving until age 30. By age 80, earning 7% a year, he will have half of Sally's lump sum with £521,983.15.

Unfortunately, John isn't likely to have as much time to enjoy this money as Sally because male life expectancy in the UK is currently 77, compared with 81 for women. However, these figures have been improving in leaps and bounds recently, so that people who make it to age 65 have a life expectancy of 82 for men and 85 for women. This is expected to increase a further three years each by 2021 so that men and women in the future will be living to 85 and 88 respectively, according to the Office for National Statistics. Just by giving up smoking, you can dramatically improve your life expectancy.

The effect of compound interest can also be clearly illustrated if you are saving on behalf of your child.

For example, imagine you put aside £5,000 for your child the day she was born (or got your parents to donate the amount). By age ten, she would have £10,000 (assuming an annual 7%

return), by age 20, she'd have £20,000, but by age 30, she'd have £40,000 – enough for a deposit on a home. This, of course, assumes that you, and she, never add to the savings pot throughout her lifetime.

The rule of 72

I worked out the first table using a clever little financial trick called *The Rule of 72*. This magic number is the easy way of helping you work out how many years it will take you to double your money. Simply take 72 and divide it by the annual percentage rate of return your money is earning. So, 72 divided by a 5% return means it will take 14.4 years to double your money, while 72 divided by 7% takes only 10.28 years – I rounded down these figures a bit for the table above.

A 12% return will only take you six years to double your money and a rare 20% return 3.6 years. But if you can find an investment that gives you 20% return consistently for three or four years without taking on massive risks like borrowing to invest then please let me know! I have some investments that have returned 20% a year, but not consistently.

Another way you can work out growth rates yourself is by looking on websites like **www.thisismoney.co.uk**, which has loads of handy calculators you can use for free. Look in the tool/ calculators section and find out how long it will take you to become a millionaire!

Sticking with it

What I found when I first started saving was that my first £1,000 was the hardest. After that, I had already created my modest savings pot and I just wanted to keep doubling it as quickly as I could. Even though I was a student, I managed to put aside around £20 a week so that I built up to my savings goal by the end of the year. After that, the challenge was to double the money I had in my savings pot. At first, I could do this annually as they were still relatively modest amounts. After all, once you have saved £1,000 in a year, all you have to do is save another £1,000 the next year and your pot has doubled.

However, as the numbers got bigger it became more difficult to double my money quickly. Now, I focus on having my assets double every ten years (as in the examples above) by ensuring my money is invested correctly, so that it at least gets a 7% return. Some years this isn't easy and you wonder if you're on the right track, but other years it is ridiculously easy and your savings fly up in value.

I also keep saving extra money, so that I'm likely to get to my target more quickly than anticipated. I think it's important with savings to always anticipate less than you will actually have. That way you get a nice surprise at the end and are motivated to keep going and save even more.

I always like to work out how much money I'm likely to have by the time I reach retirement age. There's a chance I'll want to keep working when I'm older, but I find it helpful to have a specific date in mind or deadline.

At first, retirement age just seemed too far away and I wasn't confident I would ever build my savings up enough to reach a reasonable level by that date. At that time, I just concentrated on doubling my little savings pot every year and telling myself how proud I was that it was growing. However, I discovered that the more I saved, the more confidence I had in my ability to save.

Then I realised that each year it was becoming easier and I was excited about anticipating how much money I could have at retirement. I was also building up so much money that I could think about stopping saving and just sitting back and letting my money double every decade without me adding to it. Then, all I'd have to do was just ensure it was invested correctly, and if I couldn't save for some reason, because I'd taken time off work to study or have a family, then it didn't matter because the money was still growing. Those little interest-earning gold slaves were working away for me while I slept.

Where should I keep my savings?

Any crisis in the banking sector leaves people afraid to even open up a simple savings account for fear that they will lose their money. However, there's no point leaving it under the mattress as the effect of inflation will whittle it away over time. Traditionally, we shopped around for the best rate using comparison websites (like **www.moneysupermarket.com**) and often opting for deals offered by smaller banks, which provided the highest interest rate. That strategy is now looking risky with so many smaller and offshore banks getting into trouble. Happily though, if you have your savings with a UK bank, the Financial Services Compensation Scheme ensures you will get back up to £35,000 per financial institution if the worst should happen. So, if you have more than that, try to spread your money around with different banks. It's also best to avoid having your mortgage and savings account with the same bank. If they go bust, they could use your savings to help pay off the mortgage early.

The most tax effective place to keep cash is obviously a cash ISA (individual savings account) which you can open through pretty much any bank these days. Try to get an interest rate that is higher than or at least equal to the Bank of England's base rate (4.5% at the time of writing).

JUSTINE'S TOP 10 TIPS

1) Before making a purchase, decide if it's a 'want' or a 'need'. Are designer jeans really a must-have addition to your wardrobe, or will a high-street pair suffice?

2) Sit down on a regular basis to work out if you are on track to reach your financial goals.

3) If you haven't been able to save, don't punish yourself. Just figure out how you can turn the situation around and reward yourself when you do stick to your plan.

4) Think positively and creatively about saving. Look at it as a challenge rather than a chore.

5) The things you decide to forego are very personal, so don't tell someone else how to save and don't let them tell you either.

6) It's how much you save of your income that makes a difference over the long term, not how much you earn.

7) It doesn't really matter what you invest in, as long as you can get a steady return from it that beats inflation.

8) Women live longer, so we have more time to let compound growth work for us.

9) If you are getting a return of around 7% a year, your money should double about every ten years.

10) Getting started is the hardest part. After that you might find it's addictive!

INVESTING

Getting Started

I meet so many women who are keen to learn about finance and investment but they don't know where to start. They think the stock market sounds exciting, but scary too, and sometimes they get caught up in the latest trends or some technical aspect and forget the basics of investment. Your mantra should be ***keep it simple.***

Keep It Simple!

Investment really shouldn't be any more complicated than going shopping. In fact, the skills you need to be a good investor are the same skills you need to be a brilliant bargain hunter on the high street:

* You need to be able to control your emotions so you don't get carried away at the sales.

* You need to spend some time comparing the different products on offer so you know whether you are getting a good deal.
* You have to be interested enough in what you are buying so that you understand what's important. For example, what makes one pair of shoes better quality and more likely to last than another?

A lot of the basics of investment are the types of things your grandmother used to tell you, like:

* Don't put all your eggs in one basket.
* Spend less than you earn.
* Don't buy anything you don't understand.
* Don't buy something risky if you can't afford to lose that money.

Some people get so excited by the idea of investing that they jump in the deep end before learning how to swim – there are safer ways of doing it! Start off slowly and just dip your toe in the investment pool, then take your time learning as much as you can about the area you want to invest in.

Increased knowledge leads to better returns

Another reason it's important to at least know a little bit about investment is that, even if you decide to get some advice from a professional, you will better be able to understand whether that advice is right for you or not. Often people listen to everything their banker, accountant, financial adviser or friend tells them and don't stop to analyse whether the idea makes sense to them or not. All too often, the so-called tips you get from these people lead to a loss rather than profit. Only when you have more knowledge will you be able to recognise whether any tips or advice you get are reasonable. That way, even if you still lose money, you will feel more in control about your decision and are more likely to learn from the experience, rather than be frightened off the whole idea of investment.

You can build up your knowledge by reading books, magazines, newspapers and websites. Your knowledge will also grow from your initial experiences. Don't jump in feet first by throwing all your life savings into one investment. Start small and gradually build up your investments as your knowledge and profits grow. If you are slow and cautious to begin with, you are much more likely to become a successful, wealthy investor. Sure, it takes time (and many first-time investors are very impatient), but no skill that is worth having can be learnt overnight. You wouldn't expect to be able to become a professional ice skater after just one lesson, so take your time with investing as well. Dribble the money into investments and pay attention, so that you learn as much as possible from your experiences.

Later on I will explain a simple way you can dip your toe in the investment waters with a relatively small amount of money.

What is an investment?

There are many things people spend their money on and call investments. Your dad's vintage MG, your auntie's teddy bear collection, your stash of French Bordeaux surreptitiously hidden at the back of the wine cabinet. The trouble with some investments, though, is that they aren't always good ones. In financial terms, they are liabilities, not assets. In other words, they end up costing you more money, rather than providing you with an income you can live on in retirement. So, for the purposes of this book, we are going to define an investment, or an asset, as anything which puts money into your pocket rather than taking it out.

AN INVESTMENT IS ANYTHING THAT PUTS MONEY INTO YOUR POCKET RATHER THAN TAKING IT OUT

A surprising number of people have trouble getting to grips with this simple idea. They will argue for hours that yes, it all makes sense for other people, but *their* wine collection, vintage car or investment property – which hasn't made them any money in years, costs a fortune to maintain and doesn't seem likely to ever make money – is different.

This is because it's so easy to let your emotions get tangled up with your investments. It doesn't matter whether you're 18 or 80, or a man or a woman (yes, men can be just as emotional, if not more than us, at times). In fact, I have been as guilty of this as anyone at times. It's the same feeling you get when you know you really shouldn't have bought that green velour tracksuit that you'll never wear because it was half price and you were just caught up in the excitement of the January sales.

As you will see throughout this book, one of the most important things you can do to become a better investor is to learn how to control your emotions around money. That may mean feeling terrified about putting your money into the stock market, but doing it anyway. Or it could mean reigning in your enthusiasm at times when all your friends are buying stocks and you feel left out (like at those sales). It doesn't matter whether you are simply trying to stick to a budget or juggling a multi-million dollar portfolio. Having control over your money, by being in control of your emotions, is important if you don't want money to start controlling you.

It is critical to *focus on the numbers* before you make any investment. Ask yourself whether you want to buy this investment for profit reasons, or for emotional reasons.

Believe it or not, it is possible for an investment to provide you with a regular income stream, grow in value over time and not cost very much to hold in the meantime. There are three essential elements:

* Regular income.
* Growth in value.
* Cost of buying and selling or holding the investment.

A bad investment will offer little or no income, never grow in value and possibly fall in value and in the meantime charge you fees and penalties so that you end up with less money than you started with. Let's have a look at these three essential elements in detail.

What type of return does your investment provide?

In order to compare different investments and find which one is the most profitable and simply works best for you, it's important to compare like with like. Unfortunately, different investments pay you in different ways. Some rise in value with time, like a good wine. You buy it at one price and sell it at a higher price, pocketing the difference. Others provide a regular income stream, like the goose who laid a golden egg each day. Still others can provide both price growth and income, so you get a double whammy effect – like a property which rises in value as land prices go up and can also provide income in the form of rent.

So, the first thing to do is look at what type of return you will get from your investment – is it growth, income or both?

Here are some common examples:

Income Only

* Cash in the bank (pays interest)
* Bonds you buy directly and don't trade (pays coupons)

Price Growth Only

* Art (unless you are charging someone to look at it)
* Wine
* Gold

Income + Growth

* Shares (share prices rise plus income as dividends)
* Property (property prices rise plus income as rent)

THE MAIN ASSET CLASSES

Normally, investment professionals focus on four main investment classes. These are listed in order from the least risky to the most risky:

* Cash
* Bonds
* Property
* Shares

As we've seen, the first two normally only provide one type of return (income), whereas shares and property can give you an extra boost by providing both growth *and* income. (Although bonds can also provide growth if you are buying and selling them, this is not so common among private investors who buy bonds in the traditional way and hold them until maturity.)

DEFINITIONS

Before we continue, I'd like to clarify the different types of investments and exactly how they work.

Cash

For most of us, this simply refers to cash in the bank, whether that's a current account or a savings account. Investors with larger sums to put aside can often access more sophisticated products which try to provide the stability of cash; that is you are guaranteed to get your money back – with a little extra return. There are lots of different ways this can be done, but for most of us cash is just money in a savings account – preferably one that pays a high interest rate.

You may be asking yourself – why is cash considered an investment? After all, isn't cash just, well, cash? The reason I have included this as an investment is because my definition of a good investment is *anything* that will put more money in your pocket, and the interest you earn from keeping cash in the bank will obviously do that. Also, later on you will discover that low-risk investments like cash or bonds can be very handy in reducing the overall risk of your portfolio. Therefore, they are just as important a tool as higher risk and more exciting investments.

Bonds

A bond is like an IOU. Traditionally, bonds were created when the government needed money to pay for a war, so they asked investors for a lump sum, promising to pay back the money within a certain period. In exchange for the money you handed over, you received a bond certificate, a regular income payment, plus your original amount back at the end of the period.

Bonds can be created for short periods of three to five years or you can agree to lend your money out for up to 50 years. In a way, it's like we get to play banker for a while.

The main characteristics of bonds:

* They are normally created for a set period (between 1-50 years).
* They usually pay you an income every half year (called a 'coupon').
* They can be bought and sold.

You can tell immediately how much income a bond will pay you because it's always in the name: e.g. the 4% Treasury Gilt 2016. The 4% tells you how much interest (coupon) the bond will pay per year. This is usually split into two payments, the first after six months. Treasury Gilt tells you it's a UK government bond and 2016 tells you what year you will get your lump sum back. If this was a 20-year bond, you could also calculate that the government first offered this bond to investors in 1996.

Bonds sometimes seem confusing because they are given so many different names. The UK government's bond certificates used to be edged with gold (gilt-edged) so over time they have become known as *gilts* – however they are simply just UK government bonds. Similarly, in the US, government bonds are known as *treasuries* – because they are issued by that government's treasury department. In Germany, government bonds are known as *bunds*. Bonds issued for shorter periods of time, or by state or regional governments and local authorities have different names. Companies can also issue bonds – known as corporate bonds. You may also have heard of junk bonds – these are bonds issued by companies or governments that are considered very high risk, such as a company that doesn't make much profit or a war-torn country in Africa.

Usually, UK government bonds pay a relatively low return (e.g. 4%) because they are high quality. A corporate bond (issued by a company) is likely to pay a higher return (such as 8%), but obviously there is more risk that the company will go bust and you will lose your money. The UK government is much less likely to go bust!

Normally you buy bonds via your stockbroker, but if the government is launching a new gilt, you can buy it directly from the Debt Management Office (**www.dmo.gov.uk**) and in this case you won't have to pay any sales commission. Once you have your newly issued bond, you can hold it until it matures. So for a 20-year bond you can keep it for 20 years. However, some people prefer to trade their bonds, which can also be done via your stockbroker. For example, if you bought a bond when rates happened to be higher than usual (bond rates go up and down the same way your mortgage rate does) and you were able to get a UK government bond for 6%, then a few years later rates dropped dramatically and new bonds were only offering a 4% return, you could sell your bond early for more than you paid for it.

This is mostly what bond fund managers do. They try to time the bond market and buy when bonds are offering high rates, then sell when the rates fall. They also often buy a mix of different types of bonds, some of which are very risky, so have a higher rate, and some safer ones with a lower return.

Property

For most people, the main property investment they make is their home. However, to really exploit the advantages of property (and receive an income as well as growth in the value) it needs to be rented out.

Property comes in many forms:

* Residential – houses and apartments that people live in.
* Retail – everything from small corner stores to huge shopping malls.
* Office – office blocks, sometimes referred to as 'commercial property'.
* Industrial – warehouses or factories.
* Property investment can also cover buying hotels, parking lots or simply land for agricultural or other uses.

For more details, see the *Property* chapter on p259.

Shares

Shares, stocks and equities are all the same thing. They refer to what you receive when you give your money to a company to help it operate its business. As a share- or stock-holder you become a part-owner in the company so can benefit by receiving a portion of the profits (known as 'dividends'). Plus, if the value of the company grows over time, the value of your shares will also increase. Of course, as a part-owner, you will also suffer if the company fails and goes out of business. These days, you will only lose the money you invested (if it is a limited liability company). Historically, investors were much worse off: they could not only lose their investment, but also debt collectors could come chasing them for more money.

These four assets are like your base colours in a paint palette. By investing some money in each of these investment classes, you can reduce your risk and still achieve a decent return on your money.

However, you may be wondering how you can afford to invest in all of these asset classes at once with the amount of money you have. It's for this reason that investment funds were created.

Funds

A fund is simply a ready-made investment portfolio. Different investors pool their money together and give it to a fund manager, who makes all the decisions on where the money should be invested. By investing this way, you can have access to a diversified investment portfolio for much less than it would cost to build one up yourself. For example, you could give around £1,000 to a fund manager and, because the money is pooled with other investors, you could have access to cash, bonds, property and stocks from all around the world.

Most investment funds that you find for sale are based on these four assets – either different versions of them, or else mixed together in different ways.

For example, a fund manager might try to sell you a 'package' of some bonds, some shares and some property which he then manages for you.

Or he might sell you an investment which uses one of these assets in a different way. For example, instead of buying shares in a company listed on the stock market, he buys part of a small company which is not yet listed (in the hope that one day it will).

Often, fund managers are not so much selling you the real assets but their skill in managing them. So, he might say that his skill lies in trading (buying and selling) different assets well. You are hoping that he knows so much about the investment markets that he knows when to buy and when to get out before it all crashes. Unfortunately, history has shown that this is an incredibly difficult thing to do.

These days, it is becoming increasingly common for professional investors to dabble in a fifth investment category known as:

Alternatives

This category is basically all the things that private investors have been buying for years, but which the investment industry has turned its nose up at for a long time. It includes things like wine, artwork, antiques, cars, boats, racehorses, unlisted companies, licences, agricultural commodities, gold and precious metals, gems or jewellery, timber, film rights, music rights, virtual property rights etc.

Often, these investments only provide growth rather than income. Private investors can obviously invest directly in these things as well, but in order to evaluate whether or not they are really good investments, we need to look at another aspect – costs! This is the third essential element of investing that we discussed earlier – income, growth and costs.

HOW MUCH IS YOUR INVESTMENT COSTING YOU?

If the first step in assessing an investment is to look at what type of return it gives, the second step is looking at how much it is costing you. After all, it doesn't matter if your investment is rocketing up in value if it's costing you so much to keep that you don't make any profits.

Here is a list of different costs you might have with an investment:

* STORAGE – especially for gold, paintings, wine.
* MAINTENANCE – i.e. having to paint your house or get the roof fixed.
* INSURANCE – for things like jewellery, but also housing and cars (where it's often compulsory).
* MANAGEMENT FEES – if you need someone else to keep an eye on it, for whatever reason.
* BROKERAGE FEES – the costs of buying and selling.
* INTEREST PAYMENTS – if you borrow money to buy something like a property.
* TAXES.
* EARLY REDEMPTION FEES – if you need to sell your investment earlier than planned.
* MARGIN CALLS – only for investments where you have borrowed money, where the value of the asset falls below the amount you borrowed and the bank decides it wants its money back!

If you want to compare your investments accurately – and check whether or not they are any good – you need to look at your total estimated costs, as well as the likely return you can make.

One way of doing this is to draw up a table like this one to look at the pros and cons of investments you are considering. This will ensure you carefully analyse each type of investment to see which is the most expensive and which is likely to give you better returns.

	INCOME	GROWTH	STORAGE	MAINTENANCE	MANAGEMENT FEE	BROKER FEE	INSURANCE
Property	Yes	Yes	No	Yes	Possibly	Yes	Yes
Shares	Yes	Yes	No	No	Possibly	Yes	No
Bonds	Yes	Possibly	No	No	Possibly	Yes	No
Cash	Yes	No	No	No	No	No	No
Painting	No	Yes	Yes	Possibly	No	Yes	Yes
Wine	No	Yes	Yes	No	No	Yes	Possibly

Most people are attracted to investments that they like and that they know a bit about, which is not a bad thing at all. In fact, it always surprises me when I meet people who work in a certain field, like technology for example, but never invest in companies or other assets related to their field. Instead, they go searching for something exotic, which they know absolutely nothing about and often end up losing money. So, the first tip here is: BUY SOMETHING YOU UNDERSTAND.

You might have grown up with a dad who spent his weekends restoring old cars. If so, you already have insider knowledge about that market, which you could build on. Or you might work as an interior designer and have an affinity for property investments. Or you might work in a department store where you often see the types of products which sell and those that don't.

If you are interested in something, you are more likely to spend time researching it and learning more about it. Of course, this could make you a little more emotional about it too, so that's why it's important to look carefully at the three essential elements

– income, growth and costs. By focusing on those numbers and determining if your investment is profitable and if so, by how much, you can control your emotions surrounding it.

Once you've found one or two types of investments that you find interesting, go through this process of evaluating where the money is coming in from and where it is likely to go out, and see if you can see a way to increase the return while decreasing the costs.

The reason property and shares have been very popular investments with people for so long is because they provide both growth and income, so it's easier to get a good return. Also the fees related to shares tend to be relatively low (as a percentage of the amount invested) because so many people are investing in this market, so it's possible to reduce costs. With more obscure markets, you might have less competition from other investors but also higher entry and exit costs.

For example, investing in wine might sound like a good idea if you are optimistic about the returns that could be made from this investment. However, once you analyse it using our three essential elements of investment (income, growth and costs) you may decide it is not worth the trouble:

* INCOME – not possible.
* GROWTH – possible (do further research to estimate how much growth is likely in the future).
* COSTS – buying and selling costs low, taxes apply, storage costs necessary, must be kept at a particular temperature which could lead to further costs, insurance costs possible etc.

Go through each of your investment ideas and analyse them each way to help you weigh up whether or not each is worth the time and costs necessary.

Don't forget that it's never a good idea to pin all your hopes on one investment, so feel free to experiment with a few different ones. Over time you will get an idea which suit you best. Once you have done more research, or have more experience with a certain investment, you may discover that it is more expensive or time-consuming than you initially realised, while other investments seem to provide wonderful returns without all the fuss.

What type of investor are you?

Many women have certain qualities in common when it comes to investing – that's what makes us good investors. However, we are all individuals and often have very different approaches to the same problem. For example, some financial advisers split their clients up (whether male or female) into two broad categories: active and passive investors.

Active investors love trading shares and taking an interest in their investments, but sometimes suffer from overconfidence. It's true that men frequently fall into this category, but not always. Passive investors sometimes feel helpless with their money, so hand it over to someone else to take care of and then worry themselves sick when things don't seem to be going well. Quite often, women fall into the category of passive investors because they are afraid to take responsibility for their investments and hope someone else will rescue them.

Advisers come up with these stereotypes so that they can determine whether or not their client is going to freak out if they suggest a potentially high-risk investment, like emerging markets. If the client has never invested in the stock market before and suddenly discovers that the precious savings they handed over to this adviser have halved in value, he or she may be tempted to sack the adviser – and that's not good business. Consequently, many advisers are terrified of recommending something a bit risky for fear of losing nervous or inexperienced clients. Even if this adviser has a pretty good hunch about what they think the market is going to do, they will be extremely cautious in how they phrase it. The risks of losing clients, and even worse, of being sued, are too great.

So, before you go to see a financial adviser or stockbroker, or even just for your own information, it's a good idea to know where you stand on the scale that stretches from the nervous passive investor who is scared to move out of cash, to the aggressive risk-taker keen on dabbling in the options market. Most people are somewhere inbetween, and as you get to know yourself better as an investor over the years, you can reshuffle your assets so that they better suit your needs.

The following questions may give you some idea of where you stand on the passive/active scale.

Questionnaire

The market drops 20% in one day and you have invested in a fund that tracks the stock market. You:

a) Feel OK and confident it will come back.
b) Don't feel great but are prepared to wait and see.
c) Go into panic and immediately call your broker to sell.

The stock market is:

a) A legitimate way to make money.
b) Scary, but probably necessary.
c) A legal form of gambling that is the ruin of many.

How much would you be prepared to borrow for a property?

a) 100% +.
b) 90% max.
c) 80% or less.

Your ideal portfolio has:

a) 90% stocks or property, 5-10% cash.
b) 30% bonds, 30% stocks, 30% property, 10% cash.
c) 50% bonds, 20% stocks or property, 30% cash.
d) 100% cash.

Pension money should be:

a) Invested as aggressively as possible.
b) In a mix of different assets, but switched into cash a few years before retirement.
c) In the safest possible investments, preferably cash.

Options are:

a) Something you are either already invested in, or would consider.
b) You've looked into them but think they're too risky.
c) Have no idea and wouldn't touch them with a bargepole.

If you answered mostly *a*'s you probably take quite an aggressive approach to investing. However, this questionnaire is really designed just to give you an idea and get you thinking about your own attitudes towards investing; it may take some time to understand yourself completely as an investor. Once you do, however, it will help you control your emotions and fine-tune your investment strategy.

Increasing your knowledge of the market is likely to encourage you to take on more risk, as things always seem scarier when we don't understand them properly. However, you may still have a certain level of risk tolerance that was developed when you were too young to think about it. For example, I have a friend who knows an awful lot about the stock market and investments and has the know-how to do very well in this market. Yet, she has much of her money invested in bonds. This is because, when she was young, her parents successfully invested in bonds when they were saving for her university education.

Sometimes, you don't discover until after you are invested what your risk tolerance is. Therefore, if you are pondering a certain investment, it's a good idea to just put a toe in the water with a small investment and then see how it goes. Over time, as you build up experience and confidence, you may discover that you have an affinity for this particular investment and do very well from it. Whatever you do, don't rush into anything or let others push you into something you don't feel comfortable with. Investing is a very personal thing. Yes, you may miss out on this deal, but it doesn't matter too much, another one is sure to come along and the next time you will hopefully be experienced enough to recognise it early and act in time.

Investing for the long term

As an investor, it's better to take the slow and steady approach, rather than letting your excitement run away with you. This sounds simple enough, but it's astounding how often I've seen women let their emotions take control and forget this point.

If you are investing to replace your income in the future, then it obviously helps if you start young. The earlier you start, the lower your level of risk as well, because you have time to ride out the market's busts and booms – and recent events have shown this can happen at any time. It doesn't matter as much if you make a mistake either, because you can make up for it later. Using the benefit of time really is a major asset, particularly for women – who live longer on average – so use it as best you can.

Nevertheless, life is always throwing up obstacles and your situation can change radically in just a few months. You could get divorced, have a baby, lose your job, have your partner or another relative fall ill, start a degree or decide to get married. All of these things could have a significant impact on your financial situation.

When these life changes happen, it is incredibly tempting to sell off one of your investments to raise extra money. You may have bought with the intention of holding for the long term, but have only been invested for a year or so. I know exactly how quickly circumstances can change because, a few years ago, I got divorced. At the time, I had two mortgages, so suddenly found myself struggling to pay all those debts with half the money. Somehow, I managed to struggle through without having to sell anything, but it wasn't easy. Of course, it's not always possible to do this, so if you must sell, then do. However, try to hold on to as many assets as possible. It's a pretty safe bet that one day you are going to be older, may not be able to work any more, and will probably wish you had some money tucked away. So think long and hard before you decide to break open the piggy bank that you have put aside for the long term. Don't kid yourself that you will make it up later, because there will always be other catastrophes on the horizon.

Several years ago, a close friend asked me to recommend a fund to invest in. I warned her that she needed to invest for the long term and shouldn't buy unless she was prepared to hold it for several years. Of course, her response was, 'Sure, sure, just give me the name.' Despite this initial enthusiasm, it took her several months before she got around to actually buying the fund, and it was only when a financial adviser recommended the same one that she invested her money. About three to six months after this the market took a dive. She called me and asked what to do. I said there was no guarantee that the market would rebound in the short term, but she should be in it for the long term anyway so just leave it there. She asked her financial adviser (who got a fee every time she bought or sold) the same question. The adviser said if she was that panicked about it (I was used to hearing her panic, so had ignored this) she should sell. She sold at a loss and, of course, a few months later the market went up again.

To me, this story illustrates how different investors approach the stock market and how our emotions can have a major impact. This friend didn't trust the market, herself, or perhaps me, when it came to investing, and this made her more nervous than she should have been. Perhaps if she had done more research or was simply a more experienced stock market investor these dips and rallies might not have caused such panic.

In contrast, years ago when I had first started investing in stocks, my mother gave me some savings she had put aside and asked me to invest them on her behalf. Now, no one in their right mind is going to take any great risks with their own mother's savings, so I choose the safest stock I could – a leading bank. I thought it seemed like quite a boring stock (especially compared to the great technology stock my stockbroker was trying to convince me to buy), but I knew it had regular dividends and was a strong, well-established company that had been around for years and was unlikely to go bust in the short term. About five years later, as I was reviewing my portfolio, I noticed that this particular company was the best performing stock in the whole portfolio. Not only had it done very well, but reinvesting the fat dividend back into the company had proved to be a godsend and further boosted the value of the investment. By the way, my mum has never panicked about what the investment was worth or what the market was doing. She trusted me and had a firm ten-year investment horizon, so she simply invested then forgot about it. Even with the rocky market, this bank has continued to hold most of its value and its conservative strategy has ensured it's a safe harbour in this storm.

JUSTINE'S TOP 10 TIPS

1) Keep it simple – investing should be like shopping–well and finding a bargain.

2) Increased knowledge leads to better returns.

3) Buy something you understand and enjoy researching.

4) An investment is anything that puts money into your pocket instead of taking it out.

5) Focus on the numbers, so you don't let your emotions take control.

6) Analyse investments using the three essential elements – income, growth and costs.

7) Base your investment portfolio on the four main asset classes – cash, bonds, property and shares.

8) Consider using funds if you don't have a lot of money to build up your own portfolio.

9) Diversify. Don't rely on just one investment. Spread your bets so you are covered if one of them doesn't pan out.

10) Work out what type of investor you are and then invest for the long term.

SHARES

WHAT IS A SHARE?

'Res tantum valet quantum vendi potest.'
from the Latin for
'A thing is worth only what someone else will pay for it.'

As I explained earlier, shares or stocks allow you to become a part-owner in a company. If that company does well, the value of your investment goes up and you also receive a share of the profits – known as dividends. However, if the company does poorly, the value of your investment could fall or the company might go out of business altogether, so you lose all your money.

As a part-owner you have certain rights. You are invited to attend the company's annual general meeting, where you can question the management on how business is going and raise any concerns. Also, you have the right to vote for any new board members or significant changes that affect the business, such as a change in the dividend policy. Similarly, if the company is being taken over by another firm, you have the right to vote on whether you agree with this takeover or not. For any unusual business, like a takeover, the company normally holds an extra meeting – known as an extraordinary general meeting.

Sometimes companies also offer certain benefits to their shareholders. For example, it might offer shareholders its products at discounted rates. Or occasionally it might allow current shareholders to buy extra shares in the company at a discounted price. If you don't want to buy these extra shares, or don't have the money, you can sell your rights to another shareholder who wants as many shares as possible at this discounted price.

WHY INVEST IN THE STOCK MARKET?

There are several benefits from buying shares:

* Returns
* Diversification
* Liquidity (how easy something is to sell)

Returns

Most people buy shares because of the money you can make. Being a part-owner in a dynamic, fast-growing business can be extremely profitable. As we've noted, investing in shares gives you two types of return – growth when the share price rises, and income when you receive part of the profits via dividends.

However, you shouldn't overestimate how much money can be made, or treat the stock market like a casino. Yes, you can make a lot of money, but getting high returns in a very short time means taking a lot of risk – which means you also might lose money. A lot of people think stock market investing is just about taking this high-risk approach, but it's not. There are several ways of investing and this is only one strategy.

Some stocks, usually small companies in a new field, will jump up in price almost overnight and make their owners millionaires. These are the companies that the media love to write about and which get a lot of publicity. But as we saw in the dotcom boom, some of these company bosses became millionaires for a year or so, only to lose all that money when the market crashed. It's often the case that when something jumps up in value very quickly it can also come down just as quickly.

Fortunately, there are other companies – large, respectable names – that watch their share prices rise steadily every year. They might be slow risers, but they are more predictable, reliable and longer lasting. These are usually big companies with experienced management who have proved over the years that they know how to do their job well. These companies don't always get a lot of publicity, and sometimes they're in boring sectors, but they provide good returns in a safer way.

Diversification

Another benefit of buying shares is that you don't have to buy the whole company. In contrast, when you are a small business owner or a property investor, you normally have to buy the entire asset yourself, which is expensive and risky. With the stock market, you can invest a small amount in a number of different companies and so spread your money around – not pinning all your hopes on one investment.

You can also get exposure to completely different industries. For example, you might have shares in a company that makes medicines and drugs, one that sells children's toys and one that mines gold. These are completely different businesses, often operating in different parts of the world, so even if one area is not very profitable, you can still make money from another area. For example, let's say the UK goes into recession and shops in the high street are losing money. These days, people can still make money by being invested in companies that have operations overseas, in countries which are not affected by the recession. And they don't even have to be foreign companies. Companies like British Petroleum have operations in far-flung areas of the world, protecting them from local problems.

Liquidity

If you have a house as an investment, it will probably take you several months to sell it and if the market is going through a bad patch, it could take even longer. Also, the price you tried to sell you house for in January might not be the final purchase price you receive in December if the market has been falling.

One of the great things about the stock market is that the companies listed on it are priced every day. Every day, investors collectively decide how much a certain company is worth and they are constantly being analysed to make sure they keep up to scratch. This way, if you really need to get your money out, you know you can sell immediately and get the cash into your bank account within a few days.

Knowing that different investments have these different aspects allows you to manage your entire investment portfolio more effectively. For example, if you want to buy a property or a small business and the price you finally agree on is slightly more than planned, you can always sell a few shares at the last minute to top up your cash reserves. Owning shares (or funds, which we'll discuss later) gives you flexibility and that puts you in a stronger position as an investor.

EXPECTED RETURNS

How much money can you expect to make from investing in the stock market? Top investors like Anne Sheiber and Warren Buffett have been able to get average returns of more than 20% per year. That's certainly much better than what you'd get from leaving the money in your bank account. However, while such returns might certainly be possible during good times, over the longer term your annual returns are likely to be lower.

According to the Barclays Capital Gilt-Equities study, over a period of more than 100 years UK shares delivered 5.2% a year after taking the effects of inflation into account. That might not sound like much, but compare it with the returns from cash in the bank, which have been only 1%, or government bonds (gilts) which have returned 1.2% a year. Viewed in this light, the returns look quite good.

Knowing how stocks perform over the long term may also give you some indication of whether or not we are in a bull or bear (rising or falling) market. In 2004, the return from UK stocks was 8.8%; in 2005 it was a whopping 18.9%. If you know that returns of 20% a year for the UK market are unusual, then seeing that figure should give you a clear signal that prices are getting expensive and, even if the market doesn't fall immediately, a crash is not too far away.

Also, if someone is saying they can sell you an investment that gives you a return of more than 20% a year, then your ears should prick up with suspicion. Not many investments can do that consistently and if they do have consistent high returns, it usually means that there is more risk involved. For example, if you were to invest in an emerging market like China, you could see your investment jump 40% in one year, but don't expect it to keep rising at such a rate every year. At some point it will crash and then you could see a 20% drop! Similarly, investing in small companies can give you a higher return, but there's an increased chance that they will go bust and you'll lose all your money.

A final reason why some people invest in the stock market is because it's a challenge. Trying to outwit the market, which effectively means trying to beat the crowd and outwit all the other investors, is often difficult. Personally, I think it helps to know a bit about psychology and specifically crowd behaviour when investing in the stock market.

HOW SHOULD YOU INVEST IN THE STOCK MARKET?

Once you've decided that you would like to have some exposure to stocks, there are two ways you can do it. The more difficult way, in my view, is to invest directly. This means you choose your own companies and monitor their performance, and it's true that many people find this route intriguing and immensely rewarding.

The slightly easier way is to simply buy an investment fund (such as an index tracker), which I'll explain how to do in the next chapter.

Of course, a third option is to do both – which is what I do.

Challenges of Going Direct

* The time it takes.
* The work involved.
* Dealing with stockbrokers.

DEFINITION OF BULLS AND BEARS

This is a classic bit of finance jargon that some women have told me always confuses them. I think the trick to remembering which means which is to have a clear image firmly planted in your mind. When you imagine a bull, think of one at a bullfight tossing a hapless bullfighter into the air. **Bull** markets are markets that are **rising**; bulls often fight this way, starting with their horns very low to the ground and then tossing them up.

In contrast, a **bear** market is one that's **falling**. I usually imagine a bear pulling a man down out of a tree (gruesome, I know), but you can see that the movement here is down. Bears also have this tendency of tackling their prey by standing up on their hind feet and then knocking them down with their paws (exactly the opposite movement to bulls).

I often imagine bears frowning too, which reminds me of the depressing state of a falling stock market. On the other hand, a bull tossing its horns into the air is quite a joyful movement, and if you've ever seen a photo of the metal bull statue in front of New York's stock exchange on Wall Street, you'll know what I mean – that's one happy bull!

For other easy explanations of financial terms check out **www.investopedia.com** or see the Jargon Buster section at the end of the book

Buying your own stocks will take up a bit of time, but you don't have to make it a career to do it well. Most of your research should be at the beginning. The more time you spend analysing which are the best companies, rather than just rushing in to buy some stock tip, the more satisfied you are likely to be longer term. Of course, you often learn as you go so it makes sense to just choose one or two companies first and then monitor both the companies' progress and your own level of nerves. My first stock was considered to be very 'safe' because it was a big company with steady (although cyclical) earnings. But I found it very boring and frustrating. Although it didn't lose any money, it didn't grow much either and, as I was relatively young at the time, I was more interested in a younger company that would grow with me and keep expanding. This stock would have been better suited to a retired person who just wanted to live off the dividends (income) paid by the company.

Once you've bought, you'll most likely want to hold onto the stock long term (especially if you've chosen well), so you don't have to watch every day to see how your company is doing. However, do keep an eye on the newspapers or TV in case there are any big stories surrounding your company or trends that could influence it. A few years ago, there was a bit of a scandal surrounding one of my companies. The company was very well respected but had suffered from management problems. This had disappointed investors and many were selling. Fortunately, the company had quickly realised its wrong turn and was putting in place new, but experienced, management and solving the problem. I took the view that it was still fine to hold on and that decision has served me well.

As I've said, trading in and out of stocks frequently costs a lot of money and cuts into your returns so it's really better to do enough research initially and then hold on for as long as the company continues to please you. It's a bit like hiring staff; you don't like to sack them unless they really mess up big time and you think there's no chance they'll improve.

The third challenge is dealing with brokers, but these days you can buy online, which makes things a lot easier. In *Dealing with People in Finance* I discuss some of the difficulties that can occasionally arise with brokers and other finance people and how you can deal with them more effectively.

Benefits of Going Direct

* Sense of ownership and pride.
* Can be very profitable.
* More control.

Knowing that you own a little bit of a household-name company is a good feeling and makes you feel like you're participating in the economy. And, if you think the company is very well run and provides a valuable service to the community, that's great too. But beware of becoming too attached and not being able to sell when it's necessary.

Of course, the main reason people buy stocks is for the *profits*. Over the long term, stocks and property provide the strongest returns, far outperforming bonds or cash. And, if you are investing for your child or a pension fund, you really need the extra kick stocks can give your portfolio, otherwise your savings will be gobbled up by inflation.

A third reason some people prefer investing directly in stocks, as opposed to funds, is because they simply hate paying other people to do a job they think they could do themselves. Men are particularly prone to this! But, like the last time your guy tried to fix the computer and ended up being unable to put it all back together, taking the easier option (just hiring an expert) can often be more effective. However, don't let this put you off. There are a couple of women in my club who really get a thrill out of participating directly in the stock market. Also, women often make excellent stock-pickers because we usually like shopping. We know what's in fashion and what all the latest trends are, so we can often see if a company is heading down the wrong track because it's out of touch with its customers.

Ready, steady, go!

So, let's assume that you've decided that, yes, you'd like to invest directly in stocks. You're probably feeling excited but also a bit nervous. After all, there are so many complicated terms and jargon thrown about when people are discussing the stock market – how do you make sense of all that? Remember, the important thing is to KEEP IT SIMPLE. Focus on the key factors and don't get caught up in all the market froth. Often, you'll find that stockbrokers and people working in the finance industry confuse you with the words they use. Sometimes, this is because they are trying to show off about how much they know, and other times it's simply because they've been speaking the language of finance for so long that they don't realise it's quite complicated for others. Don't be afraid to stop them mid-sentence and ask them exactly what they mean. In my work as a journalist, I've found that often the people who really understand a subject can explain it well, whereas someone who is trying to give you the impression that they know more than they do will probably bluster and keep speaking in even more jargon! That's the moment when you should walk away and find someone who can explain things better.

It's Like Shopping

Don't worry too much, because the good news is that buying stocks is just like going shopping! Think about it: when you're looking to make an important purchase, like a new coat or a good pair of shoes, there are usually two main things you look for – COST and QUALITY.

Sure, sometimes you get carried away and make an impulse purchase, but when you're spending a significant amount of money (and most people would say that £1,000, which is the minimum for direct share investing, is a significant sum), then it pays to do a bit of thinking first.

So let's have a look at these two points – COST and QUALITY – and see how it works in stock market investing.

COST – WHY THE COST OR PRICE OF A SHARE IS IMPORTANT

Quite often, stockbrokers and other people involved in investing will try to convince you that price really isn't that important a consideration. Just like a used car salesman, they'll try to make you see that what you should be focusing on is 'future growth' or the 'potential' of this particular investment. It's a bit like a cosmetics saleswoman playing on your fears of getting older by telling you this magic cream will erase all your wrinkles and make you look years younger. What they're really selling you is HOPE – and quite often the price of hope is extraordinarily high.

So, be a savvy investor and, even when you're convinced that you've found a really amazing, once-in-a-lifetime, opportunity investment, stop and consider the cost.

A very successful investor once told me that even the best stocks that are top in their field, high quality and very profitable, are *not* good investments if the price is too high. At the time, I was chatting to him about a mining company that was extremely popular and a household name in those days. I was convinced that this company would always be a good investment. But he disagreed. 'Justine,' he said, 'look at the cost. There should be a limit to how much you're prepared to pay, even if it's for a quality investment.' Of course I ignored him and went ahead and bought the stock anyway. Sure enough, a few months later the company that people thought could do no wrong, announced that business wasn't going quite as well as they'd thought and people were so disappointed (they'd built their hopes up so much) that the they sold their shares and the share price plunged.

So, how can you determine if something is expensive or not? When it comes to shopping, it often depends on how much money you have. Something that seems expensive to me is reasonable for my investment banker pals. Fortunately, when it comes to the stock market, things are a bit more clear-cut. Looking at a company's share price (e.g. if Marks & Spencer shares are trading at 397p per share) won't necessarily tell you if it's expensive.

Some of my friends say things like, 'Well, this mining exploration company is only 10p per share, whereas M&S is 397p, therefore M&S must be expensive. But it doesn't work like that in the stock market. The figure you need to look at is the Price Earnings Ratio.

The Price Earnings Ratio or PE

It sounds complicated, but it's simply the share price compared with the amount of money the company makes – its annual earnings per share (divided by the number of shares issued). After all, if a company is earning lots of money and is very profitable, it's a much better investment than one which is losing money and likely to go bust in a few years. So, if a company is making lots of money and still has a low (cheap) PE ratio, you know you've found a bargain.

In our example earlier, we might discover that the little mining company has very little earnings because it hasn't found much gold yet and is spending a lot of money looking for it. Its PE would look like this:

Price = 10p/share
Earnings = 0.4p/share
PE (price/earnings) = 25x
So, it has a PE of 25 which is quite high, making it a rather expensive investment.

In contrast, the calculation for M&S looks like this:

Price = 397p/share
Earnings = 39.30p/share
PE = 10.1x

Because M&S makes more money from its business, its PE is lower, and you can see that it is cheaper and a more attractive investment.

Having said that, it is a little unfair to compare two companies in such different industries – it's like comparing apples and oranges. You'd be better off looking at the PE ratios for two companies like Marks & Spencer and Tesco, as they are in a similar business. Of course, if you discover that they are on very different PEs, then you need to ask yourself why one company seems so much cheaper than the other – and that brings us to the next question which is QUALITY.

However, before we talk about that, you might be wondering why I wrote a little 'x' after the PE figure. Normally, people say a share has a PE ratio of 13 *times*. This means that a company would have to earn 13 times the amount of money it made that year in order to justify the price of the shares. Or that the price is 13 times the company's annual earnings (per share). You can see quite clearly from this that the stock market is always looking ahead, always anticipating how much money a company is likely to make in the future. Of course, that's what makes it so difficult because no one really knows what's going to happen in the future, and the further into the future you have to project, the more difficult things become. That's why it's important to focus on the price and not pay too much today.

Incidentally, a good rule of thumb to see if a PE ratio is high is to look at what the PE ratio for the whole stock market is – so you get the average PE for all the stocks in the market. Normally in the UK, this ranges between about 12 to 18 for the main index, the FTSE 100 (this is made up of the UK's 100 biggest companies – see glossary for more info). If the whole market is trading at the upper end of this range or higher, it's a sign that the market is getting expensive and a fall could be on the way.

To find PE ratios for your stocks easily, look at **www.digitallook.com** or **www.morningstar.com**.

QUALITY – WHY IT PAYS TO BUY GOOD QUALITY COMPANIES

Or does it? There is a bit of a debate about this question. Some investors (such as Warren Buffet's former mentor, Benjamin Graham) think that price is the most important thing and it doesn't matter what type of company you are buying, or whether its business is any good, so long as it's cheap enough.

But as any savvy clothes shopper knows, there's no point buying a new pair of shoes at the market that are dirt cheap if they're going to fall apart within a few days. You've wasted money! In my opinion, it's a good idea to look at the quality of a company as well.

But how can we tell whether a company is really high quality or not? Sometimes, they seem to look good, only to be hit by a scandal. Here are some of the factors to consider:

Management

It's a good idea to get some idea of who is running your company. You can read or watch interviews with them, or even go along to the company's annual general meeting if you're keen enough. Do they seem trustworthy or convincing?

Most importantly, do they do what they say they are going to do? There's nothing the market hates more than a company boss who promises and never delivers.

Brand Name

Is this a well-known and respected company? How long has it been in business for? Usually, if a company has a strong brand name, then it can attract business just on the basis of its name and make more money than another company that is less well known. However, sometimes if a company is large and old and is used to having things easy, the people running the company get lazy. Instead of working hard to ensure they have a quality company that makes lots of money, they rely on the fact that they've done well in the past. If they're a very big company they become like juggernauts, huge ships that, once they get into trouble, take a long time to turn around and get back on the right course.

Also, if you already buy the products of the company you are investing in, you will see more quickly whether they have a decent brand or not. If you and your friends hate their products, how good can they be?

Company Size

This is very much like brand name, but there's another factor. During difficult times, like in a recession, it's safer to be a large company with lots of spare cash and savings. That way if problems come along, the company can handle them better. However, when the economy is doing well and there are lots of opportunities to be had, a smaller company can usually move more quickly and their share prices zip up the charts. A large company is more likely to be a steady grower, with a share price that increases gradually over time. A small company can see its share price jump almost overnight, so investors can make money more quickly – but they obviously take more risk doing this. While a small company might see its share price jump up quickly, it can also see the share price fall just as fast.

Industry Outlook

Do you understand, or even like the industry the company is involved in? If it's an area you already have a personal interest in, you are more likely to keep an eye on events that affect that industry and also affect your investment. For example, you might have a passion for luxury brands like Versace and YSL. This is a sector of the stock market with investors who focus on companies producing luxury goods. Or you might be very interested in the environment and know about solar panels and the latest energy-efficient heating systems and want to consider these companies as investments. Some of the stock market sectors in Britain are:

* Retailers
* Banks
* Gold Mining
* Oil & Gas
* Diversified Industrials (this is a general term that covers a lot of different companies that manufacture, produce or distribute goods and services. For example, Yell which owns the yellow pages online.)
* Pharmaceuticals

One of the things I try to do is focus on sectors that I think are likely to do well in the future. There's a bit of crystal-ball gazing with this, but it's not too difficult. For example, you might look at the increasing number of old people in our society and analyse how that is going to affect the way we live in the future and which industries will benefit. Some industries would be the health/pharmaceuticals sector (because older people use more medicine and hospital facilities than younger people), also banking (because older people tend to have more in savings, and need investments and pension products to live on once they've stopped work).

Once you've decided on an interesting theme or sector of

the market, then you can drill down to look at which companies operate in that sector, whether they are quality companies, how large they are and how much they cost.

Number of shares

Having too many shares is a bit like having too many cousins – you can't keep track of them all, and you even start forgetting their names. If you have decided to invest directly in the stock market, rather than own a fund, you will probably be interested in analysing your companies and keeping an eye on them to see how business is doing. If you have too many (more than about 12) you will spend far too much time monitoring their progress. That's fine if you're retired and have nothing better to do, but for most people it sounds like too much work. My portfolio usually doesn't get below six or above 12. More than that is too many, less than that and I don't feel it's diversified enough. Professional fund managers often hold a lot more stocks than this. Some will buy up to 100 stocks but, just like you, they might be biting off a bit more than they can chew, so don't expect fantastic returns from them. Also, they are often investing as a team, or have several analysts on hand to do most of the research work for them.

Crowd behaviour

I mentioned earlier that I think it helps to understand a bit of psychology when investing in the stock market. Psychologists have often noted that people in a crowd will sometimes do things which are completely illogical, simply because they are caught up in what everyone else is doing. For example, if there's a fire in a theatre, the crowd will panic and all stampede towards the one exit at the back, crushing and harming each other in the process.

Similarly, investors sometimes stampede towards the exit when there's a panic in the market. A classic example was after 9/11, when investors sold almost any share. Certainly some companies, such as airlines, suffered as a result of the catastrophe, as fewer people were brave enough to get on a plane immediately after this event. But why would you sell a bank? As you may have noticed, in a financial crisis where investment banks are mostly affected, people sell every type of stock, no matter how good their quality, in their rush for the door.

Another interesting phenomenon is known as the 'war effect'. Philip Fisher wrote about the effect of wars on the stock market. He was the author of *Common Stocks and Uncommon Profits,* first published in 1958 and the first investment book ever to make the *New York Times* bestseller list.

Among Philip Fisher's top ten recommendations for investors was: 'Don't be afraid to buy on a war scare.'

He wrote that, with one exception, every time war had broken out anywhere in the world, and particularly where American forces were involved, the US stock market had plunged. The exception was the outbreak of the Second World War, when initially the US market rose because people realised many American companies would make a lot of money from selling arms. However, it soon dipped again once people's horror at the idea of war set in. Fisher describes this as, 'a psychological phenomenon which makes little financial sense'.

He said that even when there is merely a threat of war, the stock market tanks. Interestingly, stocks usually rebound once the war scare subsides and even if war breaks out, by the time it ends stocks have usually risen much higher.

Although he was writing in the 1950s, Fisher's words are still relevant today. Just before the US declared war on Iraq in March 2003, I rang up Philip Fisher's son, Ken Fisher, who has his own investment management firm on the West Coast of the United States. At the time, the market was in a slump as investors worried about the possibility of a war, so I asked Ken if he thought his father's ideas about war still applied. He wholeheartedly agreed and predicted that, once war in Iraq commenced, the market would settle down and might even rally. To my astonishment, that's exactly what happened.

As you can see, smart investors are those who are prepared to go against what the rest of the crowd is doing, and make sure they don't get caught up in all the panic when markets are falling or the euphoria when markets have risen too much.

Keeping your head and following a simple investment strategy that focuses on the numbers (like a company's price earnings ratio) and the quality of the asset, is the best way to go.

THINK LIKE A FARMER

I once read an article written by a reader of America's *Forbes* magazine called, 'How Mr Womack Made a Killing'. This is an incredibly simple story about a pig and rice farmer who, over the years, never lost money on his stock market portfolio.

Mr Womack viewed the stock market in the same way that he viewed the pig market. At certain times, perhaps because of a glut, the prices pigs were selling for were obviously too cheap. At other times, perhaps during a drought, they were quite expensive. His technique with stocks mirrored his approach to the hog market.

He bought stocks when the market was down and everyone was very nervous and worried about even further falls, and he sold when there was lots of optimism and stock market analysts were coming out with predictions on how high they thought the market would reach that year.

He didn't worry about whether he was buying exactly at the bottom or selling exactly at the top. He just bought and sold when he could see what the general mood of the market was. He was happy not to invest for a couple of years and just patiently waited until the mood changed again, which it always did. When buying, he was careful to always try to get a bargain and he bought some quite boring companies, but they all paid a dividend. One or two might bomb, but he would buy about 30 stocks at a time, just putting a little money into each one, so on average he always made money.

I have only been investing for about 15 years, but in this short time I have seen quite a few moves both up and down in the market. Occasionally, there have been opportunities that I would call a 'screaming buy' and where I was very confident that I, or other investors, could make money. At other times, there has been a bit more uncertainty, but it was still possible to see the general trend. Unfortunately, there have been occasions when I thought the market looked like it was at a good price but I simply didn't have the cash to invest.

That's another reason why regular savings are fundamental if you want to become wealthy from investing. One of the things I really like about Mr Womack's story is that it shows that you don't have to be a rocket scientist to make money from stocks, or any other investment for that matter. In fact, I think that sometimes being too clever works against you. You just have to think like a farmer and be able to control your emotions, rather than letting that stampeding crowd drag you down.

Where do I sign up?

Assuming you are convinced you want to get into the stock market, what's the next step? If you want to invest via a fund, I explain how to do that in the following chapter. If you want to invest directly, you need to hire a stockbroker. You can either make an appointment to go and see one in person, or do this online. Normally there are two types of brokers:

* Advisory brokers
* Discount brokers

The first give you advice on which stocks they think look good value, so are a bit more expensive. Normally, you pay your broker a fee (usually a percentage of the amount you are investing) plus everyone must also pay stamp duty (which is basically government tax). If it's your first time, you might like to see an advisory broker (there are more and more female brokers around these days too), so you can ask any burning questions you have about how the market works.

Brokers giving advice are:

* Charles Stanley & Co
* Red Mayne Bentley

The second type of broker (more common with online brokers) doesn't give you any advice, but the fees are obviously cheaper.

Some UK-based discount stockbrokers include:

* TD Waterhouse
* Charles Schwabb UK
* Barclays Shares Online
* Halifax
* Sharepeople
* iDealing

To get a full list of stockbrokers go to **www.apcims.co.uk**.

If you want to join an investment club to share ideas on stock-picking see **www.proshareclubs.co.uk**.

JUSTINE'S TOP 10 TIPS

1) If you understand your market very well, you will be able to recognise quality and notice cheaper than normal prices more easily.

2) Invest in companies you understand. If shopping is your passion, then analyse retailers. If you know which banks have the best deals on savings accounts or mortgages, then consider the banking sector.

3) Just because a stock or a sector seems boring doesn't mean it isn't a good investment. Like people, the boring ones are often the most reliable.

4) Only sell if you realise you've made a mistake, or the outlook for the company changes.

5) Sell your poor-quality stocks and hold on to your winners

6) Gradually build up your portfolio by consistently investing a little bit every month or year no matter what the market is doing. This is known as pound cost averaging – *see pg 227*.

7) If you can, think like a farmer and unemotionally take advantage of slumps or jumps in the market.

8) If it seems too good to be true, it probably is. Getting a return of more than 20% *every* year is quite difficult to do, although it can be achieved in certain years.

9) Don't fall in love, but buy quality stocks and patiently wait for your investments to perform over the long term.

10) Work out your own investment personality, so that you can rely on yourself and don't rely on stock tips from others. However, go easy on yourself; you can't always get it right.

FUNDS

What is a fund?

Funds are a bit like investment clubs. They allow different investors to pool their money together and then hire someone to manage it full-time. With a relatively small amount of money, each individual investor has access to a ready-made portfolio, which may hold hundreds of stocks, bonds, property or other investments.

This way, investors don't have to be rich to start investing, they can access investments that would otherwise have been out of reach and they take less risk because their money is diversified across a number of different investments.

The first fund in Britain was created in 1868 by Foreign & Colonial (a company still in operation today). It was created so that small British investors could profit from exotic investments in the colonies. At the time the return on UK government bonds was quite low (between 3.5% to 4.5%) so the smart men at

Foreign & Colonial decided to create a fund (or 'trust' as it was called then) to allow ordinary British investors access to US, Australian, European and even South American government bonds.

WHY FUNDS are GOOD FOr WOMEN

For the women in my investment club, and for many other women, funds make an ideal investment. This is because they allow you to access the stock market in a less scary way. Many of the women in my club feel quite intimidated by the idea of buying individual stocks which, we are led to believe, require lots of research, hours of reading the *Financial Times* and analysing complicated ratios. In contrast, a fund allows you to buy a ready-made investment portfolio for much less than it would cost to build one up yourself. This means you are instantly diversified, which reduces your risk – and women are wary of taking risks with their money.

The next question that arises, of course, is which fund? After all, these days buying a fund has become a lot more complicated than it used to be, simply because there are so many on offer. Should you buy something invested in your home country, or something more exotic like an investment in emerging markets? And what if you end up with a fund manager who isn't any good and actually loses money?

I have been writing about investment funds for most of my career and have also been invested in them for many years. In fact, the second investment I ever made was into a general fund, which held a combination of stocks, bonds and cash and performed quite nicely over the years. As a result, funds have become my speciality, but this has meant I've often seen the bad side of the industry, as well as the good. Fortunately, I still believe that funds make an excellent investment for many women as long as you follow a few simple rules:

* Pay as little in fees as possible.
* Buy a simple product like a tracker, index fund or ETF – these charge low fees.
* Make sure you understand what the fund is invested in.
* If you don't want to take too much risk, don't buy a really specialised fund; rather, opt for one that's more general.

Pay as little in fees as possible

The Effect of High Fees

Let's say you have invested £5,000 in a fund which grows in value by 7% a year on average. Assuming you don't pay any fees, after 20 years that investment should have grown to £19,348.

However, if the total fees you are paying are just 1% a year, your performance after 20 years will be reduced to £15,839. There is a very useful calculator on **www.thisismoney.co.uk** which you can use to help you work out the effect of fees on your own investments:

Investment of £5000

	0% fee	1% fee	3% fee
Year 0	£5,000	£5,000	£5,000
Year 5	£7,012	£6,670	£6,034
Year 10	£9,835	£8,899	£7,284
Year 15	£13,795	£11,872	£8,791
Year 20	£19,348	£15,839	£10,610

Source of calculator: www.thisismoney.co.uk

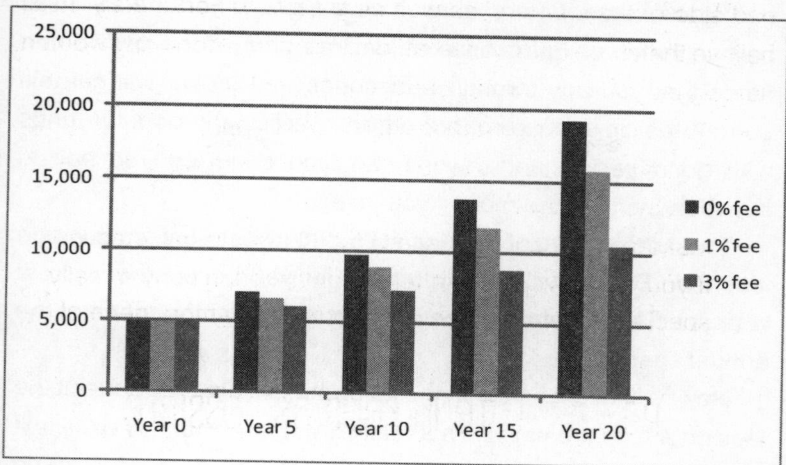

You can see how an increase of just 1% in fees really eats into your profits and why it's important to pay attention to fee levels. If a fund is not performing very well (because the fund manager hired isn't any good) *and* you are paying high fees, you'll quickly lose money.

Most traditional funds that use a fund manager – hired to choose the stocks or other investments in the portfolio – charge a lot more than 1%.

According to Morningstar, the median level of annual managment charges for all UK funds was 1.5 % in 2008. Around 57% of UK funds charged this amount whereas US funds only charged 0.67% per year. Stock market funds tend to be the most expensive, charging around 1.6% on average, and those based in Luxembourg have the highest prices.

If you were paying total yearly fees of 3% on an investment of £5,000, your performance after 20 years would be dragged down to just £10,610. So, £8,738 would be taken out in charges over the period.

It gets worse. Often, when you buy a fund you are asked to pay an initial, or upfront fee as well as annual charges. Some funds that you buy through a discount fund broker will cut this upfront fee down to zero, but others, particularly popular funds with good performance, won't. So, you could end up paying between 3-6% of the money you invest.

That means that, of your initial £5,000 investment, on average less than £4,750 will be put to work for you because of upfront charges. That's before you even start to look at the effect of the annual charges.

Now, you might be thinking that perhaps it doesn't matter if the fees on a fund are high if it's a really great fund that has excellent performance. Sure, that's reasonable. After all, if a fund is giving you a return of 15% a year, and charging 3% in fees per year, you still end up with a healthy 12% return.

But to get a fund which provides such a high return, you usually need to take a bit more risk, and most of us start off with a lower-risk fund where the returns are less spectacular. The important thing to remember is that, over the long term, even just a small change in your return of 1% can make a big difference.

BUY A SIMPLE TRACKER OR INDEX FUND

Tracker Funds

Fortunately, there are funds available that do have very low fees and quite reliable performance – index tracker funds. These are funds which are designed to track (or follow) the performance of a stock market index such as the FTSE 100.

An index is the average price of a group of shares. When you hear people say that the FTSE 100 has risen 20 points today, they mean that the average value of all the 100 largest stocks in Britain have risen by 20 points. Of course, some may have fallen and others done better than this but the overall trend was positive. The index's name tells you how many companies are being included – the FTSE 250 or the S&P 500 (in the US) have a much larger range of shares in their group.

Instead of having to choose which British companies are the best investments, you simply buy a portfolio of 100 of the country's largest and best-known companies.

Websites for Tracker Funds:

* **iShares.co.uk**
* **www.morningstar.co.uk**
* **www.trustnet.com**

If it has been created well, a tracker fund should give you almost exactly the same performance of the index it is following. If the UK stock market rises 20% one year and falls 5% the next, then that's exactly what your fund should do. You won't have to worry about your fund manager having a bad year or making a mistake and getting it wrong, but you also won't have the chance to 'beat the market'.

If you choose a fund that tracks the FTSE 100, you will have a ready-made portfolio with companies like HSBC, Vodafone and BP. The fund either buys shares in all of the stocks in the index, or buys enough of a sample so that its performance is the same as the performance of the index. So, if a company gets into trouble, and it shrinks and is no longer one of Britain's most valuable companies then it is sold.

I like tracker funds because they were designed to allow the little guys to get into investing, beat the dismal returns on their bank account, and get a taste for the market. They do exactly what they say they are going to do – track the market – which reduces certain risks to you as an investor.

John Bogle created Vanguard, the world's first tracker fund provider, in 1974, and it is now the second largest funds management company in the world. His philosophy is that 'simplicity underlies the best investment strategies' and he believes that investing for the long term is the only way to go.

There is a long and complicated debate that has been running in the City for years about which is better – tracker funds or funds that are managed by active, stock-picking fund managers.

But if you know that a certain fund is a good one, that it has had consistently good returns over a long period, that the fund manager currently running the fund is responsible for this and that he's not likely to leave the company in the short term, and you think the fees are reasonable, then go ahead and buy it. It's your money after all.

However, if you don't know much about funds or the stock market and don't have a lot of money to waste, then why not make your life a bit easier by choosing a 'tracker' or 'index' fund?

Personally, I like to have a mix of different funds – this is a strategy followed by most of the big pension companies. They take the money from their employees' savings plans and invest most of it in tracker funds. They then buy a few funds that are more expensive, but could possibly have a higher return, and sort of use this as 'play' money. It's the same strategy that people often use with their stock market portfolio: have most of your money in reliable stocks and investments, and then if you want to take a bit of risk invest 5% in something a bit sexier.

Tracker funds are also great for women because they are a way to **just get started**! You know you're buying something cheap and relatively simple, so you have no excuse to put it off anymore. And you can tell all your friends you're invested in the stock market. Also, it's a great way to dip your toe in the investment waters and get a feel for how you react to market rises and falls, without spending too much money. Normally, you can get started with about £1,000, but if you don't have this much money, most fund companies offer savings plans which allow you to invest as little as £30 a month on a regular basis. This is known as pound cost averaging and is an excellent way to invest because you avoid having to worry about whether your timing is right.

Tracking Error

When checking out which tracker fund to buy, you should look at:

* Which stock market index it is following.
* How low its fees are (some are lower than others).
* The tracking error.

The tracking error is simply the way fund managers assess how well the fund is able to track its chosen index – that is, give you a performance as close as possible to what the actual index did. Some funds do a better job than others.

Fee Trends

The beauty of a tracker fund, in my view, is the low fees it charges. Because there is no 'star' manager being paid to pick stocks – just a computer program – you pay a lot less for what is usually a pretty good investment.

Research from Fitzrovia, a London-based firm that analyses fund fees, shows that fees for tracker funds have been diminishing even more over the past few years. As these funds have more and more money on their books, they can use economies of scale to reduce the costs to investors.

At the same time, fees for funds that use a stock-picker have been rising. This is a somewhat bizarre situation since these stock-picker funds have also been benefitting from economies of scale. The reason these active funds have been able to charge more and more for their services is because they have become increasingly specialised. Whenever a new fashion hits the market, like technology stocks or gold stocks, investors rush in like teenage girls buying the latest colour lipstick and the fund managers put up their prices.

The best tracker funds have no upfront fee and charge less than 1% in annual fees, with some as low as 0.35%. There are tracker funds that charge more than this, but since you are not paying for a fund group's expertise, it's best to go with the cheapest possible.

ETFs

Another option are ETFs – or Exchange-Traded Funds. These are tracker funds, where the fund itself is listed on the stock market. These have become very popular in recent years because there is far more choice and they are more specialised. For example, you could buy an ETF which just tracks water companies. Basically, they work in the same way as a traditional tracker and are sometimes even cheaper than a normal, unlisted, tracker fund. See **www.iShares.co.uk** or **www.etfs.com**.

Some tracker fund providers are: Fidelity, Liontrust, M&G, Barclays Global Investors (their product is known as iShares) and Legal & General. At the end of this chapter is a list of websites that will help you compare the cheapest tracker funds. Be warned, some unscrupulous fund houses charge 1% or more per year, which is really too much for such a simple product.

MAKE SURE YOU UNDERSTAND WHAT THE FUND IS INVESTED IN

Which Tracker?

Once you have decided which tracker fund provider to use, you can then think about what the tracker will be invested in. Most of the women in my club start off with a tracker fund that's invested in the main stock market index of their country (we're a pretty international bunch, so not all of them are invested in the UK). Usually it makes good sense to buy a fund that is invested in the stock market of the country you are living and working in, because then you don't have to worry about changes in the currency.

Nevertheless, it is possible to buy a fund that is based in the UK (so you're buying in pounds) but gives you access to a country overseas. You could start off with a UK stock market fund like the FTSE 350, and then as your portfolio grows buy some in Europe, in America, in Poland – whatever you like.

If you want to stick with the UK market, there are a couple of main indices, but the largest is the FTSE 350 (pronounced 'Footsie'). As the name suggests, this is made up of the UK's top 350 companies. It provides you with more diversification than the FTSE 100, and also allows you to invest in some medium-sized companies which could be tomorrow's leaders.

Interestingly, while you might think that it's safer, or that you'll get better returns from buying the FTSE 100 because, after all, it has the largest, and therefore some of the best companies in Britain, this is in fact not necessarily the case. It's actually a better idea to buy a broader index like the FTSE 350. The reason for this is because it's more diversified – which lowers your risk – *and* research has shown that it has done better over time than the FTSE 100.

How can that be so? The 350 is less risky and better-performing at the same time? The reason is because it includes some smaller and medium-sized companies, and these companies tend to grow at a faster rate than the big fat companies at the top of the list.

You could also invest in the Eurostoxx 500. This is an index that follows the 500 largest companies all across Europe, so you have access to German car companies, Irish banks and French pharmacy groups, as well as top UK brands.

Once you've dipped your toe in the water with a UK or European tracker fund, you might decide to build up your portfolio with some other funds which could potentially give you a more exciting return.

They can be funds based on:

* ASSET TYPE – so you can buy property, bonds or gold, rather than just shares.
* SIZE – so you can buy very small companies or ones that are not even listed on a stock market yet (private equity).
* COUNTRY – funds invested in emerging markets like China or other developed countries like the USA or Europe.

The huge variety in the types of funds available has also led to some advisers and brokers encouraging people to trade their funds, jumping in and out of different funds to try to make quick money. For the average person, trading is usually a loss-making game and in the funds business, where fees are higher, it's even more risky.

Some people actually look up which funds had the best performance during the year and then leap in and buy them the following year – often with disastrous results. When it comes to emerging market funds, the fund which did the best in one year is likely to do the opposite the following year. Sometimes you're often better off taking a very contrarian view and buying the worst-performing fund in the hope that it will recover the next year.

But why try to guess like this? It makes investing too much like gambling. A much better strategy is to start slow, buy a UK FTSE 350 fund, get a feel for how the markets work, monitor your emotions when the fund goes up or down and then, when you feel comfortable, add something else. Keep most of your money in larger, safer countries like the UK, Europe and US and put a small portion in dynamic areas like emerging markets, smaller companies, or alternatives like gold or oil.

With emerging market funds it makes sense to buy a fund that gives you access to a couple of different countries – not just one. So, rather than putting all your money in China, you could buy a BRIC fund. This gives you access to four major and fast growing emerging markets – Brazil, Russia, India and China.

Another option would be to buy a whole region – like Asia Pacific. This way, if the Beijing market falls you still have some performance from Singapore, Malaysia, Taiwan and even Australia.

BUY A GENERAL RATHER THAN A SPECIALISED FUND IF YOU DON'T LIKE RISK

As you will see in the chapter on portfolios, diversifying your investments (not putting all your money in just one investment) is a key way to reduce risk. By deciding to buy a fund instead of just one stock, you will already reduce your risk. If you buy a fund that's invested in a broad index (like the Eurostoxx 500) instead of a narrower index (like the FTSE 100), that will reduce your risk further.

Another way to reduce risk, which is particularly helpful if you don't have much money to invest, is to buy a fund that invests in a number of asset classes. So, rather than just having exposure to the stock market, you also get some bonds, some property and even some cash. These funds are like a ready-made portfolio and are usually called 'diversified', 'balanced' or 'general' funds. The first fund I ever bought was a fund like this.

Unfortunately, these types of funds are less common these days because more and more people want really specialised funds, so they can pick and choose exactly what investments they have and build up their portfolios themselves. They like having more control. Also, many of the diversified funds are more expensive because you have to pay a fund manager to choose which asset class to buy, as well as which stocks.

If you are very keen on this type of fund, then the following section gives some tips on how to narrow down your search when buying an actively managed fund (one that uses a professional fund manager to pick and choose the investments). Many of the oldest funds in Britain are still managed in this way. However, these funds often have a slightly different structure (they are called Investment Trusts), which can actually work to your advantage if you take the time to understand them properly. For more information check out the website **www.aitc.co.uk**.

In general though, my point is that, if you are a beginner, be wary of buying highly specialised funds such as those invested in just one small emerging market (like Thailand or Chinese technology). Once you have built up some knowledge of investing, you can put a small portion of your money into something more specific like this if you want to have a bit of fun. However, for now keep things simple and go for something like a Eurostoxx 500 tracker or FTSE 350 tracker, where you know you will get a broad range of quality companies at a very cheap price.

Buying actively managed funds

When you first try to invest in funds, whether it's a tracker or an actively managed fund, you might be overwhelmed at the incredible number of choices available. They go on for pages in the *Financial Times*. There are funds that only invest in Bordeaux wines, funds that invest in water companies, funds that buy residential property, funds invested in small countries you may have never heard of and obscure mining operations in far-flung corners of the world. To simplify things, try asking yourself the following questions:

Which Asset Class?

First choose which asset class you want. Most likely it will be an equities (stocks or shares) fund, but you can also buy funds that invest in property, bonds and the money market – which is effectively cash. Some funds, often called 'balanced funds', provide a mixture of all these asset classes. This can reduce your risks and is often a good place to start.

Which Size?

If you have decided on a shares fund, which part of the stock market do you want to focus on? Large UK companies, small UK companies, companies in other countries? If you're going for a bond fund, what type of bonds? Reliable government-backed gilts, or higher-risk, higher-return bonds?

Who is the Manager and How Much Do They Charge?

If it's a tracker, you should look for one with the lowest fees. Firstly, search for the most respected fund manager and then evaluate if the charges are reasonable.

Once you have narrowed down your search a bit, you should focus on the top five (or even top ten) best-performing funds in a certain category, once you have decided which category to focus on. This can be done by looking on some of the websites listed below, or at tables printed in the personal finance sections of most major newspapers.

If you decide to use a table of this year's top-performing funds found in a newspaper, then make sure you study the companies involved thoroughly. They may have had good performance this year but was it a fluke? How did they perform last year, or over the past three or five years? Who are the managers involved and what's their reputation? Is it a company that has spent a lot on building up a strong brand name and neglected its performance, or is it a respected smaller company?

If you aren't buying a tracker, then it's important to really get to know who the most respected fund managers in this field are. I'd start off with looking at Citywire's top ten managers in your chosen sector (they should be AAA rated), then do lots of reading to see what people are saying about a particular manager and how long they have been doing their job. This is easy enough; if you just google the fund manager's name, you should come up with any articles that have been written about them if they're reasonably well known.

To a certain extent, the funds management industry is a bit of a boys' club. Not only are there very few female fund managers, but often it's a case of who you know. Once you start researching this field, you'll find that there is a relatively small group of fund managers who are acknowledged by fund experts and their peers as the cream of the crop. These guys consistently outperform the market. Sure, they might have bad years, but over the long term they have the patience and aptitude to get results. However, you need to do your homework – not only to find these people but also to keep up to date with changes. Many of the best ones stay in the industry, and often with the same company, for a long time but you never know when they might decide to retire.

Here are some things to consider if you decide fund investing is your thing and you want to become really good at picking the best managers:

* How long has the fund manager been investing or been with this company and do they have a good reputation?
* How is the fund rated by rating agencies like Morningstar, S&P, Lipper, Citywire (**www.citywire.co.uk**) or the *FT*?
* How much money is the manager in charge of? It can be harder to manage a very large amount of money.
* What is the reputation of the funds management company? Do fund managers tend to stay long term, or is there high staff turnover?
* What is the long-term performance of the fund? Look at the performance in each individual year so you can see if

the manager has been consistent.

* The type of assets the fund is buying – e.g. the fund may be invested in the shares of very small companies (less than 100 million market capitalisation).
* How much risk is the manager is taking? E.g. with 'focus' funds the portfolio may have only 20 stocks making it more volatile.
* What stock market sectors is it invested in? Look at the top ten stocks that a fund holds to see if he is too focused on one risky area.
* What are the entry and exit fees? Can you get a discount on this by buying through a discount broker such as BestInvest?
* What is the annual management charge or total expense ratio (TER)?
* Is there a performance fee?

Whichever fund you choose, you should be able to buy it inside an ISA wrapper, which will make it much more tax effective for you. An ISA (Individual Savings Account) is a tax-free account that allows you to invest up to £7,000 a year without having to declare your returns to the taxman. You can put your tracker fund inside an ISA wrapper, or you can use it for stock market investments or other funds. For more information have a look at: **www.hmrc.gov.uk/leaflets/isa.htm**.

Getting started

OK, so let's say you're sold on the idea of buying a tracker fund. Where do you go? Well, the supermarket of course! Or more specifically, a *fund* supermarket.

Fund Supermarkets

These allow you to buy many different funds online quickly and cheaply. Some of the fund supermarkets available in the UK are:

* Funds Network (operated by **www.fidelity.co.uk**)
* Fund Choice
* Money World
* iii Network

Alternatively, you can buy funds through discount stock or fund brokers. For a comprehensive list of discount brokers see **www.uknetguide.co.uk**.

Finally, I think it's important to know that funds in general can be good investments, particularly for women who are looking for a first step into stock market investing.

JUSTINE'S TOP TIPS

1) Funds are a great way of getting diversification.

2) There's a huge amount of choice in the funds industry, so keep it simple by choosing a fund that simply tracks the performance stock market – known as trackers, index funds, ETFs or iShares.

3) The average fund doesn't return enough to beat the stock market. Some do much better and some do much worse.

4) Trackers are cheaper than the average fund because they use computers rather than people. They simply buy all the stocks in the index – or a representative sample.

5) High fees mean your investment has to perform much better than average just to keep up.

6) Funds make it easier for investors to access the stock market and buy a whole portfolio of investments with less money than it would cost to buy lots of shares individually.

7) Funds also allow you to access difficult investments, such as companies in China or Brazil.

8) Some fund managers who are specialised in a particular area – such as smaller companies, private equity, environmental stocks – can add value because they know a lot about these very specific investments

9) Buy a tracker on the FTSE 350 rather than a narrower one like the FTSE 100 to get more diversification and keep a close eye on fees.

10) If you are choosing an actively managed fund, make sure you do lots of research to find out what the fund manager is like and if they are any good.

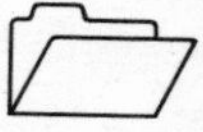

PORTFOLIOS

WHAT MAKES YOU RICH?

When researchers looked into the main factors that influenced how wealthy people became in later life, they discovered that there were three key factors:

* How much people saved.
* How many years they were able to stay invested (starting young).
* Which assets they invested in (known as asset allocation).

We've already talked about the importance of saving and living below your means. And you know that the earlier you start to invest, the more chance your money has to work for you, so the larger the pot you'll have in retirement. In this chapter I'd like to focus mostly on the third point – asset allocation. This is about why you need to stash your money in something more than just the bank, and which assets are best for you or best for getting a high return (which is not always the same thing).

The effects of inflation

The other day, a new member joined our investment club, who told me she was an excellent saver. She's a single mum, but earns a good living, and for years she has been putting some money aside in a savings account for her future. Yet, despite this, she still couldn't afford to buy a flat for herself and her daughter in the area where she lives.

The reason you need an investment portfolio, or investments in general, is so that your savings work hard for you (meaning *you* don't have to work as hard!). The other crucial reason is so that you can beat the effects of inflation.

In the same way that a very light exercise programme might not work your body hard enough to give you visible results, buying assets that don't give you a high enough return means your investment portfolio is either standing still or going backwards. This is because inflation (and therefore the cost of living) creeps up over time, so your investments have to provide a return that is better than the rate of inflation or you will actually lose money. Over the long term, inflation can have a devastating effect on your savings if you don't take care.

Ironically, although this woman saw herself as a low-risk investor who preferred to have her money in cash, she was actually taking a high-risk strategy. She had too much money in cash, so was risking her money to the inflation monster.

For the last decade inflation has been pretty low (between 2-4%). Now, it's creeping up to between 4-5%, but in previous times it has been even higher. In 1972, for example, the rate of inflation was around 9%. This means that, if you had left £100 under the mattress in 1972, it would be worth the equivalent of just £12.64 today. So, you could have bought an awful lot more with your £100 in the 1970s than you could today.

According to the Barclays Gilt-Equity study, in the 50 years from 1955 to 2005, money left in a building society account beat inflation by just 1.7% on average per year. If the money was in government bonds, it would have returned 2.1% over the rate of inflation. But if the money had been invested in the UK stock market it would have beaten inflation by 6.6% per year.

So if you had put your £100 into shares in 1972, given a return after inflation of 6%, you would now have £768.61 – a much better result. Just think, if the interest rate on your bank account today is too low, you may already be earning less than the rate of inflation and watching your money get eaten away. That's why it's important to have some 'growth' assets like shares or property in your portfolio.

Also, you should remember that, even though inflation has been low over the last ten years or so that doesn't mean it will stay that way. In the early 1990s, inflation was around 7%, and if you go back to the 1970s, it was in double digits! Currently inflation is rising – you will certainly have noticed the price of food and power has been going up. Although the Bank of England has a policy of trying to keep inflation low, it is not always possible to control it.

Why you need to manage your investments

Apart from inflation what else do you need to worry about? Well, once you start investing, it's easy for things to get a bit out of hand. Most people find that, after a few years, they have a random collection of funds or shares or pension products. The documents are all stuffed into a drawer and rarely looked at, and they're not even sure what they have any more or how much they're worth.

By working out how your investments are currently structured (I do this by creating a pie chart) you can see what you have and, in particular, identify whether you are taking too much or too little risk. Then you can decide whether you want to build up your investments in one area, or reduce them and switch the money into something more profitable.

What should my portfolio look like?

Really, this depends on you. After all, different people have a different tolerance for risk, a preference for a certain type of asset, or a particular time horizon for how long they plan to stay invested.

My friend Alice is an interior designer and a keen property investor. She's quite young at the moment (26), so happy to have most of her assets in a 'growth' investment like property, rather than bonds or cash. She obviously has some money in cash for emergencies and some in a stock market tracker fund for diversification (and because she's not interested in stock-picking). Her portfolio looks a bit like this:

Alice's portfolio

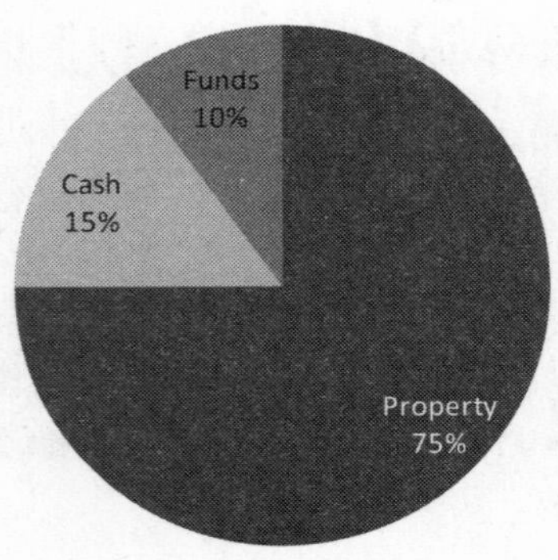

Another friend, Karen, has shares in the company she works for. She's a high-flying city type, but also owns her own home and is a keen bond investor (because her parents did well investing in bonds when she was growing up). Her portfolio looks a bit like this:

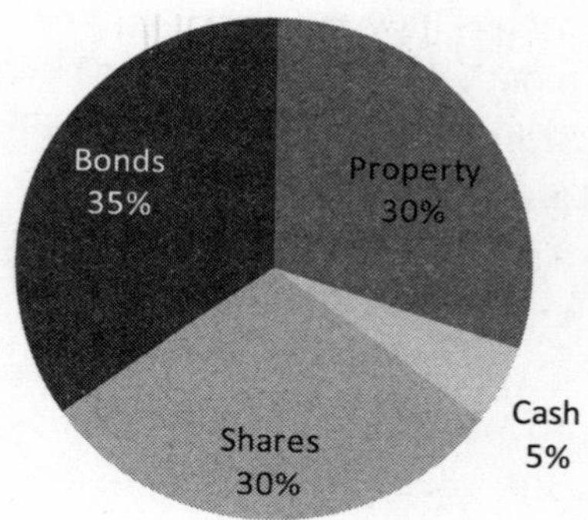

Although these portfolios show the current position for these women, they may not be ideal for them when they are getting ready to retire or when they are living in retirement. That's why it's important to spring-clean your portfolio every now and then to make sure you are still on the right track and that it suits your current and future needs.

Generally, most people want their assets to be fairly diversified because it reduces risk. At the moment, Alice is quite young, so doesn't mind having most of her money in one asset class but this might change as she ages. Having most of your money in high-performing assets (like shares or property) will increase your returns. This is especially so if that asset does well. But it also increases your risk. That's not such a problem when you're young, especially if you don't plan to touch the money for a while. When I was younger, I had about 90% of my money in the stock market – either via direct shares or funds that invested in shares. When I decided to buy a property, I took a bit of money out of my funds for the deposit and now my portfolio is much more balanced. At the moment, I don't have much money in bonds, but as I get closer to retirement and more concerned about holding on to my wealth, rather than building it up as fast as possible, I will switch some money into this area. I also have too much cash in my portfolio currently because I'm preparing to buy another property, so that has skewed my portfolio a bit.

For someone already in retirement, or close to it, their portfolio is more likely to have a traditional mix like:

* Cash 20%
* Bonds 20%
* Shares 30%
* Property 30%

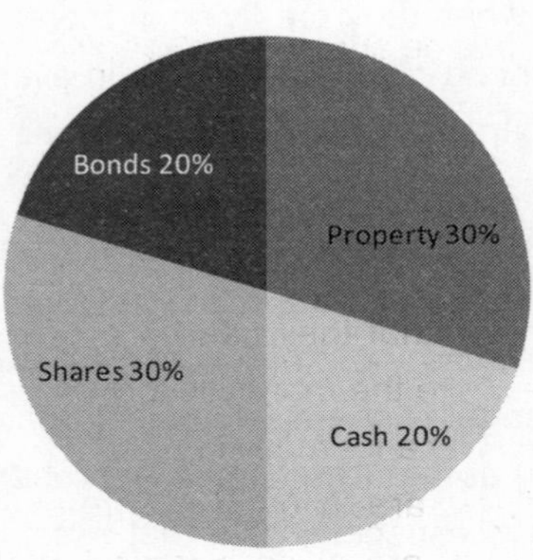

Once you're in retirement, your needs will change, so your portfolio will too. But what about professional investors? How do they structure their portfolios?

Professional investment portfolios

David F Swensen is seen as a kind of fitness guru for many people in the finance world. He is the chief investment officer at Yale University in the US and manages pension and life assurance money (endowments) on behalf of the college. OK, that might sound pretty tame compared to your personal trainer with a deep tan and bulging biceps, but what gets finance people really excited is that, over the past 20 years, David has had a great track record providing a return of around 16% a year.

His job is to hire fund managers from all around the world and decide which assets the college should be invested in. Needless to say, he knows a thing or two about investing and creating a portfolio which will give the best returns.

In his book *Unconventional Success*, Swensen describes a 'basic' portfolio of assets which is designed to provide good returns, but which can be adjusted depending on how much risk you feel comfortable with and how long you plan to be invested. This portfolio is pretty similar to the breakdown of assets that many financial advisers recommend to their clients. Although it's interesting to look at what professionals do with their money, you should remember that they can be a bit more aggressive than you or me because the money is locked in for a number of years, so they can hold a lot more in stocks.

Also, professionals are in quite a different position to the average women. They are given a large lump sum of money and then asked to invest it in the most profitable way without taking too much risk. They aren't gradually increasing their savings to invest as they already have the lump sum! Although this portfolio works for them, it may not work for you.

Professional's portfolio:

* Local stocks (i.e. from your own country) - 30%
* Stocks from foreign, but developed, countries - 15%
* Emerging market stocks (e.g. China) - 5%
* Real estate - 20%
* Long-term government bonds (e.g. Gilts) - 15%
* Inflation-protected bonds - 15%

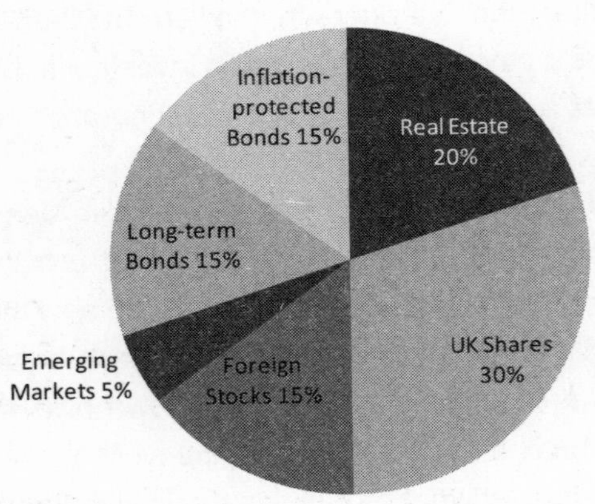

Notice that this portfolio is mainly made up of the four key asset classes – except cash. As a pension fund manager, rather than a personal investor, they don't need to keep some cash for emergencies (although they probably have some in their private portfolio).

As Swensen is based in the US, the first component of his portfolio would be US stocks, but if you live in the UK you could switch this to UK stocks. The second part would then be invested in stocks from Europe or the US. The third part could be a diversified emerging markets fund, or just one or two specific emerging market funds – such as Brazil, Russia, India or China.

This 5% component is designed to give the portfolio a bit of spice and higher than average returns. Swensen has chosen emerging markets to do this but you could also choose something risky like small companies, unlisted companies (private equity) or an alternative investment like gold. Alternatively, your UK stocks component could be made up of some larger, safer stocks and some smaller, riskier stocks.

He also has around 30% of his total portfolio in bonds, and I'll explain in a minute why this is quite an important aspect of the portfolio.

Investment money you can get your hands on quickly (liquidity)

Swensen is also invested in property, but his real estate component is made up of property funds (called REITs) that provide a regular income and can be sold very quickly and easily.

People often find that property makes up a huge chunk of their portfolio because of their home. However, not all homes are good investments and property can take a long time to sell. For this reason, it's handy to have some shares or funds as well. These investments can be sold almost immediately (in a day or two), so they're great in an emergency and give your portfolio much more flexibility while still, hopefully, giving you high returns.

If you are creating a portfolio with the objective of having really high returns, or because you want to have as much money as possible in retirement, it's a bit like cheating to include your home as an asset. You are not likely to sell your home to buy food when you are retired and you are less likely to rent it out to other people and gain an income from it (because you need to live in it).

Also, you could find – as many elderly women do – that your home could actually become a drain on your finances when you need to fix the roof or pay to get the grass cut.

Think of it this way: if you cheat a bit now by including the value of your home and telling yourself that you're rich, it means you will take less care about providing for your future. Your laziness will be paid for when you are old and possibly ill, and in a much worse position to deal with any problems.

So think carefully about all the assets you are including in your portfolio and whether they are really likely to help you reach your goal – or whether you are cheating yourself out of future income.

The Benefits of Time

As I mentioned earlier, how rich people become rich is often influenced by the assets they are invested in. If they have all their money in cash or bonds, they will get a lower average return over the years than if they have all their money in the stock market and property. However, getting higher returns often means taking on more risk and some people are not prepared to do this.

The other key factor is time. If you are young, you are in a brilliant position! You have more time to let your investments grow, so you can take more risk and buy investments that an older person wouldn't dare touch. The same applies if you are investing on behalf of a child – where you might have an 18-year time frame, for example. If you are able to leave your investments untouched for, say ten years, you can buy riskier investments.

Harry Markowitz and the benefits of bonds:

How bonds can reduce your risk without eating into your returns

Harry Markowitz is an economist and Nobel Prize winner from the University of California. In the 1950s, he wrote a book called *Modern Portfolio Theory* and invented a graph called the Efficient Frontier, which investment professionals and financial advisers love to talk about.

The graph shows how a portfolio of shares only can be quite risky, but if you add some bonds it reduces the risk without cutting into your returns too much. At a certain point, the amount of bonds versus the amount of shares is perfect for balancing risk and return.

However, if you keep adding bonds, the portfolio's performance starts to go down and the returns you make are less interesting. If you add too many shares, your returns might go up, but they won't go up enough to justify the amount of risk you are taking. It's a bit like a see-saw. Too many stocks and the see-saw tilts to the left; too many bonds and it tilts to the right.

The goal is to have the highest possible returns, with the lowest possible amount of risk.

You can see why it's handy to have a number of different types of assets in your portfolio. Some provide liquidity (you can get your hands on the money quickly), others boost your returns, and others reduce risk. How much you put in each asset really depends on you: on how much risk you want to take and your personal preferences for certain asset classes.

Allocation within asset classes

Once you've identified how your assets are split (asset allocation), you can then drill down to more detail and break them up further. For example, within your shares/funds component you can identify how they are split in terms of sector, country or type of company.

One of my friends, Katya, is originally from Poland, so she likes to have quite a few investments in stock markets in Eastern Europe where she can also, happily, make higher returns. She doesn't hold any property because her husband owns a couple of apartments as investments so her portfolio looks like this:

Katya's portfolio

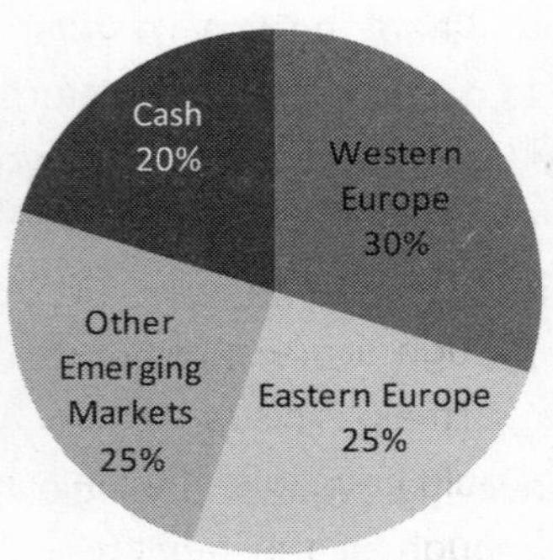

Katya has decided to focus on one asset class – shares – and to invest in them via funds. But within this asset class she has spread her money around different countries and different sized companies. By doing this, she reduces her risk.

You can see how, if Katya had just put 80% of her money into one company (perhaps the one she works for) it would be much more risky for her than putting 80% of her money into several funds or a whole portfolio of shares. If her company were to go bust, she would lose all her money. But, if she's invested in a number of companies or funds, one of them could go bust and she'd survive relatively well.

I should point out too that Katya has been investing for a long time and works in the finance sector, so in her case this portfolio is less risky than someone who has had no experience of investing. This is because understanding what you are buying and increasing your knowledge of investing can significantly reduce your risk. If she had no idea what she'd bought or how markets worked I would be quite worried to see her investing so much in emerging market stocks. She also has a well-paid job and can afford to leave the money invested for the long term, plus has a good portion in cash in case any emergencies arise.

a well-balanced portfolio

Generally speaking, though, it's a good idea for most of us to have a well-balanced portfolio. This is a bit like preparing a well-balanced meal. You should have lots of variety and make sure you're getting enough of the healthy things your purse needs, and not too much of the sugary, exciting, but risky stuff that isn't in your long-term interest.

The four key asset classes (shares, property, bonds, cash) are like the main food groups. You want a good mix of the healthy stuff that might seem a little boring but provides regular, reliable returns, and maybe just a small portion, around 5%, of something riskier, or which you don't understand as well – like wine, art, gold, hedge funds etc.

risk

Once you have started to build up your portfolio, you can see more clearly how much risk you are taking on and then decide whether you want to increase or decrease that risk. As I explained earlier with the exercise example, an older person or someone with less time to invest might want to take less risk, whereas someone with plenty of time can afford to take on a lot more risk – and get a better return.

There are many ways to increase or decrease your risk, but here are some examples:

Reducing Risk

* **Diversify** – don't put all your eggs in one basket: buy a range of assets with different qualities which perform well at different times of the economic cycle.
* **Increase your knowledge** – if you understand some of the principles behind investment explained in this book, then you are more in control and less likely to make a mistake.
* **Thoroughly research your target investment** – if you know a particular area inside out you are less likely to get taken for a ride by unscrupulous operators and can more easily identify a bargain. If, after researching something

thoroughly, you still feel you don't understand it properly, don't buy it! Find something easier.

* **Reduce the costs/fees of buying or selling** – paying too much in fees will be a big drain on your money over the long term.
* **Don't overpay** – make sure you are not paying a premium for an investment because the market is at a high, and that you are not being charged for bells and whistles that you don't really need.
* **Add value** – buy something that you can add value to yourself or where you have more control. This could be a property that you renovate, or shares in your own company. Having more control often reduces your risk as long as you know what you're doing.
* **Low/No borrowing** – either don't borrow at all, or minimise the amount you borrow and the borrowing costs – i.e. get a low rate of interest.
* **Pound cost averaging** – this is where you buy a small amount of an investment on a regular basis, say once a month. As the price fluctuates, over time you end up paying an 'average' price, and it ensures that you keep investing in good times and bad and don't let your emotions get in the way. Often, people get scared of investing at exactly the moment when they should – i.e. when prices are cheap. By pound cost averaging you take away the risk of 'timing' the market – and getting it wrong.

At other times, you may actively want to increase the risk you take in your portfolio because it means you increase your returns. This can be sensible as long as you are taking calculated risks that you understand, not foolhardy ones. Borrowing to invest, for example, is one calculated way of increasing your risk and therefore returns. However, not doing any research into an investment is a rather foolish way of increasing your risk, and probably won't help your investments in the long term.

Increasing Risk

* **Gearing** – in other words, borrowing money to invest.
* **Building a small, concentrated portfolio** – this is done by not diversifying too much. For example, you could hold a small number, say half a dozen, of very good-quality stocks or specialise in just a couple of areas of investment.
* **Investing in less liquid assets** – if an investment is hard to sell, it is less attractive to other investors. In buying these neglected assets you may be able to find a bargain. Examples include: a company that is not listed on the stock market (if there is not an organised market for buying and selling something, it's sometimes more complicated to buy); a stock which is listed, but the majority of shares are owned by a family (so fewer shares are available for other investors and they are not traded as often); alternative investments like art, where there is not a big market for a particular painter's work, so it takes longer to find a buyer.
* **Emerging markets** – investing in smaller, less regulated economies adds risk because often these countries are quite volatile so their returns skyrocket one year and plummet the next. Also the local government could decide to seize the assets of a company, effectively stealing your money.
* **Small companies** – investing in small companies with little or no track record. These companies are more risky because often their management is often less experienced or it's not clear yet whether their business idea will work. The majority of new companies go bust within five years

whereas a larger, more established company has proven that it can handle business difficulties. You can find even smaller companies among those not yet listed on the stock market. You can invest in these via venture capital and private equity funds.

* **Derivatives** – these are investments like futures or options which you could be offered by your employer.

What Is Your Risk Appetite?

Until you are invested, you probably don't know how you are going to react to a market fall. That's why it's better to take it slowly and not invest too much for your first investment. Do a patch test to see what your own emotional reactions are to the way your investment performs over a few months. Be particularly observant during any falls in its value. This may not be easy with some investments such as property which moves in longer cycles. In any case, ensure you always have some money in cash, particularly if you sense that you won't feel good about any loss.

Ask yourself what things would make you feel afraid or confident/secure about your investments. What is the worst case scenario and could you handle that? How does this investment fit in with your goals and what is important to you? What is the most important thing in your life and could an investment loss affect that?

DON'T COUNT YOUR CHICKENS

Life is full of ups and downs; sometimes you feel rich, then suddenly you can start to feel relatively poor. You may have more assets than when you were younger, but if they are costing you a lot (such as a house with a leaking roof), or your living standards are such that your income can't keep up, you can feel poor. You might decide to take on a big expense, like private school education for your kids, when you're feeling flush, only to lose your job and suddenly discover that all those bills seem insurmountable.

That's when having a cash cushion to fall back on comes in handy, and also making sure that your investments are working hard for you, that you're not taking on too much risk and you aren't wasting money on an inefficient investment.

Knowing you have budgeting skills behind you, a nest egg of savings and a well-diversified portfolio makes you a lot less stressed during the difficult times. So 'don't put all your eggs in one basket' and 'save for a rainy day' because you can bet there's one hovering on the horizon.

WHAT NOT TO BUY

Apart from ensuring your portfolio is protected from inflation and has a nice balance of assets to reduce the risk, it also helps if you don't buy any dodgy investments! Sure, you can buy some higher-risk assets (although it helps to limit them to 5%–10% of the portfolio), but don't go buying something that is going to damage your returns.

Our guru Swensen believes there are a number of assets that are a waste of time for most investors. He describes them as: 'superficially appealing but ultimately performance-damaging'.

Many of these investments are products created by finance companies to try to achieve the seemingly impossible – low risk with a high return. Normally, if something is low risk, such as a bank account, your returns won't be very exciting – whereas a high-risk investment is supposed to compensate for the sleepless nights by giving you a better return.

These new products remind me of the dieting merchandise companies also try to sell us – yes, you too can eat a caramel and peanut chocolate bar and actually lose weight! Not surprisingly, some of these dieting products have been found to contain chemicals that actually *harm* your health and can even make weight loss more difficult. It's pretty similar with many of these financial products. My personal opinion is that the reason the industry keeps coming up with these products is because it is essentially sales-driven (like any industry) and needs new products to get us to buy more. In the same way that you probably don't really need a new electric toothbrush, remote-controlled light switch or 'scientifically tested' lipstick – you don't really need some of the new-fangled investment products which are launched every year.

Expert after expert has extolled the virtues of keeping your investments as simple as possible. This way, you understand what you are buying and are better prepared if things go wrong.

So, if you don't really understand how a bond fund manager is going to make you money or what he's really up to then keep things simple and buy bonds directly – such as UK gilts that you can get from the Post Office.

When it comes to building your portfolio, fill it with assets that you understand and diversify across the four key asset classes – shares, bonds, property and cash.

JUSTINE'S TOP 10 TIPS

1) Make sure your portfolio is structured so that it beats the inflation rate over time.

2) Design your portfolio so that it fits your needs now, but be prepared to re-evaluate it on a regular basis as your needs change. Like a healthy diet, you should have a good balance of different assets. Don't hold too much of the sugary, high-risk stuff in your portfolio. Risky assets shouldn't be more than 5–10%.

4) Ensure you are taking on the right amount of risk given your time horizon and consider whether you need to increase the risk you're taking or reduce it.

5) Evaluate whether you need some lower risk assets like bonds.

6) Plan for the long term and you will be able to afford to buy more aggressive investments that give you a better return.

7) Ensure you aren't paying too much in fees to buy, own or sell your investment.

8) Buy investments you understand and that do their job, not complicated investments a financial company talks you into.

9) Build up your knowledge of a particular asset to improve your returns.

10) Keep some money in cash for emergencies.

Property

Why property is a good investment

Property is a very girly investment. There's something about buying your own nest and feathering it that strikes a chord with most women. Ever since the 1882 Married Women's Property Act, when we were finally given the same rights as men to buy properties and hold on to those inherited from parents, women have been taking advantage of this freedom.

Research by the Office of National Statistics shows that young women move out of the family home at an earlier age than men and also jump on the property wagon at an earlier age. If done correctly, this can give them a fantastic financial boost. According to the Centre for Economic and Business Research (CEBR), women are set to represent more than half of Britain's millionaires by 2020, largely due to property price rises.

For many women, property has provided not only security and independence, but also good investment returns. Whether it's your own home, a flat that you rent out or a commercial property investment, it's possible to make good profits from property if you follow a few key rules. Below are the main reasons why property is a good asset to add to your portfolio.

Growth and Income

Like shares, property can provide you with two types of return. You can make money from an increase in the value of the land and building, plus earn a regular income in the form of rent.

Gearing

Another key benefit is that you can borrow quite a significant amount of money to buy your property. The effect of this 'gearing' will boost returns further.

Here's an example. Let's say you have £10,000 to invest. If you put it all in the bank or in shares and it rises 10% over a year, at the end of the year you'll have £11,000.

But, if you put that money down as a deposit on a property worth £100,000 and that investment also rises 10% in a year (to £110,000), your initial cash outlay will have doubled to £20,000. So, the return on your investment is not 10% but 100%.

Of course, this ignores the costs of that debt, i.e. mortgage payments, and your buying and selling costs. But you can see how gearing can rapidly improve your returns. It's possible to borrow money to invest in the stock market too, but you won't be able to get such a big loan (e.g. 90% or even 100% of the value of the investment). Also, if the shares fall in price the lender will demand you pay a 'margin call'. This is when the lender asks you to start paying back the debt faster because he is nervous about the performance of your asset. In contrast, if your property falls in value, your bank rarely asks for its money back, especially if you are still making the normal monthly payments.

If the value of your property does fall, your loss will of course be greater than if you hadn't borrowed at all. A house you bought for £100,000 cash will only lose £10,000 if the market falls 10%, but if all you had to start with was a £10,000 deposit, your deposit will be wiped out. Fortunately, as long as you haven't lost your job and can still keep making your mortgage repayments, you can keep your home.

Adding Value

One way investors can improve the returns they receive on any asset is by increasing their control over it, or by adding value to that investment. For example, if you buy an old car and do it up, you can sell it for more money. This is the same strategy used by some entrepreneurs who buy struggling companies. They cut costs and make them more efficient, and then either reap the higher profits the company is making or sell it for a higher price.

A key feature of property is that you are able, quite easily, to improve this asset if you buy carefully and know a few tricks. Some ways you can add value to property are:

* Renovating or improving rooms (especially the kitchen or bathroom).
* Adding an extra bedroom.
* Adding an extra toilet or bathroom.
* Adding a garage.
* Landscaping the garden.
* Building a second property on the same block.
* Improving the general quality of the decorations – e.g. a fresh coat of paint in a neutral colour throughout.

However, before you race off to B&Q, it's important not to get too carried away with decorating. Only make renovations that are vital and don't cost too much.

There are other things you can do to increase the return you receive from your property investment without spending any money:

* Increase the rent (especially if it is below the market average).
* Ask tenants what they want, for example increased storage space, and then provide it in exchange for higher rent.
* Reduce the insurance costs you are paying.
* Reduce your mortgage costs by refinancing.
* Ensure you are claiming everything you can tax-wise.

All these features make property a very good asset to hold. However, as with other types of investment, you still need to follow a few rules if you want to make a profit. It is still possible to lose money investing in property, usually by buying in the wrong area, or at the wrong time, and selling too soon.

How to find a good investment property

Because many women are naturally drawn to property, they might find it difficult at times to keep some emotional distance and look at their property purely as an investment, rather than a home. When you find a gorgeous little flat or house it's easy to fall in love, and that's usually when you pay too much for it – consequently reducing your investment returns! I have a friend who has done this with several properties. Each time she falls in love, sure that this property is 'the one', only to get bored a year or two down the line and sell for a loss, or the same price.

It's true that some properties can be like an awful boyfriend. They demand your attention all weekend, suck up all your spare cash and leave you feeling disappointed and drained.

So how can you keep your emotions in check and ensure your property investment works for you, rather than you constantly working to keep it in shape?

Don't Overpay

The first rule is the same for men. Don't jump into a long-term commitment until you have checked out the goods properly. You must get an inspection done to have an accurate assessment of how much repair work will be needed, and you should always be careful not to overpay – otherwise you could become resentful later on.

A study by the Council of Mortgage Lenders found women pay more for their properties than men do. This is because they were more likely to buy a property that had already been renovated and was in good condition – which bumps up the price. However, buying properties where you can't add value through renovations will reduce the returns you can make when you sell.

With any investment, whether it's property or something else, it's always important not to overpay. If you buy something for a good price, you have already made money. You don't have to wait for the market to go in your favour or try to figure out a way to add value to the investment. To make sure you are getting a good price:

* **Look at what the market is doing** – are prices considered quite high and has the market been performing well recently, or is there lots of doom and gloom?

Obviously, during a boom there's a higher risk that you are overpaying and it's easier to get caught up in all the hype.

* **Ask yourself if the asset is being discounted for a particular reason which could change in the future.** For example, you may find a property that is in bad condition, so not selling; if you fixed it up, you could sell it for more. Similarly, you may have just been through a market crash and investors are all being extra-cautious because they lost money. If you didn't lose money, then you are perfectly positioned to take advantage of the bargain prices around.

If property prices are in free fall, it's obviously a good idea to hold back until you can see that the market has bottomed. But keep looking at properties during this time, so that you are aware of property values. That way, if a real bargain comes along, you will be able to identify it quickly and snap it up. If prices are stagnant, it may still be a good idea to buy if it's as a home and you are currently renting. But don't struggle to pay for an expensive mortgage – only buy if you can realistically afford it. It is obviously more difficult to make money from a property in a flat or falling market, particularly if you are impatient and can't hold on for the long term, but it's not impossible – you just have to work harder. In a market where prices are very cheap, you might only have to look at ten stocks or properties before you find a good one. In a market where there's lots of froth and bubble, you might have to look at a hundred and monitor your emotions carefully. I bought my last property at what was close to the peak in prices and sold it when prices were already starting to come down, yet I doubled the money I invested by adhering to the following rules.

If you think property prices are set to fall or stagnate, it's important to:

* **Do your homework** – visit as many properties as possible before you buy and ask estate agents lots of questions about the market and what's selling. Some will be more helpful than others.
* **Negotiate hard** – if you are a first-time buyer or have enough cash to buy a property outright (without a mortgage), you are in a stronger position. Always offer less than the asking price (around 20%) – you can always increase your offer later if it's rejected. If it is winter, or the market is weak, use that to your advantage.
* **Don't take on too much debt** – you shouldn't be spending more than one third of your take home pay on debt repayments. Avoid 100% mortgages or interest-only mortgages.
* **Find a property that is discounted for the wrong reasons** – (e.g. it needs some renovation) not for a good reason (it's in a horrible area).
* **Add value to the property** – either by adding another room or renovating. This way you can make money even if prices go nowhere. But be careful to carry out only renovations that improve the value. Don't spend too much on pretty decor just because you like it – other people might not. There is also no point renovating a property to look like a castle if it's in an area of modest family homes where there is no demand for something so flash.
* **Be prepared to hold on to the asset for the long term** – at least five years, preferably ten years or more.

Hold for the Long Term

As I explained earlier, property investment should be a long-term commitment, especially if you want to make money safely and reduce your risks. Spending a lot of time in the market is a safer way to make money than trying to time when you enter or exit. Sometimes, people try to dip in and out of the property market by buying and selling after only owning the property for a year or even less. This strategy is just as foolish and risky as trying to trade stocks. Occasionally it works, but it has more to do with good luck than good management. You will incur high transaction costs and you may not get it right and end up losing money. Besides, trying to trade property might work in a market that's going up, but in a slow-moving or stagnant market it simply won't work as it takes so much longer to sell properties. It's like trying to get rid of that dodgy boyfriend who simply won't move out.

The property market cycle is similar to other market cycles, except that it's much slower. Just when you think prices are too high, they will keep going up for another year or two. Similarly, just when you think prices are cheap and the worst is over, they will keep falling or stay stagnant for a bit longer until the general public are finally convinced that they should start thinking about getting back into property.

A good way to tell what the market is doing is simply to listen to gossip. When a market is getting frothy, or turning into a bubble, every man and his dog will be talking about it. Your taxi driver will be giving you share tips, or your sister-in-law will be raving about how much money she and her husband have made from buy-to-let property investing. These people all make it sound so easy and encourage you to jump in too. Beware! This is exactly the time when you should be getting scared that the market is too expensive. If everyone seems to be making money, then the smart money has probably already moved on to somewhere else.

Don't Fall in Love

One of the hardest parts of buying a property for investment is stopping yourself from falling in love. Because you can see, touch and smell a property, it often seems more real than a stock market investment, so controlling your emotions can be harder. You might start out planning to buy something cheap, spend very little on renovations and rent it out for maximum gains. However, once you walk into Ikea or your local B&Q, you get carried away by the look and feel of all those beautiful things. Suddenly, you have spent a fortune on building the latest stainless steel kitchen with all the trimmings and your profits have halved. Look at all the people who find it impossible to follow Sarah Beeny's advice on *Property Ladder*. She consistently advises them not to overspend, but they rarely resist.

Falling in love can also hit you before you even get to the renovations stage. Once you're smitten with a property, the sellers know they have you and you can't negotiate effectively. You always have to be prepared to walk away from a deal, no matter how good it looks. Otherwise, you will end up paying too much, selling for too little, or buying something that ends up costing you a fortune in maintenance costs. You have to work out not only whether you can afford the property, but also its upkeep. Don't think of your first property as your dream home unless you really don't plan to ever move. Buy something you can live in, certainly, but think of it more like a stepping stone.

Keep Costs under Control

If you are just buying a home, rather than an investment property, it is still sensible to reduce your costs as much as possible. Because a home isn't usually providing you with an income, it can be a less efficient investment than some others, so it's important to minimise the amount you spend on it. That way, you will have more money left over to put into other investments that could provide you with an income. If you want to install a jacuzzi in your bathroom or buy a luxury rug for your living room, go right ahead – but don't try to tell yourself it's an investment. It's as much of a toy to make you feel good as your partner buying his fancy new car that costs a fortune to insure.

Fortunately, studies show that women are usually quite sensible about these things because we don't like to take too much risk. For example, a study by the Council of Mortgage Lenders found women pay a deposit that is 4% higher on average than men when they first buy a property. This ensures the cost of your mortgage repayments, as well as your stress levels, are lower.

When to Sell

As with stock market investing, deciding when to sell can be fraught with problems. Fortunately, most people hold their properties for longer than their stocks, so this helps ensure they don't make a loss. Obviously, you may decide to sell for many personal reasons due to a change in your life – marriage, divorce, retirement, a larger family, moving towns or cities. Even in these cases, it can be possible to hold on to a property that might be valued at less than what you paid for it – for example, by renting it out when you move town. Another alternative is to extend your home to make room for a growing family, or convert it to flats if you need to scale down. This means the flexibility of your chosen home is another important factor when buying. Even if you are currently childless, you might want to start a family in the next few years. Buying near a school, or buying a home that can be extended could save you a lot of money if the market takes an untimely dip.

With investment property there are some experts who simply never sell. They buy a property that earns enough rent to give them a healthy return. Then, they either save enough from this or other income for a deposit on a second property, or, assuming the property has increased in value, release some equity from the first property, by remortgaging, to pay for the second. In this way, they are able to build up a portfolio of properties without ever having to sell and release the capital gain or profit. If all your gains are only on paper, you don't have to pay tax on them.

What's the yield?

Of course, this strategy only works if you can minimise your mortgage costs and ensure you are getting a healthy return from rent. For this reason, professional investors scrutinise the yield on a property very carefully. The yield is the percentage annual return that your investment property is giving you. For example, let's say you buy a flat for £250,000 and are able to rent it out for £1,000 per month. Your annual rent is £12,000 which (divided by the £250,000 and multiplied by 100) means your annual return is 4.8%. That's not much better than you'd get from a bank account, which is why many UK buy-to-let investors pulled out of the market or went looking overseas. If the numbers don't add up, there's no point rushing into an investment.

VOID PERIODS

If you do want to become a hotshot property investor and join the increasing number of landladies around the country, then you also need to think about void periods, when your property is left empty and can't be rented out. This could be caused by an electical fault, flood, necessary renovations or even just a slow market. You also need to have a decent savings pot to cover things like the washing machine breaking down, agency fees, and mortgage rate increases if you don't have a long-term fixed rate loan.

By keeping a sharp eye on what the yield is on a given property, you can keep your emotions in check when buying. If a property is only yielding 5%, then you may be better off leaving it in cash for a while – especially if prices aren't going up, so you wouldn't benefit from an increase in the capital value in the short term. Keeping an eye on the yield properties are providing, can also give you an early indication that properties are getting too expensive and that the market might be heading for a fall.

The good news is that many women have already taken to property investment like ducks to water. According to Landlord Mortgages, since the start of 2006, women have bought more than 24% of all buy-to-let properties and there has been a big increase in the number of female landlords. All this property investment is already boosting fortunes.

The studies show that women can be very good landladies. They are more professional, keep their properties in better shape, better understand the needs of female tenants (who are generally cleaner), so have lower void periods and build good relationships with tenants and contractors.

Below is a list of things you should keep in mind when buying a property. When you go to see one, bring this along to keep you on track, as well as a list of your particular requirements – e.g. must have a garden for the kids.

PROPERTY CHECKLIST

* Buy the worst house in a good street.
* Keep a hold on your emotions – buy a property you like but ensure it makes financial sense as well.
* Buy within a 20km radius of a major town/city centre.
* Study your market. If it is a family home are you near good schools? Think about who you would sell the property to later.
* Calculate carefully how much renovations are likely to cost.
* Look at who the property will be sold to – e.g. if you are targeting young families, are there good schools nearby? If you're aiming at young professionals, are there good transport links?
* Renovate bathrooms and kitchens first – these add the most value.
* Some renovations can be a bad investment, such as a swimming pool or fountain which are costly to maintain. Even the popular choice of a loft conversion may cost more to do than the value it adds.
* Decorate in neutral colours. Buyers like to see the property as a blank canvas that their furniture is more likely to match.
* Look at bonuses – e.g. if you have an inner-city apartment with parking, you can rent out the parking space separately.
* Don't underestimate the effect that a nice and neat garden can have on the appearance of your home, and this can be relatively cheap to do.
* Preferably buy in an established suburb. Up-and-coming ones

may never up and come, and their prices are more volatile (both on the way up and down).

* Buy when prices are low and everyone is negative about the market.
* If you must buy when prices have already risen, make sure you do your homework. It's possible to get a good deal, but realise you must work twice as hard and not let yourself get caught up in the hype.
* Hold for the long-term like any investment. Don't buy for a quick profit – property market cycles are much slower than shares.
* Make sure you know what maintenance costs are involved. These can be prohibitive on a large property and send you broke.
* Only deal with agents, brokers and lawyers you trust, preferably recommended by a friend. Sometimes paying a bit more for someone you really trust and who will do quality work can save you thousands if it means the contract goes through smoothly, quickly and at the right price.
* If it's a rental property, don't buy something just because it's what you would want to live in. Buy something with low maintenance costs, good transport links and decent security. Don't overpay! Do you want to spend all your weekends or lots of money repairing things?
* The market is usually strongest in spring/summer, so buy in winter when houses (and gardens) don't look as good. It will give you an idea of how good the heating is too!
* Check how noisy the street/neighbourhood is, by visiting at different times of the day. Values will be lower if you are next door to a pub or school.
* What parking is available? Is it on the road or private?

MORTGAGES

* Don't overborrow. Repayments shouldn't be more than one third of your take-home pay.
* Don't take out an interest-only mortgage or 100% loan.
* If interest rates are low, lock in for the long-term.
* Shop around for the best mortgage deals; don't just take the one your local bank offers.
* Avoid mortgage gimmicks unless you know you understand very well what is being offered (such as interest-only mortgages where the extra repayments are invested in the stock market).
* Preferably choose a mortgage that allows daily interest calculation (rather than annual). This allows you to pay off your debt quicker and you pay less interest over the life of the mortgage.
* Preferably choose a mortgage that allows you to make over-payments with no penalties. This can save a lot over the long term.

> **'A banker is a fellow who lends you his umbrella when the sun is shining, but wants it back the minute it begins to rain.'**
>
> **Mark Twain**

Property Millionairess

There are now many examples of women who have made themselves millionaires, or at least quite rich, from investing in property.

One of my favourite stories is that of Jan Somers, a housewife and former school teacher. She began investing in property in the early 1970s and became a millionaire by the age of 35 –

long before the last property boom took off. The secrets to her success were a strict savings discipline, keeping a close eye on all the costs, seeing property as a long-term investment (she basically buys rental properties and never sells) and also using the local tax rules effectively.

Her first property was a very modest home in an unpopular suburb bought just after her wedding when she was still a struggling teacher. She and her husband were forced into becoming landlords when they had to move house because of his job. After that, her savings discipline and sheer appetite for owning homes saw her continue to buy more properties long before the first one was ever paid off.

Jan took advantage of negative gearing, which involves making a loss on your rental properties (i.e. your rent isn't enough to cover the mortgage and other costs), so that you don't have to pay as much tax on the income from your job. She also took out interest-only mortgages at times.

Although some of these techniques might be considered too risky for many investors, there is still a lot that can be learned from her experience. For example, she doesn't live beyond her means and never gets into debt unless it is related to property investment. She has also paid quite large deposits on her homes, largely because she is so good at budgeting and saving.

Jan believes that you don't need wealth to start, and that it's possible to build up what you already have in order to get what you want. Then, the trick is simply to hold on to your investments and not 'trade' them by trying to buy and sell over a short period.

Holiday Homes – Following the Sun

Over the last few years there has been an interesting change both in demographics and in people's lifestyles. The baby boom that followed the Second World War has meant there are now an increasing number of people of retirement age. Many of the baby boomer generation have already retired and many others plan to do so in the next few years. As they retire, a large proportion of these people are moving to coastal areas where it's warmer and they can enjoy a view of the sea.

This is an interesting phenomenon which reverses previous trends we have seen over the past century. Industrialisation led more and more people to move away from country areas and to the cities to look for work. Now the opposite seems to be occurring. The Internet revolution allows more people to work from home, so many of these people are choosing to buy homes in either coastal or country areas, where they can have nicer views and a more relaxed lifestyle. If you can work from anywhere, why not work from a house on the beach or from a lovely old farm where you can go for long walks in the afternoon?

Some commentators argue that it's unlikely that a lot of people will give up their jobs in the city and move inland or to the coast. Yet the trend has already started. At a recent commercial property conference I attended, one speaker stood up to voice his concerns about the long-term impact this decentralisation was going to have on the value of office blocks and shops in European city centres. Similarly, a recent European property market report by RICS (Royal Institute of Chartered Surveyors) showed that in certain markets holiday homes by the sea had increased at a faster rate than principal residences.

It's possible that this rapid increase is partly due to the fact that Britons (and many other Europeans) are wealthier these days, so can increasingly afford a second home. Many have downsized, remortgaged their main home, or made money from property investing so that they can afford to buy a holiday house. The lower cost of flights to sunny climes has also boosted the holiday homes market. However, the increased number of retirees moving to the sun is yet another factor that is having an impact.

As with many long-term trends, the impact of demographics is going to continue to influence where people buy property in the future. Over the long term, as the baby boomers retire they are still likely to want to do so in sunny places. Certainly, some properties in coastal areas that have been overdeveloped – or badly developed – have seen their prices crash. This clearly illustrates the importance of analysing carefully all the possible risks. Usually, the holiday homes market is more volatile than other markets because people who have bought a second home as a luxury will sell it before they sell their main residence – especially if they are finding the mortgage or maintenance costs are a drain on their finances. The only exception is where that home was bought for their retirement, in which case they might move out of their main residence first. In any case, the secrets of buying in a coastal, holiday home area are the same as for other types of properties. Quality property with a lovely view is likely to hold its value over time, whether it's on the Costa del Sol or in Cornwall.

The risks

The massive numbers of northern Europeans buying properties in southern parts of Europe, helped by the formation of the European Union, has led to very strong price rises in places like the south of France and Spain.

Between 1998 and 2005, the number of UK households with second homes abroad doubled to around 280,000. Almost half of these homes were located in Spain and France.

Unlike the UK, where housing and land supply had been somewhat restricted by bureaucracy, France and Spain saw a big jump in housing construction. Whenever you have a greater supply of property than there is demand, you have a fall in prices. We have already seen a significant correction in the Spanish market and France is coming down too, though at a slower pace. The message here is that any market will tumble if it is overbought and there are few restrictions on the supply of properties. The same happened in Ireland, and the weather is far from sunny there! It's a classic supply/demand scenario. When there's lots of demand, builders increase the supply of properties, but often they overdo it and pretty soon there's too much supply. Then something happens in the economy and demand falls away as well, so prices fall even further. You might be used to seeing this happen in the UK, but remember that building regulations (which sometimes limit supply) are not the same abroad, so markets can behave differently – either in a more extreme or in a more restrained way than at home.

There are a number of other risks associated with holiday homes that you might not have thought about. As the owner of a holiday home myself, I have experienced some of these problems first hand so I know what a hassle these properties can be.

Holiday homes can be great because you have your own little piece of paradise where you can just hang out and not worry about curfews or check-in times, or if you can bring your kids/pets. But they can also be a lot of work. If your home has a big garden, you may find you spend all your holiday cutting the grass, as well as cleaning, weeding and trying to repair crumbling terraces or damage to your roof, rather than hitting the beach.

Another problem is the increased risk of being broken into, particularly if your property is isolated. I once arrived at my property to discover squatters had been living there. Alerting the authorities or asking your neighbours to keep an eye out can only do so much if you are away for extended periods. Insurance can be difficult to get, if not impossible, and your home and belongings are at a great risk of being damaged in a fire or fierce storm if you are not actually there.

Buying the property can also be fraught with problems. In countries like France, you must pay a 10% deposit to secure the property (so no other buyers can come in), and agents and legal fees can add up to around 10% of the value of the property. In some countries, these upfront costs can be even higher at around 12.5%. Then, you have the difficulty of working out which taxes and other bills you have to pay in a foreign language – needless to say, it helps if you can speak the local language, which I didn't when I first bought.

In some countries there are different rules regarding titles, so you may discover belatedly that you have bought a house with no rights to the land underneath it. Other countries that only offer leasehold purchase may do so because they don't like the idea of foreigners actually owning anything in their country. Beware of such attitudes! If the country is not particularly developed, you may discover down the track that the government has decided to reclaim all land owned by foreigners to give it back to the locals and your investment will be worthless.

If you decide to rent out the property, you may be able to get a very good return in the high season, but nothing at all in winter. It's safer to assume that you will only be able to rent it for about half the year when you are working out your figures. A good idea is to speak to local estate agents before you buy about how much properties are usually rented for and for how many weeks of the year. You may find that in your area you can only get holiday tenants for two months of the year. This of course means you can't take your own holidays during that time and can only use the property in the off season.

If you are considering longer-term, non-holiday lets, then be sure to investigate the rights for local tenants, or you may find it difficult to regain control of your property. In countries like France it is not possible to evict a tenant during the winter months, and certain tenants, such as farmers, have more rights so may lock you in for a long-term lease and then refuse to leave. Unfortunately, buying a holiday home in a sunny, foreign land might sound idyllic but it can be a nightmare if the locals resent you being there. The local community or government can make life difficult by refusing to allow certain renovations, or push through changes such as constructing an airport or highway not far from your plot.

Despite all these problems, I am still happy with my purchase and have made very good money from it. When I first bought my holiday home, my friends told me I was mad and that 'everyone' knew that property prices in France simply don't move because the French all rent. Luckily, the last few years have supported my contrary decision. As with other types of property investing, if you remember the basic rules of buying for a good price, minimising your costs, and adding value to your investment, you should do well over time. Most investments are quite forgiving over the long term, and property especially so.

Whenever you are able to influence and exert some control over an investment, rather than simply relying on market movements or the expertise of others, you can potentially boost its performance. This control aspect is another reason why property is such an incredibly popular asset for many small investors.

For more information

There are a number of specialist overseas mortgage advisers now in the UK who can advise you on some of the difficulties with this type of purchase. Also, if you are considering a property in Europe, the RICS European Housing Review (which is usually available on the Internet) has a detailed breakdown of residential property trends in a number of countries.

JUSTINE'S TOP 10 TIPS

1) Be careful not to overpay, especially in a strong market.

2) Don't fall in love, and stay as unemotional as possible.

3) Look at lots of properties but set yourself a deadline so that you actually make a decision.

4) Have a clear idea of who you would sell the property to before you buy or renovate.

5) Be clear before you buy which renovations are needed and how much they'll cost. Only make renovations that will add value.

6) Buy with the aim of holding for the long term.

7) Don't take on too much debt or you will find it hard to sleep at night.

8) Search for properties in an area you are familiar with and don't mind living in.

9) If you buy a holiday home, know exactly what you can rent it for and how often, and be prepared to visit it only in the off season.

10) Focus on the figures if it is an investment, not the gorgeous décor.

PENSIONS

Why don't more women take an interest in finance? Well, quite frankly because much of the information you read about it is boring! Especially if you look at the way people try to talk about and sell pensions. If you're a busy woman, like most of us, you probably don't have time to pore over articles in the weekend financial press, to decipher the industry's jargon or compare thousands of different investment products, pension rules, tax implications etc. Even bank savings accounts offer so many bells and whistles these days it's difficult to compare products. I get confused trying to work out which is the best mobile phone package, so I'm sure many women just close their eyes and point when they're asked to choose a pension product. However, pensions don't have to be so complicated. After all, they're just another form of savings and one that can be very tax-effective. Unfortunately, the government and others have covered up pensions with red tape and rules which are now growing like weeds over a once-healthy plant.

Below are what I consider to be the most important points when planning for your retirement.

JUST SAVE SOMETHING

Despite all the rules and jargon, a pension is just another route for savings to ensure you are not poverty-stricken in retirement. Given that one in five single female pensioners are in exactly that state in their dotage, it's important to take it seriously.

Fortunately, you don't necessarily have to take the standard approach. The important thing is simply to save in some form through small, regular amounts and start early, so you benefit from the incredible benefits of compound interest. Your goal is to have as few fixed expenses as possible by the time you reach a certain age (so have your mortgage and other debts paid off) and as much income as possible. When you think about how much income you can get from a particular investment, it really changes the way you look at it. Some people go for investment property, some buy shares, funds or bonds. But the best policy is to diversify – get a few *different* sources of income so that you are not reliant on just one. Of course, getting a standard pension product via your employer or directly is still a good idea because it's fairly tax-effective, but you don't have to have all your future retirement income wrapped up in just one product.

DIVERSIFY YOUR ASSETS

Your income during your working life probably only came from one source, but in retirement there's nothing wrong with having income from a number of sources. In fact, this diversity will reduce the risk of something going wrong and one income stream drying up. Also, different investments behave in different ways and grow at different times of the economic cycle, so it pays to be well covered. Some may provide purely income, others may 'grow' in value as well as providing income. Even just having investments that pay you at different times of the year or month can be helpful. Here are some sources of income:

* Investment property – rental income (plus you could get some growth if the property rises in value).
* Shares – dividends (plus growth if the share price rises).
* Cash – interest (just income, no growth).
* Bonds – held directly, these provide income via coupon payments.
* Funds – provide income plus possibly asset growth (depending on the type of fund). These can be bought tax-effectively through an ISA.
* Company pension provided by your employer.
* Private pension that you make your own private contributions to.
* Company shares/options – that your employer provides you with through a company savings scheme (again, these can be quite tax effective).
* State pension benefits from the government.
* Income from part-time work.
* Gains from alternative investments such as art, antiques, wine, timber, private companies, royalties, gold etc.

If you have changed jobs quite often, as I have, you may discover that you already have several different pension schemes from various employers. It's a good idea to have a good look over these funds and choose which ones you think are the most reliable and have the best investment performance, then merge the money into just a couple of funds where this is possible. This will reduce the fees you are paying on each fund that can really cut into your returns in the long term.

However, don't put all your pension money in just one place. Over the years there have been scandals where people have put all their savings with one company, only to be left destitute when that company went bust and lost all their money. Even if the government or regulator tries to bail out these companies, you often only get back a relatively small portion of your original savings, so don't take the chance.

HOW MUCH SHOULD YOU SAVE TOWARDS RETIREMENT?

This will depend on a lot of things such as:

* How far away you are from retirement.
* What your investment return is.
* How much you want to live on in retirement.

If you are relatively young, a good rule of thumb is to save at least 10% of your pre-tax income and preferably 15%. So, if you are earning £25,000 a year, you should be saving £2,500 towards your retirement. A lot of companies will make contributions on your behalf so, if your company is putting in 5% for you, top it up to 10%.

Don't forget this money doesn't have to go into a standard pension product, but make sure it does go somewhere. Standard pensions (such as the **stakeholder** pensions) can be good because the money is locked up so you don't blow it before retirement, and you get a tax break. Make sure you check out the product thoroughly for fees and charges, though, and also how well the money is invested. Stakeholder pensions have to meet certain criteria so that they don't overcharge on fees, but you still need to make sure the money is invested well. If you are retiring in 20 years there's no point having the money sitting in mostly cash-type investments that aren't growing very fast. You have the benefit of a lengthy savings period on your side, which significantly reduces your risks, so you might as well exploit that.

Save regularly and avoid taking breaks

One of the main reasons British women's pensions are in their current disastrous state is because women take breaks to have children, or for other reasons, during their lifetime. If you are taking time off work for your children, make it a priority to get your husband to keep up contributions for you. Whine, cajole or beg, whatever it takes, but get that extra £2,500 a year out of him for your pension. It will add up to much more than that over the long term, and he is probably still making his own pension contributions while you are at home with the kids. Don't rely on the idea that he'll take care of you in your old age just because he's doing that now. That's the strategy our mothers and grandmothers used and it didn't work very well for many of them. Even if you stay together and his pension is set up to provide for you, he is likely to have a pension policy that only pays a small portion (perhaps a third) to you on retirement. If he dies, your entitlement will most likely be less than his full pension as well (if any). Not to mention the fact that you will most likely live longer, so your pension has to be bigger than his so it can last longer.

When in a couple, people tend to look at their finances together as a family rather than as individuals. That's perfectly understandable but with pensions it's crucial that you have your *own, separate* retirement income. Why? Because:

* You live longer.
* You are more likely to have responsibility for the kids.
* You are more likely to take responsibility for elderly parents.
* Something could go wrong in your relationship.

As a journalist, I have heard countless horror stories about elderly ladies who have found themselves with very little in retirement just when they needed it most. It's always so heart-breaking and frustrating when some little old lady looks up at you and says something like: 'He told me it was all taken care of and not to worry about it. He always took care of the finances, and I loved him and trusted him so of course I never questioned it. I thought that, because he was a doctor and earning good money, that I wouldn't have to worry, but he never started a pension and now I find out he didn't even have life insurance.' Traditionally, it has always been the man's job to take care of us financially, so it's not surprising that most women don't raise this issue until it's too late. If your partner won't speak to you about these things, then at least set up your own pension for your peace of mind.

Invest aggressively

OK, this one sounds controversial, but hear me out. If you are in your twenties, thirties or even forties you have a fair bit of time before you are going to need to live on that money. If you are 40, you are probably going to retire at 60 or 65 – that's in another 25 years. You can certainly afford to be invested in shares. You should look at shares if you have around a ten-year investment horizon. If it's more than ten years you can afford to invest not only in UK shares but in other areas like emerging markets and smaller companies as well. That's why, when your company asks you to tick a box deciding where your pension money will be invested, you should choose a fairly aggressive one. Of course, if you are going to panic and lie awake at night worrying about it, then choose the default option which is usually more diversified with some bonds in it. But don't choose the most cautious option if you are more than ten years away from retirement. Many women describe themselves as 'cautious' investors because they fear they don't know much about the financial markets and don't want to make a mistake. Unfortunately, in the long run this seemingly 'safe' option could turn out to be the least safe and will cost you money.

For example, you invest £200 each month for 30 years in a 'cautious' investment fund that gives you a yearly return of 5%. At the end of this period you would have £167,425.

However, if you had invested the money in a fund or pension that achieved a yearly return of 7%, you'd have £242,575 at the end of the period, and if it was managing to return 9% a year, you would end up with £356,580.

Stock market investments are risky in the short-term because you might need the money, but pension money is 'set and forget' money. If it's locked up for twenty years and you can't touch it, what's the point of having it in cash? Worse, if you leave it in cash, it's more likely to be whittled away by inflation.

Let's look at a specific risk, such as the market crashing just before you retire.

> Julie, aged 40, invests £200 a month, or about £2,400 a year for 20 years and gets a nice 9% return each year. This gives her a lump sum at retirement of £133,834. Then, at age 60, the stock market falls 23%, as it did in the US on Black Monday in 1987. She's left with £103,052.
>
> Amanda, aged 40, invests the same amount at 5% a year over 20 years with no loss at age 60. Her lump sum at retirement? £83,326.

Of course it is risky to keep all your money in the stock market right up until retirement date. That's why many advisers recommend gradually shifting some of it into bonds or cash-type products in the last few years before you reach retirement. Some pension providers do this automatically for you: these are often called 'lifestyling' pension products because the investments change as your life does.

In any case, if you have 20 or more years left until retirement, you shouldn't be wasting those precious years by keeping too much of your money in conservative investments, otherwise you will lose out in the long term.

Work out how much you want to live on in retirement

To work out how much you need to save for your pension, it's a good idea to work backwards. Ask yourself, what age you would ideally like to retire, and what level of income you want to be living on in retirement? Don't just say you want to be rich. Could you live adequately on the same level of income you are currently on? Some expenses will go down if you are no longer going into the office, but others will go up (such as health care and heating bills), so it's a good idea to assume roughly the same income that you are on now.

Many of our grandparents live on an income provided by the state, so they didn't have to worry about calculating their future income requirements. But for us it's likely to be different. If you have private pension savings (or a pension through your company), you are likely to end up with a big lump sum of money in your pension pot at retirement. Assuming you don't blow any of this money on a cruise around the world, you can then transfer it into what's called an **annuity**.

An annuity is like a reverse insurance product. With insurance you pay small premiums over your lifetime, so that when you die your heirs get a big payout. With an annuity you pay one big lump sum which is turned into a regular income that is designed to last your whole life – no matter how long you live. So, if you live until 100, you won't be eating cat food and struggling to pay your heating bills. You can buy an annuity which ensures that your lump sum is turned into a set amount of income that you are guaranteed to receive every year until you die. You can even buy one that's linked to inflation, so that even if the cost of living goes up you are still covered.

Now, how big a lump sum do you think you'll need to get a decent income that's going to last your whole life? Well, the bad news is that because we're all living longer we need a bigger lump sum if it's going to stretch that far. These days, people might only work for 40 years (from age 25 to 65) but then could live in retirement for another 30 years which is almost as long. That means your lump sum can really get stretched.

According to the Annuity Bureau (**www.annuity-bureau.co.uk)**, a woman who decides to retire at age 55 with a pension pot worth £100,000 would be able to get an income for the rest of her life of around £3,000 a year (these figures are subject to change and were correct at time of writing).

If she decides to retire a bit later at age 65, she'll have fewer years to live, so could buy an income worth around £4,000 a year with the same lump sum. These figures assume your income keeps up with inflation over the years. So, if you want an income in retirement of £16,000 a year, you need to have a lump sum by age 65 of around £400,000.

For many people I know, a target of around half a million is what they're aiming for with their retirement funds. This is likely to get you a reasonable income in retirement and should be on top of having paid off your home or flat.

Another way to look at it is to ignore annuities and, instead of putting all your money into this type of reverse insurance product, you just invest it yourself. Of course, this strategy is much more risky and also requires that you have a much bigger lump sum.

But let's assume that you've been a great saver and savvy investor, so you have a big pot of money and want to just invest in a low-risk way when you reach retirement age. We'll assume that you are able to get a 5% annual return on your money by leaving it in something safe like bonds. If your money is invested in bonds or cash and is earning a regular return that keeps up with inflation, you could live on the interest and not have to eat into your lump sum. The lump sum could then be left to your heirs or you could use it for emergencies.

If you have a lump sum of £1 million earning 5% a year, that's obviously equivalent to £50,000 a year in income. Half a million, earning 5% a year, would give you £25,000 a year in income. Once you come to choose where to invest your retirement money, make sure you buy investments that are indexed to inflation – in other words, they increase as the cost of living increases over time. Otherwise, your retirement years will become progressively poorer as you age, and as inflation whittles away your savings.

Let's say your goal is half a million – how are you going to get there? Work out what your assets are worth today, work out what they could be worth in the future if they double every ten years (this assumes around a 7% return each year) and see if you are over or below your target.

Jane's story

Jane has a flat in London that's currently worth around £250,000, but has a mortgage on it of £200,000. She's 35, so has calculated that her mortgage will be paid off in 25 years when she turns sixty. She thinks she'd like to retire at age 65. If her flat doubles in value every ten years (assuming 7% growth per year) it will be worth £500,000 at age 45, £1 million at age 55 and £2 million at age 65.

Of course, there is no guarantee that her flat will perform quite like this, but even if it does, she will only have one asset, a property that she'll be living in – what's she going to eat? If it was a big house, instead of a one-bedroom flat, she could rent out a room to help pay for the heating bills and dinner, but it's not. Jane needs to diversify and invest her savings in something else that is going to grow at a decent rate. Plus she needs to make sure all her credit card and other debts are paid off before that date.

If you are far behind on your goal you need to:

1) Increase the amount you save.

2) Improve the returns on your investments.

3) Increase the time you have before retirement (i.e. retire later).

Or all three!

Jane has a small pension from a previous employer, but she's not sure how much money is in there (she thinks not much). We take a look at it and discover that yes, it's not much, but also she opted to invest in the most conservative option, so the money isn't even growing very fast.

Fortunately, Jane's new employer offers quite an attractive pension scheme. It's a stakeholder pension which means it follows government recommended rules of providing low costs and fees, so that more of the money works for her rather than being eaten up by high fees. The big plus is that Jane's company has offered to make contributions on her behalf worth 5% of her salary. She decides to top this up by adding another 5%, bringing the total to 10%. She also has the money invested in the old pension scheme transferred into the new pension scheme, so she has less paperwork to worry about.

Jane's income is around £30,000 per year, so her new pensions savings scheme amounts to about £3,000 a year, which she plans to continue for the next 30 years until she reaches her set retirement date. This should give her an estimated lump sum of £209,000 if the money grows at 5% a year, or £303,000 if the money grows at 7% a year. Jane decides she wants as much money as possible in retirement, so this time opts for the most aggressive pension option. This means her money is mostly invested in stocks, but is diversified so she is not just invested in UK companies, but also emerging markets, Europe, the USA and Japan.

But Jane is still a bit worried about whether or not she'll have enough to live on in retirement. Then she remembers that her grandmother died a year ago and left her a lump sum of £10,000, which has been sitting in a savings account. We have a look at the bank statement and realise that the bank has been charging a ridiculous amount in fees and not paying much in interest, so the money hasn't grown very much in the last year.

She had been thinking about using the money to buy a new car or go on a trip abroad, but decides she'd rather invest it today and instead use *that* money for something fun in the future, like buying a house in the south of Spain and moving there to retire, which had been her grandmother's dream.

Jane has two options here. She could either buy the house in Spain now and rent it out, so that the mortgage is paid off by the time she retires. Or she could put the money into an ISA, which will make sure she doesn't pay too much tax on it, and have it invested in a Eurostoxx 500 fund (so that the money is invested in companies across Europe, not just the UK stock market).

The trouble is Jane isn't 100% sure if she will enjoy living in Spain. She doesn't speak any Spanish and 30 years seems a long way away. Her life could change dramatically in that time. If all her savings are locked up in a property (particularly one that's losing her money), she won't be able to get at it for emergencies. She and her husband might change their minds and decide to have a child, or her mother could get ill and need expensive hospital care. Also, she takes a look at the Spanish property market and decides that despite the huge property rises in the last decade, the market looks a bit shaky at the moment with prices crashing in many areas.

Jane decides to hold off on the property and instead puts £7,000 of her lump sum into an ISA. The Government limits how much money can be put into an ISA in any one year, so she will have to wait until after April (the end of the tax year) to invest the other £3,000 so that it is associated with a different tax year.

If Jane's £10,000 is invested well enough and gets a return of around 7% per year, roughly it should double every ten years. That means that when she's 45 it should be worth around £20,000 and when she's 55 it should double again to £40,000, so that by the time she turns 65 hopefully it will have grown to £80,000. Of course, those returns aren't guaranteed, so Jane has to make sure she chooses an investment that will give her returns that are as high as possible now.

Jane works out that, added to her new stakeholder pension, this money makes her feel much less worried about her future in retirement. Also, she's very happy that she's using her grandmother's money in a way that will make her life much better when she's her grandmother's age herself. She'll have more flexibility to take holidays, take up a new hobby or spoil her own grandchildren. She's also decided to take up Spanish, just in case the Spanish property market becomes really cheap and she decides she can afford a place there after all. However, she promises me that, whatever happens, she has decided she wants to make sure her grandmother's money is kept for her own retirement. She saw how frail her grandmother became as she aged and how much more difficult it was to cope with life as a pensioner.

Life Begins at 50

If you haven't yet started saving towards your pension and are worrying yourself sick about it all, take heart. It's amazing what we can achieve even if, and sometimes especially when, they start late.

There are countless stories of men and women who achieved their greatest success in life past the age of 50. The actor Morgan Freeman only became successful in his fifties, and since then has wowed audiences with his sensitive and endearing characters. There are countless other examples: actor Anthony Hopkins; the romance novelist Barbara Cartland; the investor and author Bernice Cohen, author and financier Jim Slater; Michelangelo, who painted the Sistine chapel in his nineties; Picasso, who created some of his best work in his eighties. If these people were able to be so incredibly productive and creative in their later years, then perhaps when you're older you might be quite happy to work for longer and put off retirement. Why not, if you really enjoy what you do and are able to keep working?

Start looking for them, and you will find inspiring stories everywhere of men and women who are refusing to accept the conventional idea that retirement should be about slowing down.

These days, retirement is increasingly a period of rebirth and renewal. A time to finally try all those artistic endeavours you put off at a younger age because they were financially hard to justify or your last chance to embark on a new career or follow a dream that you didn't have the courage to do before. Many an actor, comedian, singer or business person has launched their new career at 50 after dreaming about it for most of their life. Look at Kentucky Fried Chicken's Colonel Sanders. He was over 60 when he tried to start his fried chicken franchise. It's probably lucky he was that age, because it meant he knew a thing or two about life and that it's always too soon to quit. He was rejected more than 1,000 times before his business was finally a success. At 75 he sold his company for $15 million.

You only have to look in the magazines or on TV to see plenty of famous actresses who still look amazing, fit and sexy well into their fifties and sixties. Sharon Stone, Kim Cattrall, Goldie Hawn and Susan Sarandon are just a few.

According to many doctors and scientists, there is no good reason why the last years of our life have to be inactive, weak, sick and generally unpleasant. Also, learning to have greater control over your mind through meditation or simply by continuing to read, study and exercise your mind will also ensure that you stay mentally alert for longer.

Several friends of mine have decided in their early and mid-thirties to have a complete career change and go back to university. One of them, aged 34, decided she wanted to study medicine even though this is a seven-year course in her country of origin, the United States. She was quite nervous about this decision, even though it felt right, until a friend said to her. 'How old will you be when the course is finished? I'll tell you, the same age as you would be if you don't do it.' Surely it's better to reach that age, whatever it is, having fulfilled your dream rather than having several more years of being bored with your job and your life.

It doesn't matter what age you are: living a happy, contented life will boost your health and longevity.

So, don't stress too much about your upcoming retirement, as it doesn't necessarily have to be grim. If you take action now to ensure you are putting enough money aside and that it's growing at a healthy rate, you will be in a much better position. Also, you may find that, even if your income is low in retirement you can still focus on having fun, meeting new people, sharing your time with friends and family and just getting out there and enjoying life. If you focus on enjoying yourself and getting the most out of life, your body will be forced to keep up with you.

Today, many women are terribly afraid of facing their old age for financial reasons. They worry that their pensions won't be enough, or that they'll get sick and won't be able to afford proper medical care. The more active and healthy your lifestyle is, the less chance there is that you will get ill in later life and need to call on those financial resources. Insurers state that one quarter of your entire life's medical costs are used up in the very last year of life. This is usually when doctors spend a fortune trying to keep someone alive for a little longer when they are suffering from something that can't actually be cured. Other studies show that mental alertness in old age principally declines in the very last year of life. If you keep active and healthy, you shouldn't have to worry too much about illness. Sure, things might go wrong, but if you've followed my advice and have your savings buffer zone, plus insurance for the big disasters, then you can look forward to retirement with eager anticipation.

Make the most of living longer

As previously stated, the average UK woman currently lives to age 79, and this age has been gradually increasing over the past century or so. More and more people are now living to 100 and even beyond, so it is a fair bet that you will live much longer than previous generations could expect, particularly if you keep yourself in good shape, don't drink or smoke too much and keep up an optimistic outlook.

However, many people say that they don't really want to live a long life, just a happy one. Certainly, if your view of old age is one of declining health, vitality and mental ability, then I can perfectly understand people wishing for a quick termination. But what if it's not? The more you find joy in life and can think up plenty of exciting projects and things you want to do, then the more you are likely to be able to sustain yourself for longer. It was probably this drive to create new and better projects that kept artists like Picasso and Michelangelo so active in their later years.

From a financial perspective, living longer can definitely be in your favour if you're smart. Let's say that by the time you reach 50 you are able to build up savings of £100,000 which are completely separate from your pension or other living costs. If you are able to leave this money invested, earning around 7% a year, it will double in value every ten years. This is the effect:

Age 50 – £100,000
Age 60 – £200,000
Age 70 – £400,000
Age 80 – £800,000
Age 90 – £1.6 million
Age 100 – £3.2 million

You can see how in the later years all that doubling can really make a huge difference. If you think it's too late to start saving, that you're already too old, think again. If you are already 50 there's still plenty of time to become a millionaire. Now, you might think that having all that money is a waste of time if you are leaving it invested, not touching it and just handing it all to your heirs when you pass away. However, the wonderful thing about good investments like shares and property is that they can grow in value and also provide an income. If you keep building up your nest egg over time, the bigger it gets, the more income it will be able to pay you. If you invest well, then by age 90 you won't just have a big lump sum, but you could also have a very healthy income being generated from that cash that can supplement your pension.

If you intend to live a long time, and intention is a big part of making something a reality, then this will also influence how you invest your money at age 50 and beyond. After all, if you are only at the halfway mark and going to live for another 50 years, then there's no point just leaving your money in cash is there?

Finally, always remember that women are particularly lucky because we live longer, so have more time to allow our investments to reach fruition.

For more information

www.thisismoney.co.uk

In the calculators section of this website you will now find a programme that lets you type in what income you'd like to live on in retirement and it will tell you what lump sum you need to achieve this (based on current annuity rates). After that, you can go to their long-term savings calculator to work out how much you need to save each month to reach that goal. Who said saving for retirement was difficult?

www.hmrc.gov.uk/pensionschemes

HM Revenue & Customs is publishing monthly newsletters specifically about pensions tax simplification and has produced a factsheet for individuals, employers and those affected by international issues. You can find these by visiting the HMRC website.

JUSTINE'S TOP TIPS

1) Just save something. Every little bit counts, especially with pensions, when you usually have a long time to build up your savings.

2) Diversify. Ensure that in retirement you will have a number of sources of income so that you aren't reliant on just one company – which could go bust!

3) Save at least 10% to 15% of your income regularly, especially if you are still quite young.

4) Avoid taking breaks, but if you must, get your husband or relatives to make contributions on your behalf at this time.

5) Don't just opt for the lowest risk, cash option for your pension money. You have the benefit of time, so you can afford to invest more aggressively.

6) Work out how much you want to live on in retirement and then work backwards to see how much you need to save

7) Invest in growth assets that are likely to double in value every ten years (achieve at least a 7% return per year).

8) Don't just get depressed about getting older, think outside the box and look at fun ways you can earn money easily during your retirement.

9) Make sure you are on track to have all your debts paid off and as few expenses as possible before you reach your retirement date.

Dealing with People in Finance

Most of this book has dealt with how you can take control of your finances and become your own best financial adviser. However, given how increasingly complicated financial products have and are continuing to become, sometimes it is necessary to ask for help from someone in the finance industry. For example, you might consider yourself a stock market wizard and do all your trading online so you don't have to deal with stockbrokers. But then your mother gets ill and you find yourself trying to sort out her pension and find a decent retirement home or private hospital for her. Suddenly, you are forced to deal with finance professionals in a field which can be exasperatingly complex. In such a situation you can't do it all on your own. Even though I have been learning about finance for almost 20 years now, I can't say I know it all, or ever will. There are always going to be times when you need to deal with people working in finance. Having dealt with many of them over the years, I know they can sometimes be crafty salesmen who try to bamboozle you with complicated jargon, but at other times they are thorough, intelligent professionals who provide you with a much-needed service. The trick is learning how to know the difference and which questions to ask so that you get the best service possible. The great thing about being women is that we are modest enough to recognise when we need help and aren't afraid to ask for it. The challenge is to make sure we get the right advice and aren't overcharged for it.

Sexism in the city

In 1996 I was writing a financial column for a women's magazine. One article I put together was about investing in shares. I mentioned, as an aside, that women might have a little difficulty even getting a stockbroker because they were mostly male (especially then), young, arrogant and borderline sexist at times. However, I cautioned women not to be put off by this attitude and plunge into investing regardless.

After that article was published, I received more letters and responses than ever before and not because I was writing about stocks. One woman wrote in to say that she had rung one male stockbroker only to be asked: 'Er, shouldn't I be speaking to your husband about this love?' His response had totally disheartened her and she started to believe that perhaps he was right. Perhaps she shouldn't be thinking about buying stocks and getting involved with this intimidating, male-dominated world of numbers and complicated jargon. Fortunately, this woman was writing to tell me that after reading my article she was spurred on to try again and this time met with success. Like me, she found a female broker who was much more sympathetic and encouraging, and made her first stock market investments. I've never been so proud of writing an article in all my years of journalism.

Unfortunately, this story is not unique. Most Americans know the story of the Beardstown Ladies. Based in a small town in Illinois, they were the members of a stock market investment club composed entirely of women, most of whom were in their sixties, seventies and eighties. The ladies came to fame in the late 1980s and early 1990s when their club achieved annual returns of 23.4%. This beat most other investment clubs over a ten-year period as assessed by the National Association of Investors Corporation, which tracks the performance of US investment clubs. Unfortunately, the ladies later came into disrepute when an independent audit by Price Waterhouse in 1997 revealed that their returns hadn't been quite as high as originally thought. Instead of a 23.4% annual return, they had achieved 9.1% a year. That was still not bad considering that US stocks have returned 6.8% a year on average from 1954 to 2004, according to the Barclays Capital Equity-Gilt study, so the ladies still beat the market.

However, what struck me most about this still inspirational story of the Beardstown Ladies was their struggle to be taken seriously from the very beginning. In their book, *The Beardstown Ladies Common-Sense Investment Guide*, 77-year-old Shirley Goss described her own attempts to get a stockbroker, not only for her personal use, but also later to make transactions on behalf of the club. She describes how it took several tries before a stockbroker was prepared to take on her business, even though she obviously had plenty of money to invest. The excuses given were that the brokers didn't want to deal with retired women or someone who was an 'artist' (Shirley did some painting in her spare time, but her main income was from farming). In her frustration, she got the president of her bank to write a letter of credit and was eventually referred to a broker her brother had used for his investment club. Luckily, this broker was smart enough to see the potential in front of him and told her that there is no reason why a broker should turn down anybody if he is looking for business. Unfortunately, studies have shown that there is still a definite bias against women and minority groups.

It's true that the world of finance can be intimidating and downright sexist at times. It doesn't help that we are constantly hearing discouraging tales of women working in finance who are not treated well by their employers.

In recent years there has been a string of court cases, some of which have been successful, brought by women working in finance. They have accused their bosses of lewd behaviour, of sacking them for wanting a family or while they were off on maternity leave, or of getting rid of them because they complained about sexist treatment.

Some of these cases, against the City's top banks and finance institutions, have been brought by incredibly wealthy and high-powered women who have suddenly found themselves out of a job because they dared to complain.

Is it little wonder then, that there are so few women working in funds management? According to the Association of Investment Trust Companies (AITC), only ten women are registered on their database as fund managers compared to 190 men. Other studies of finance employees have shown similar results.

If even highly educated, powerful women can get burnt by the finance industry and not be taken seriously, then what chance do we less experienced investors have? Does working in finance and coming into contact with this world through investing your own money mean you have to be tough, ruthless and competitive? No wonder many women shudder at the mere thought of investment.

THINGS are CHANGING

Fortunately, all the negative publicity about sexism in the City seems to be having some effect, with many women winning their cases against overbearing bosses. The industry is trying, belatedly, to clean up its act.

Besides, your financial future is important, so don't let any of this behaviour put you off reaching your goals. Some women use online brokers where they only have to deal with a computer, so can sidetrack silly questions from male brokers and simply get the trade done.

Others, like me, opt for female stockbrokers or financial advisers. Although only around 5% of the UK's 25,000 independent financial advisers are women, this is changing rapidly as many clients, both male and female, find it easier to talk about their money with a woman.

I bought my first shares when I was 20 and still a student. I had become fascinated by the idea of making money and investing to supplement my income – which I knew wouldn't be overly generous as a journalist. I read every book I could get hold of on the topic and went along to an investors' evening at my local stock exchange. There, surrounded by mostly retired men, I watched many young men stand up to talk about price earnings ratios and the benefits of options and all sorts of things which at the time went completely over my head. God knows why I kept going and didn't completely lose heart, but I was crazily determined and one night I met my future broker there. She was an older woman, perhaps in her forties, and she explained the world of investment in terms I could understand. Friends have also told me about male brokers and investment advisers they use who were smart enough to recognise the potential of female clients. The world of investing is finally starting to become more female-friendly. Certainly, the changes have been ridiculously slow, but with so many determined and highly educated women out there, change is inevitable.

The right questions

Dealing with people in finance has a lot to do with knowing the right questions to ask and 'reading' the people you are dealing with correctly.

A few years ago, I was asked to participate in a radio programme where investors rang in to ask questions and our team of 'experts' answered. I was the only woman, and was sitting between a stockbroker and a financial adviser, so I felt a bit intimidated. The first caller was an elderly man who had shares in the Woolwich Bank which at the time was being bought by Barclays. He wasn't sure if he should sell his shares or hold on to them but his gut feeling was that he should hold.

The stockbroker went into a tirade using lots of colourful expressions about how banking stocks were rubbish at the moment, everyone in the City knew this – *sell, sell, sell.* I tried to chip in with some cautionary advice, saying that companies the size of Barclays Bank were unlikely to go bust tomorrow, the government simply wouldn't allow it, and that perhaps some of the selling had been overdone. However, this stockbroker wouldn't listen and simply talked over me. It's true that, at the time, banking stocks were down and a lot of people in the financial world were gloomy on their outlook, but things rarely stay the same for long in finance. Six months later, shares in Barclays had completely recovered and the banking sector was one of the best performing sectors on the market.

About a year after this incident, I interviewed this particular stockbroker and a number of other key people in the finance industry and asked them a very simple question: 'What do you invest your own money in, and how has it done?' This broker told me that he had a portfolio of shares, but he left most of the investing to his wife because his stock-picks had been disasters! He even had the cheek to tell me that if you're doing your job as a stockbroker, your own investments shouldn't be doing well because you should be paying more attention to your clients' investments. Frankly, I found this a bit hard to swallow. If you know anything about human nature, you'll know that most people have their own interests at heart. I think perhaps this broker spent too much of his time doing interviews and trying to be a celebrity rather than focusing on *anyone's* investments.

Nevertheless, this incident showed me how I had, unwittingly, stumbled across an extremely important question. If you were going to hire an architect or interior designer, the first thing you would want to see is what other projects they have worked on and even how they have designed their own homes. It should be the same with finance. In the book *The Millionaire Next Door*, the authors describe an interview with a multi-millionaire called Mr Martin. Despite earning a relatively modest income compared to most millionaires, this man had amassed a fortune through extremely good investing. His favourite trick was to ask cold-calling stockbrokers to send him the details of their own investment portfolios with the promise that, if any of them had made more money from their investments than he had, he would use their services. Unsurprisingly, he hasn't had one broker take him up on this offer. Like many other millionaires, he finds his stockbrokers and other financial intermediaries in the same way most of us hire builders – by getting a referral from someone you trust. The best person to ask for a referral is someone who is already rich. If that's impossible, ask someone who at least works in finance, such as your accountant, if you have one.

If none of these avenues are open to you, you can get a list of possible candidates from registered associations which have their own standards and ethical codes that members must adhere to. Then you simply go through the same process you would when hiring a builder, though perhaps be a little tougher. Do your homework and bombard them with questions. Ultimately, you must go with someone you trust who doesn't have a whiff of 'dodgy' about them.

Once you have your list of at least three possible candidates, it's important to interview them as if they were a prospective employee. Here is a list of possible questions you could ask a stockbroker or financial adviser and the types of responses to look out for.

Questions

1) How many years have you been working in finance?

A very good fund manager once told me that I shouldn't waste my time listening to 'pimply-faced brokers who hadn't even seen a full market cycle'. It's true that brokers, fund managers and financial advisers who have been around for a while are usually more cautious and often more sensible when it comes to money. They have seen markets rise and fall and appear relatively unsurprised whichever way the market turns. They may be more conservative than average, but only because they've discovered through trial and error that the number one rule is 'don't lose your client's money!'

2) Are you registered with an industry association?

This will hopefully weed out some of the more unscrupulous players who haven't bothered to get the correct qualifications. Advisers must be regulated by a recognised authority such as the Financial Services Authority.

3) What is your area of specialisation?

Some Independent Financial Advisers (IFAs) are all-rounders, but many others specialise in a particular field. If you are nearing retirement, you will want your IFA to have specialised knowledge of pensions and other retirement planning tools. Make sure you choose the right man or woman for the job. Ask about their other clients and check if there are any particular products they don't advise on.

4) Where do you invest your own money?

This is your key question, but it might be a bit intimidating if it's the first one you ask. If you are a very cautious investor, you might not be 100% comfortable with an adviser who is used to taking a lot of risk. On the other hand, you may decide your adviser is too cautious for your tastes. If they have a different approach, it could have a nice balancing effect, ensuring gung-ho investors don't take too much risk, and urging too-cautious investors to make better use of their money. It's important to know what type of investor, and person, they are before you establish a relationship with them. If your views are poles apart you will never trust them with your money and waste a lot of time and energy.

5) Why is this investment suitable for me?

This question can be followed up with others such as:

How does it match my investment goals? How will the investment make money e.g. dividends, interest, capital gains?; How easy is it to sell this investment if something happens and I need to get out? What are the specific risks associated with this investment, e.g. would a change in interests rates affect it? Where can I get more information about this investment, such as an independent evaluation? How many different investments did you research before coming up with this one?

6) How are you paid?

Financial planners can be paid in several ways:

* A salary paid by the company for which they work. You pay the company through either fees or commissions and this is passed on to your adviser in the form of a regular salary.
* Fees based on an hourly rate, a flat rate, or on a percentage of your assets and/or income.
* Many advisers are paid a commission by the provider of the products they sell to you. This could be a large insurance or fund company. These commissions are usually a percentage of the amount you invest.
* A combination of fees and commissions, where fees are charged for the amount of work done to develop a financial plan and commissions are received from any products sold. In addition, some planners may offset some portion of the fees you pay if they receive commissions for carrying out their recommendations.

7) How much do you charge and could anyone else benefit from your recommendation?

Financial advice is never free, even if it seems to be. Advisers are often remunerated by the fund managers and other finance companies when they hand them your money. Make sure you know the source of your adviser's income. You may decide you don't mind if they are taking commission, but you should still know. It will determine how 'independent' they truly are. Also, ask how the charges on certain investments will affect the returns you get on those investments and, if a company is offering your adviser a very high commission rate on a product, ask if they are prepared to take a smaller percentage.

8) Have you ever been disciplined or questioned for any unlawful or unethical actions?

If the answer is yes they might not tell you, but it is worth asking the question given the number of scandals we have witnessed in recent years. It may at least prompt them to explain what their ethics policy is and how they handle situations where the clients feel aggrieved.

9) Can I have it in writing?

Keep a copy of all the documents your adviser or broker gives you and ask that they put their recommendations in writing for you, so that if there are any problems down the line you have the documentation to back up your argument. This should also cover how they will be remunerated and exactly what services are being provided.

10) Can I have more time?

Don't be afraid to ask for more time to consider the investment options. Your adviser or broker should not be trying to rush you into anything. They should be happy to arrange a follow-up meeting. With many products you have around seven days to change your mind once you have bought it, but this may not be enough time for you.

QUESTIONS TO ASK YOURSELF

1. Do you know what you hope to achieve and how much you are willing to spend?
2. Do you have the documents for any investments you already hold?
3. Do you know if you need a specialist adviser, and if so what type?
4. How do you feel about commissions? Would you be prepared to pay a fee for advice?
5. Make sure you know the difference between information and advice. Advice may give you certain rights and protections. Your adviser should explain these to you.
6. Are you prepared to shop around and see three or four advisers before making your decision?
7. Did particular advisers you saw encourage you to take your time? Make you feel comfortable asking questions? Try to understand your situation thoroughly?

LEAVING IT TO OTHERS

'But with our industry we must likewise be steady, settled, and careful, and oversee our own affairs with our own eyes, and not trust too much to others . . .
Trusting too much to others' care is the ruin of many; for in the affairs of this world men are saved, not by faith, but by the want of it.'
from *The Way to Wealth* by Benjamin Franklin

Whether it's your husband, parents, financial adviser or friend, leaving all your money decisions to another person is not a good idea. Why? Because even if they take good care of your finances you won't trust them as well as you trust yourself and you're likely to become anxious. Therefore, it pays to learn a little bit about what you're getting into and keep an eye on things yourself.

Just having a stockbroker or a financial adviser (or for that matter a spouse or relative who is good with money) doesn't mean you give up responsibility for your own money. Take some advice certainly, but do your own research as well. The best person to take care of your money is *you* – no matter how incapable you might feel at the moment. When you take responsibility, even if you lose money at least you have no one else to blame and you will feel more in control.

Listen to other people, learn from them, and think through every piece of advice you receive (as with any advice in this book), but make up your own mind about what's right for you. Every individual looks at their investments in a different way so there is no one investment strategy or asset allocation decision that is right for everyone. What you choose will depend on many things – your tolerance for risk, your personal preferences in terms of investments, your financial responsibilities at home, your age and your time horizon. Someone advising you may or may not understand these needs and recommend something that goes against your instinct that just doesn't feel right. Stand up for yourself if you're not sure about something and perhaps do a bit more research into a particular investment if you don't feel comfortable with it.

Female advisers

I have a female stockbroker and some of the people I speak to about my finances are women, but I don't recommend relying solely on women when building up your team of experts – that would be far too limiting, given how few women work in finance compared to men. Besides, there are many extremely intelligent and genuinely helpful men in the world of finance. Use their many years of experience and expertise to your advantage.

Nevertheless, studies have shown many people find it easier to speak to women, whether it's a doctor or a financial adviser. This is because women are perceived as being better listeners, more understanding, professional and motivated by more than just money.

Currently, the average UK financial adviser is male and in his fifties, so if you're a young woman you may be worried he won't be able to understand or relate to you.

Caroline Anstee is a female financial adviser who has been practising for many years and is now one of the founding partners of Elements – a financial advising group made up entirely of women.

She is a good example of an IFA who looks at the bigger picture. Elements donates £10 to the women's charity WOW (Wellbeing of Women) for every client they see. The charity aids women and does research in all areas of reproductive health.

Caroline is also involved in a lot of educational campaigns around the country helping women and students learn more about money and handling their finances.

She says advisers, both male and female, can mistreat their clients and take them for granted, but she thinks it is important to put the customer first, so she trips around the country so that she can see her clients in their homes.

'I think it's too arrogant to expect them to come and see you. We're used to seeing people in their homes, where they're more relaxed and have all their paperwork already with them,' she says.

Unfortunately, it's not always easy to find a female financial adviser. Caroline estimates there are only around 1,500 female independent financial advisers out of 26,000 IFAs in the UK.

According to industry body IFA Promotion, a quarter of all firms on their database have female IFAs within their company. However, of the 17,950 individuals registered with IFAP, only 11% are women.

Many of the women working in this field are paid less on average than men, partly because they are less likely to work on commission, and are stuck in administrative roles.

However, given the demand and the large number of girls coming through university, this is expected to change. Already, female IFAs are likely to hold more qualifications than males, so many in the industry are encouraging graduates to consider financial planning as it can be not only financially rewarding, but also more flexible for working mums as well.

JUSTINE'S TOP 10 TIPS

1) Take responsibility for your money, don't just leave all the decisions up to someone else.

2) Use the same tricks as you would for a builder – interview a lot of advisers and don't go with anyone who seems dodgy. Women's intuition is often right.

3) Ask investment experts what they do with their own money and ask how long they have been doing this job; experience often counts.

4) Make sure you find someone who is qualified, regulated and a member of a professional body such as IFAP.

5) Don't take any flak from sexist brokers who insist on dealing with your partner instead of you. Even bank managers can be guilty of this at times.

7) Ask a lot of annoying questions – you are hiring them, not the other way around.

8) Build up a team of investment experts, or just knowledgeable people who you trust. That way, you are also less likely to get a one-sided opinion.

9) Do a lot of reading and researching yourself so that you are more confident, can evaluate the advice more easily and feel more in control.

10) Have a think about what you are really trying to achieve before interviewing advisers. If you really don't know just go on a fact-finding mission and don't be pushed into buying anything until you are ready.

Detox Goals

The beginning of the year is always a great time to get the women in my investment club together for a glass of wine and a chat about their New Year's resolutions. Once they are cheerfully sloshed, I hit them with the hard questions on what their saving or investment goals are going to be for the following year. This always seems to spark plenty of interesting debate and it's also a great time to look back on the year passed, take a note of your achievements (whatever they were) and give yourself a big pat on the back. It's also a time to assess what you would have liked to have done better and how goals could be more effectively achieved this year.

As I've noticed with the women in my club, the more investing experience they have, the more confident they are with the whole process, and I've been so amazed (and proud) to see how they have developed. Once nervous and frightened, they are now becoming determined savvy investors who aren't afraid to haggle with a stockbroker, or demand a better deal from their bank. Sharing our experiences with each other is also inspiring, so I encourage you to form your own group of like-minded friends. Once you see younger and seemingly more naïve friends open up an investment account, you realise it's not so hard to do after all and will be generally more determined to make the effort yourself.

To get you on track for what I hope will be a very prosperous year, here is a personal goal sheet all the members in my club fill in each year. The idea is to encourage them to *act* rather than just *talk* about investing. Writing down our goals really helps us focus on what we want to achieve in the year ahead and I hope it will do the same for you.

If you've managed to make it to the end of this book, then you certainly deserve a pat on the back for reading through so much financial terminology in one hit! Now it's time to get down to the nitty-gritty and look at what you're going to do with all this information. I hope you're feeling inspired by the stories and experiences I've shared, but I also hope you're determined to make your own story one of prosperity and calm confidence in your dealings with finance. Good luck!

CASH SAVINGS

- I currently have in savings.
- If I were to lose my job I would last for months/years on these savings.
- In one year's time I would like to have in savings.

DEBT

- I currently have in credit card/personal debts.
- I currently have in mortgage debt.
- I plan to be debt-free by .

INSURANCE

- I currently have no/the following insurance .
- I need to take out insurance.
- This will be put in place by .

PROPERTY

- I currently have properties.
- My goal is to have properties by .

FUNDS

- I currently have worth of fund investments in funds.
- I plan to have fund investments by .

SHARES

- I currently have worth of stock market investments in companies.
- I plan to have stocks, worth by .

BONDS

- I currently have worth of bond market investments in bonds/bond funds.
- I plan to have bond market investments by .

BY THE TIME I'M 50

(assuming 7% growth in assets so doubling the value every 10 years)

- I estimate that my net worth will be .
- Ideally I would like to have .
- This is a shortfall/surplus of .

BY THE TIME I'M 60

- I estimate that my net worth will be .
- Ideally I would like to have .
- This is a shortfall/surplus of .
- By age I will be a millionaire.

WILLS

- I do/ do not have a will.
- Currently if something were to happen to me the state would allocate my assets to .
- Ideally I would prefer that my beneficiary is .
- I plan to put in place a will/ update my will by .

SUMMARY

My three most important financial goals for the next year are:

1)

2)

3)

Jargon Buster/Glossary

Annuities

A contract by an insurance company that is designed to provide regular payments to you while you're in retirement. The idea is that the insurance company promises to keep paying you this agreed amount of income each year until you die, no matter how long you live. So, if you live a long time, you know you won't run out of money. To buy the annuity, you hand over a large lump sum of money from your pension pot. Obviously the bigger your pot, the larger the income you'll have to live on. Unfortunately, women usually receive a lower income than men with the same size pot because we are more likely to live a long time. People with poor health, such as smokers, can also receive a lower than average income.

Asset

I define an asset (or a good investment) as anything that puts money into your pocket rather than taking it out. The official definition of an asset is anything that has economic value and can be converted into cash. Assets can be owned by individuals (such as a house) or companies (such as a factory or office equipment).

AVCs (Additional Voluntary Contributions)

Most company pension schemes stipulate how much an employer or employee will each contribute on a monthly basis to their fund. If you want to add more, you can do this by paying in extra money known as an 'additional voluntary contribution' or AVC.

Bonds

Bonds are like an IOU. They can be issued for a period of one year or more. Federal governments, states, cities, companies and many other types of institutions use bonds to raise money by borrowing cash from investors. The bond issuer promises to repay the initial amount (principal) by a specific date (the maturity date) and also pays interest to the investor (coupons).

If a company goes bust, bond holders (and other creditors) are paid off before shareholders. The safest bonds are those issued by respected federal governments such as the UK (where they are called gilts) or the US (called Treasury bonds) because these countries are the least likely to default, i.e. not be able to pay the money back.

Bear market

When the stock market is falling.

Bull market

When the stock market is rising.

Capital Gain

This is basically when you buy something and it goes up in value. It is an increase in the price (capital value) of an investment that is above the price you paid for it. It includes your profit after taking into account any expenses. It also ignores any income you may have made on the investment while you held it. A capital gain is sometimes called capital appreciation. In the UK, investors pay tax on their capital gains (CGT). However, the government also takes into account the effect of inflation during the period you held the asset, so this reduces your tax liability. You do not have to pay capital gains tax on your home (principal residence), but if you own a holiday home or other assets you have to pay tax when they are sold. Fortunately there are various ways of reducing your tax burden, such as by holding your investments within an Individual Savings Account (ISA).

CPI

Consumer Price Index. This index shows how the value of a basket of commonly purchased goods (food, TVs, computers) goes up over time. It's an important measure of inflation or the cost of living.

Defined Benefit Pensions

Also known as ***final salary pensions***. With these pensions you know how much you will receive on retirement because your employer promises to give you a certain percentage (say 40%) of your final salary. So if you are earning £40,000 in the year before you retire, your pension would be £16,000 per year. These pensions are much simpler for you but more expensive for your employer, so they are less common these days. These pensions also depend on how long you have been with the company. As people spend less time with one employer these days, Defined Benefit pension schemes are more difficult to structure.

Defined Contribution Pensions

Also known as ***money purchase pensions***. These pension are increasingly common and are where your employer makes regular contributions to a fund on your behalf. The money is invested and builds up over the years, but you don't know for sure how much you will have on retirement because this depends on how the investments perform, how long you contribute for and how much you contribute.

Freehold

This is when you own a property or land outright, as opposed to via a leasehold (see ***Leasehold***). With freehold, your ownership is unconditional and represents the broadest ownership interest recognised by law.

FTSE

Sometimes called the 'Footsie'. Stands for Financial Times Share Indices (see index). The FTSE 100 includes the 100 largest companies in the UK.

Index

An index is a number that shows how much investors value something at a particular time. The index can show the value of a basket of shares (such as the FTSE 100) or a basket of goods (such as the consumer price index). By creating an index, investors can see how the value of their investments change from one day to the next.

Inflation

An increase in the general level of prices in the economy over time.

ISA

Stands for Individual Savings Account. These are tax-free, so you don't have to declare to the taxman any income or capital gains you receive. Individuals can save up to £7,000 each year. The financial year runs from 6th April until the 5th April the following year. ISAs were brought in by the government in April 1999 to replace Tax Exempt Special Savings Accounts (TESSAs) and Personal Equity Plans (PEPs) and are guaranteed to run until at least 2010.

Leasehold
The right to hold or use property for a fixed period of time at a given price. Although there is a lease contract, there is no transfer of ownership. Leasehold properties can be bought and sold to other investors until the end of the lease period (normally around 99 years). The leaseholder has the right to remain in the property as an assured tenant paying an agreed rent to the owner of the freehold (see ***Freehold***).

Liability
Generally, a liability is something that takes money out of your pocket, so it could be an expense or debt that you must pay. It can also refer to when you are legally bound to pay a company or settle a debt, such as when you crash into someone else's car and are liable for the damages.

Mortgages

Fixed rate mortgages:
This is where your lender fixes the mortgage repayments over a set period, so you don't have any changes in the amount you pay each month. At the end of the fixed period, your mortgage usually reverts to a variable rate. These are good because you don't have any nasty surprises; however, if interest rates fall, you might be stuck paying more than your friends.

Variable rate mortgages:
Every mortgage lender offers a standard variable rate (SVR), which it uses as the basis for all its other mortgage products. This is based on the Bank of England's base lending rate which is decided once a month (although they may decide not to change it). Every time the Bank of England raises base rates, mortgage lenders re-evaluate their position and often raise the SVR. Usually, a bank's variable rate is about 2% above the Bank of England's base rate so it can make a profit. Some banks offer a better deal because they want to attract more customers and some offer a worse deal – particularly for people with a poor credit history.

Capped rate mortgages:
These try to offer the best of both worlds: if standard mortgage rates rise, your rate will only go up until it hits the cap, then it stops. However, if rates

drop, you will benefit from this drop. Like a fixed-rate mortgage, capped rates are also set for a particular period of time.

Discounted rate mortgages:
This is a bit of a gimmick to get more bank customers in. A bank will offer new customers a mortgage that is cheaper than their standard variable rate for a limited period of time. Your rate is still variable – so it goes up and down – but you are not paying as much as other borrowers who didn't get in on the deal. For example, you are offered 6% and they are offered 7%. Rates go up half a percent, so now you are on 6.5% and they are on 7.5%. These mortgages are also only for a set period of time; after this you go on to the normal SVR like everyone else. If you want to change banks often to exploit this new customer benefit, make sure your old bank doesn't charge you a penalty for leaving.

Base rate tracker mortgages:
The interest rate tracks the rate set by the Bank of England for its base rates. These deals can either last a couple of years – then revert to a standard variable rate – or they can be set for the whole term of the mortgage and are called Lifetime Trackers. E.g. the interest rate may be set at base rate plus 0.25% for two years, or base plus 0.75% for life. Most lenders set their standard variable rate at about 2% over the base, so these deals are a bit cheaper.

Fix and track mortgages:
This is for borrowers who want to start out on a fixed rate mortgage but don't want to get stuck paying a lot of money if mortgage rates fall. It starts off with a fixed rate, say for a year, then turns into a tracker mortgage. This is where interest rates are charged at a set percentage above the Bank of England's base rate for the rest of the mortgage term.

Repayment or interest-only mortgages:
You also have the choice of either paying off your debt normally – where you pay the interest rate the bank charges plus part of the debt so that gradually it is reduced – or you can just pay the interest. If you opt to just pay the interest, you will still have just as much debt as you started with in the beginning. The reason some people choose this option is because they want to use the money that would otherwise be paying off the debt to invest

on the stock market or in some other asset. Their theory is that they can make more money by investing than paying off their debts early. Obviously this is a pretty risky strategy because you might turn out to be a terrible stock market investor and lose the money that was supposed to be used to pay off your home. Some banks have even encouraged people to take out interest-only mortgages if they can't afford a normal loan.

In my opinion, if you are so hard up that you can't afford a normal loan, then maybe you shouldn't be buying a property in the first place. A home comes with a lot of extra costs and responsibilities. If you pay a high price for a property so that you are really stretched and can barely afford the mortgage payments, what are you going to do when something goes wrong? In the UK, home ownership is seen as very important, but it's not for everyone. If buying a home reduces your standard of living or means you end up losing money, it is not a good investment; it is a very bad one.

Pensions

Self-Invested Personal Pension (SIPP)

These are do-it-yourself pensions, often set up by people running their own businesses. A SIPP is a personal pension that allows you to have more control over your investments than other pension arrangements. They offer a broad range of investment options, so you can tailor your pension pot to suit your requirements. Since Pensions Simplification came into effect in April 2006, the restrictions on which pension schemes you can be a member of have been removed. As a result, employees can be members of their company scheme, and can also opt to pay into a personal pension (such as a SIPP) as well.

Stakeholder Pension

A stakeholder pension is a type of low-fee pension. You can buy a stakeholder pension from a finance company, a bank, insurance company or building society.

Stakeholder pensions must meet a minimum standard, set by the government, which ensures that they offer value for money and flexibility. For example:

- Management charges each year can not exceed the cap on fees and charges. This cap has been set down by law. For people who join a stakeholder pension scheme on or after 6 April 2005*, the cap is an annual management charge of 1.5% for the first ten years. This reduces to 1% if members stay in the scheme.

- No charges for members transferring into or out of the stakeholder pension.
- All stakeholder pensions must accept contributions of £20 or more, though some may accept lower payments.
- Stakeholder pensions must be run in the interest of their members and either have trustees or be run by a scheme manager.

(*People who bought a stakeholder pension before 6 April 2005 will continue to be charged annual fees of 1% for as long as they remain in the scheme. However, if they move to another stakeholder pension scheme on or after 6 April 2005, the new charge cap of 1.5% will apply for the first ten years.)

PE ratio (Price/Earnings ratio)

This is the most common measure of working out how expensive a stock is. The price of the stock is divided by its after-tax earnings over a 12 month period. This is usually the past year's earnings (trailing period) but sometimes investors also estimate the coming year's earnings (forward period). A PE is sometimes referred to as the price earnings multiple.

Shares/Stocks

An instrument that signifies ownership (called 'equity') in a company. Shareholders can claim a share of the company's assets and profits. Ownership in the company is determined by the number of shares a person owns divided by the total number of shares in the company. For example, if a company has 1,000 shares and a person owns 50 of them, then they own 5% of the company. Most stock also provides voting rights, which give shareholders a proportional vote in certain corporate decisions. Only a certain type of company, called a corporation, has stock; other types of companies such as sole proprietorship and limited partnerships do not issue stock.

S&P 500

The main stock market index in the US. It stands for the Standard and Poor's 500 index and is made up of the 500 largest American companies.

INDEX